the naked truth

hans fahrmeyer

HAMBURG GROUP

First published in the United States of America in 2017
by HAMBURG GROUP, INC New York, NY

Copyrights (C) 2017 Hamburg Group Publishing
All photographs copyrights (C) 2017 by Hans W Fahrmeyer

Design by Werner Redman

Forward by Trevor Briggs

Hans Fahrmeyer's images are bold, colorful and unabashedly sensual. The intent is to evoke desire, and the intention is there in the eyes of each model on each and every page.. This energy is palatable and through his use of vibrant colors, uniquely body poses and positions, as well a creative editing, Hans channels the energy into images drenched in both intensity and urgency.

Born in Germany, Hans worked throughout Europe prior to immigrating to the United States in 1979. Although his European influences are evident within his vision, the glamour and energy embedded in his images are erotically rooted in his passion for his home in New York's West Village. Like so many of the men who journey to Hans' studio to work, like the artist himself, are not all native New Yorkers. Yet through his skill and creativity, in front of Hans' lens, they embody and channel the electricity and creativity of both the artist, and the city.

With most of the world online, images of the naked male form are now splashed all over the web. Yet, within the catalog of mediocrity that the Internet has become, Hans' work remains ground breaking through the artists dauntless desire to capture male sexuality at it's most bold and climatic. There are no filters in his vision, nothing to blur or hide the pulsing vitality of the men in their prime which Hans commemorates. Some photographers seem to want to diminish the intensity of carnality in the men they shoot, as if it's something to be ashamed of. Hans' goal is to capture the raw and naked truth of male sexuality in all of it's colorful, powerful glory.

Hans has shot some of the worlds most successful male fitness models, and many of the images captures have become iconic depictions of the male form. I believe many of the images within The Naked Truth are destined to join them. An extensive collection of work, as you turn each page, a new theme and visual experience is unveiled. Hans beautifully pairs each page with models, pose, energy, color and motif creating dynamic visuals and interplay between the images on the page.

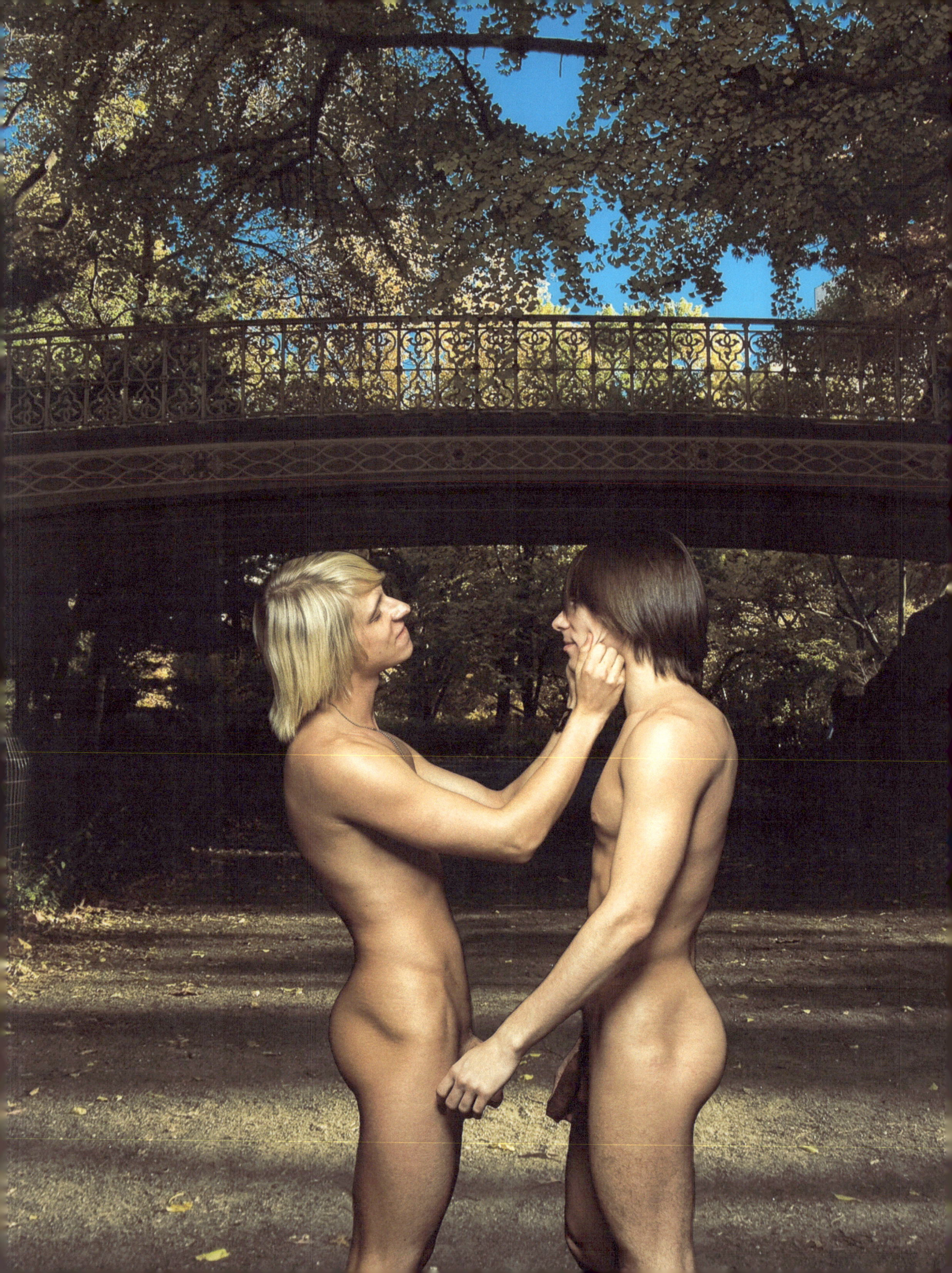

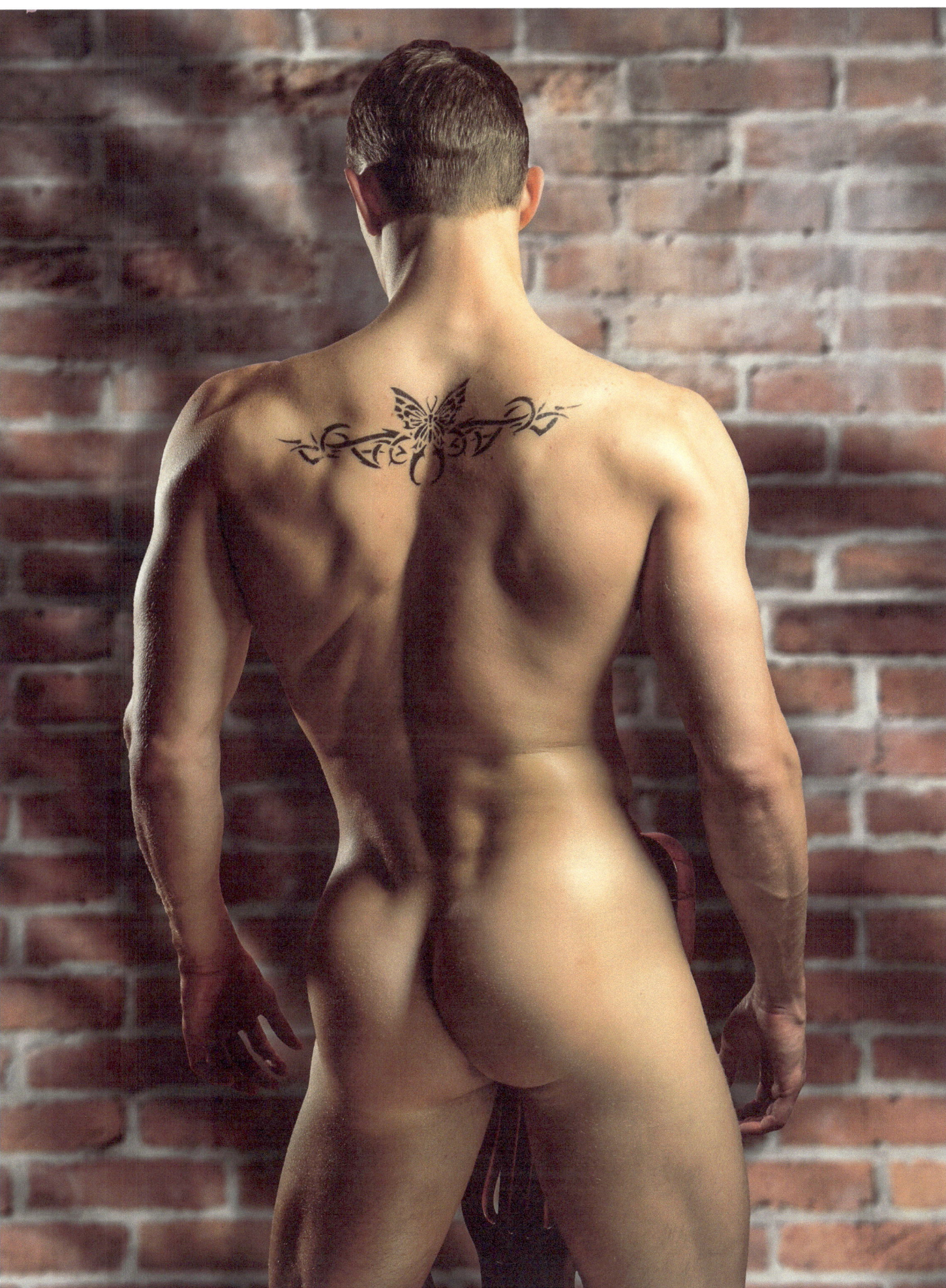

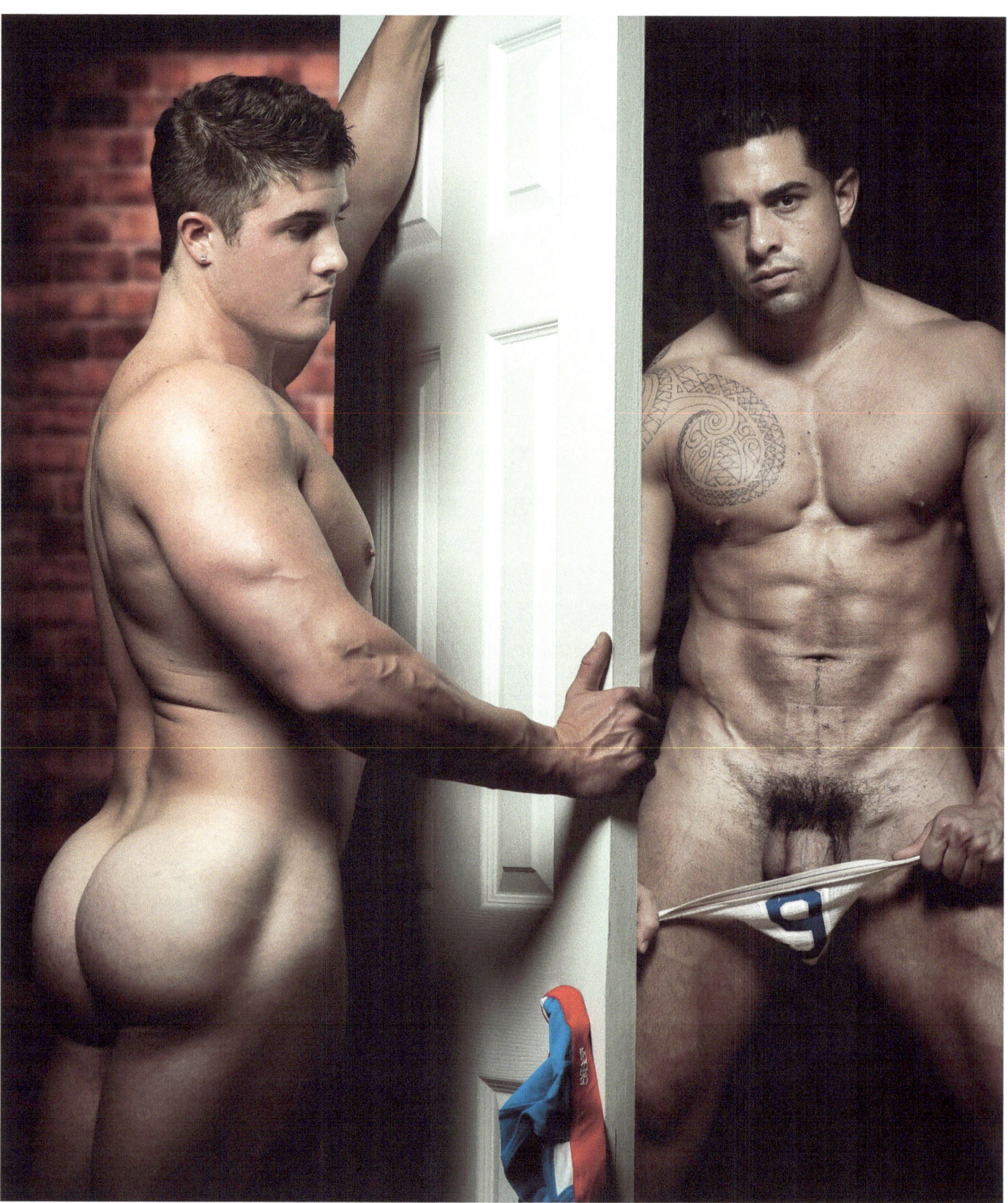

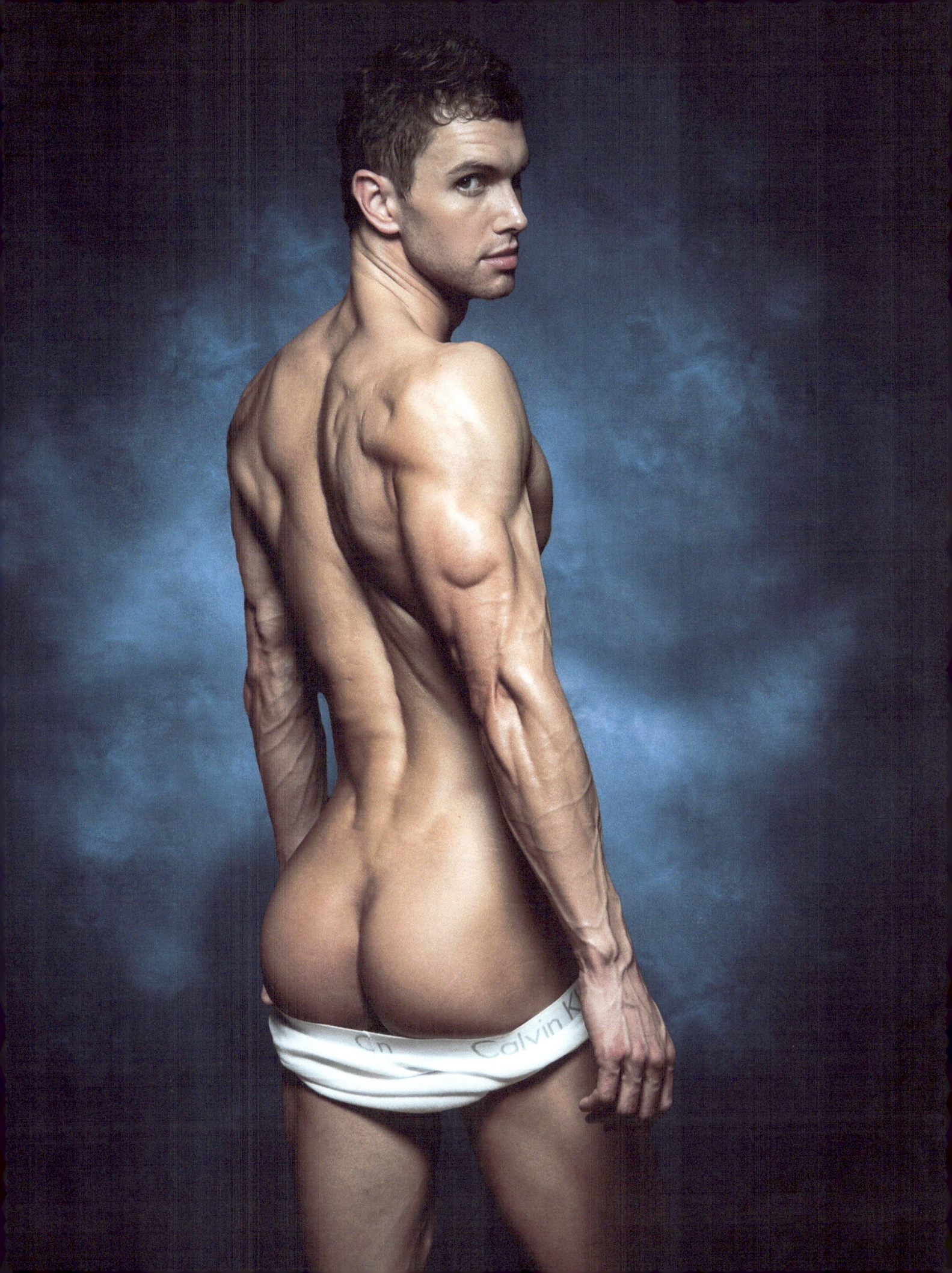

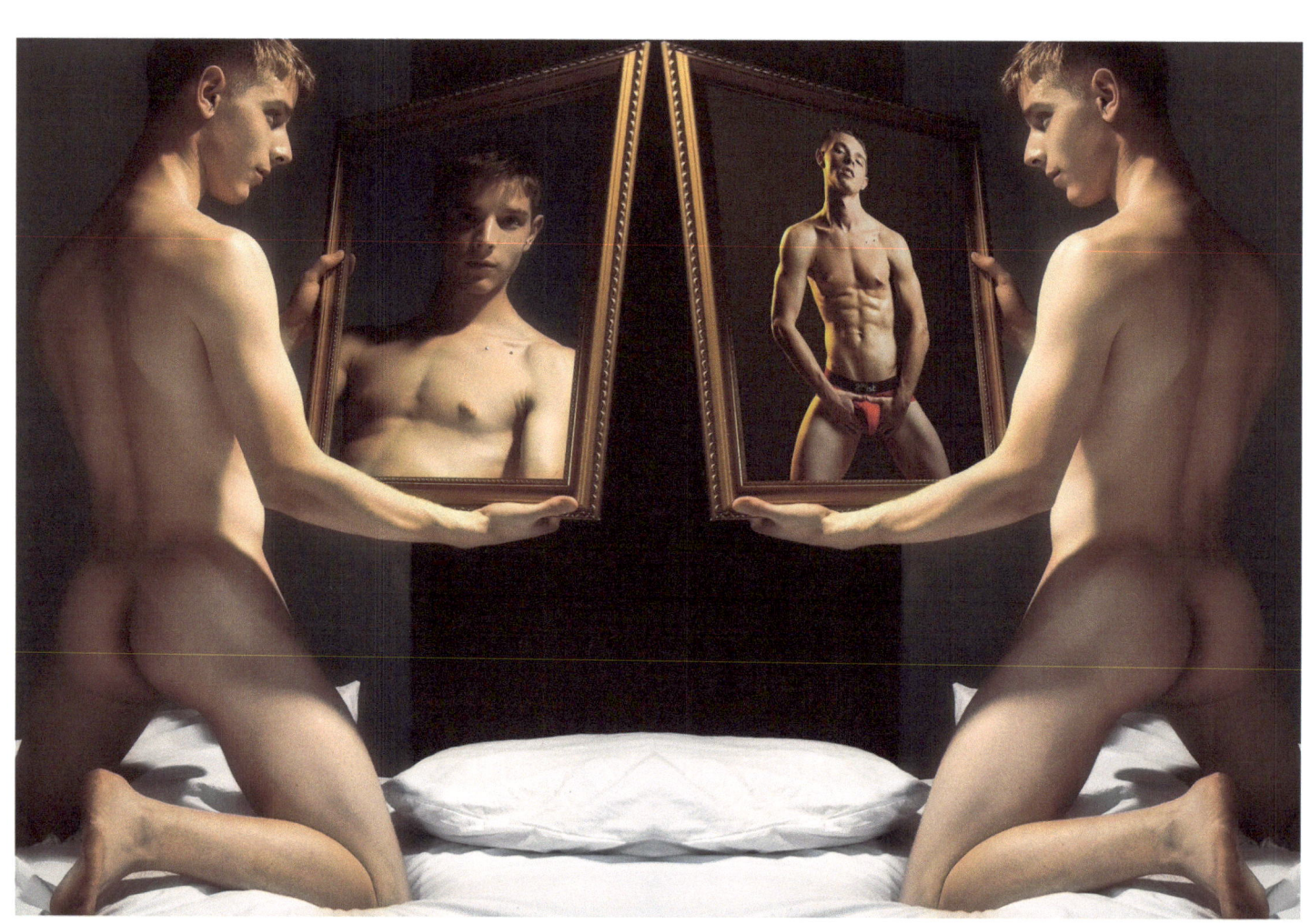

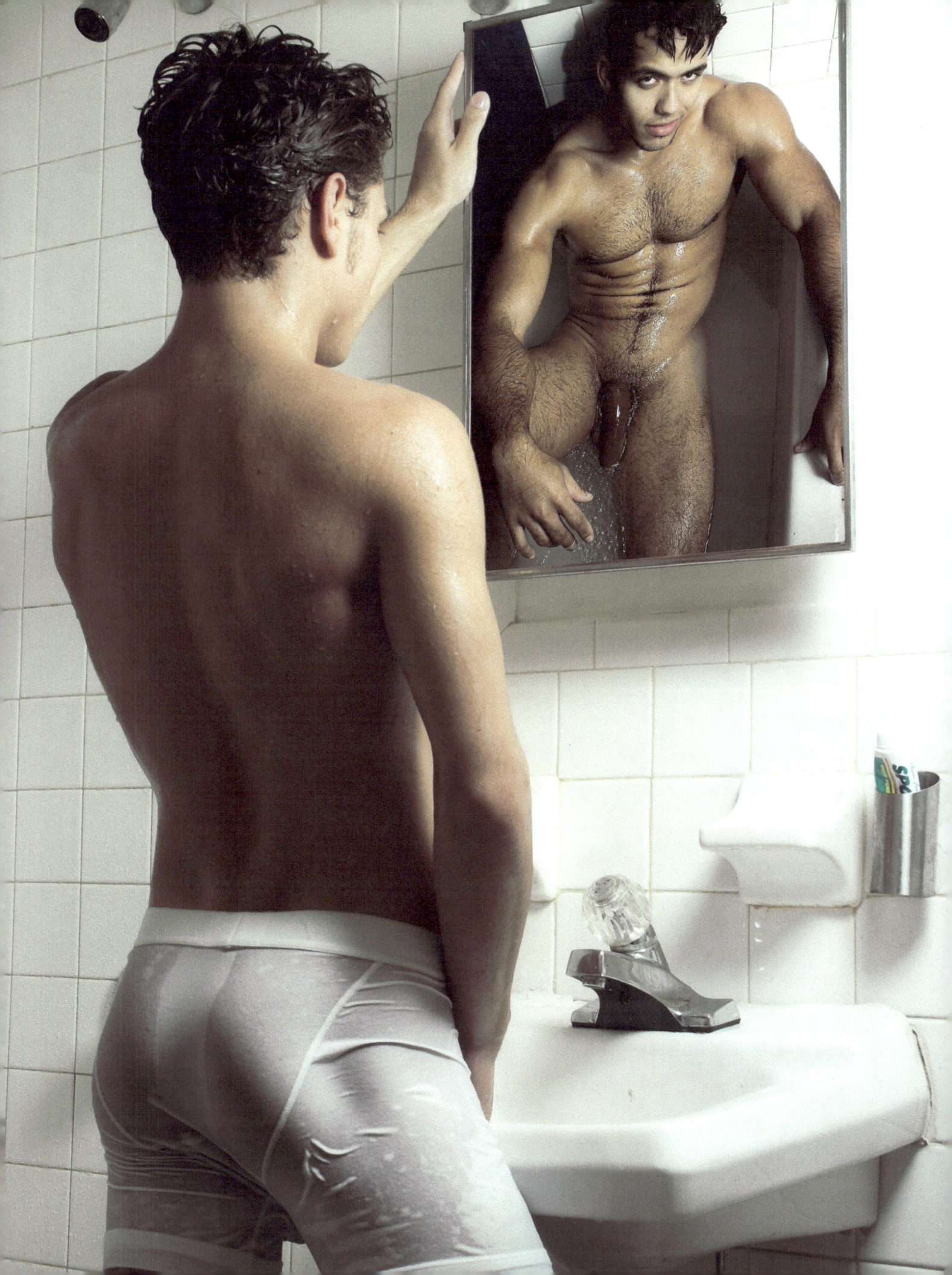

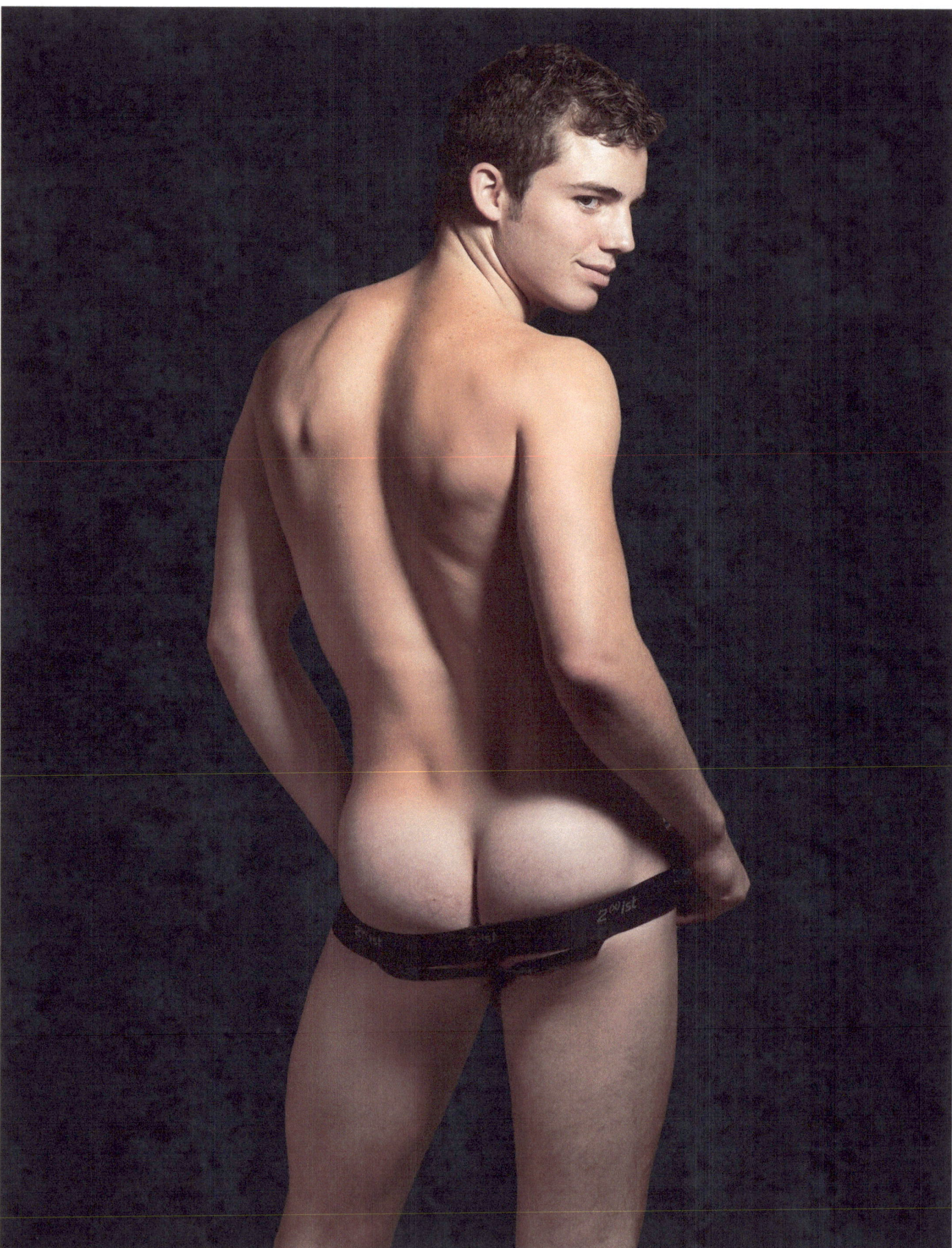

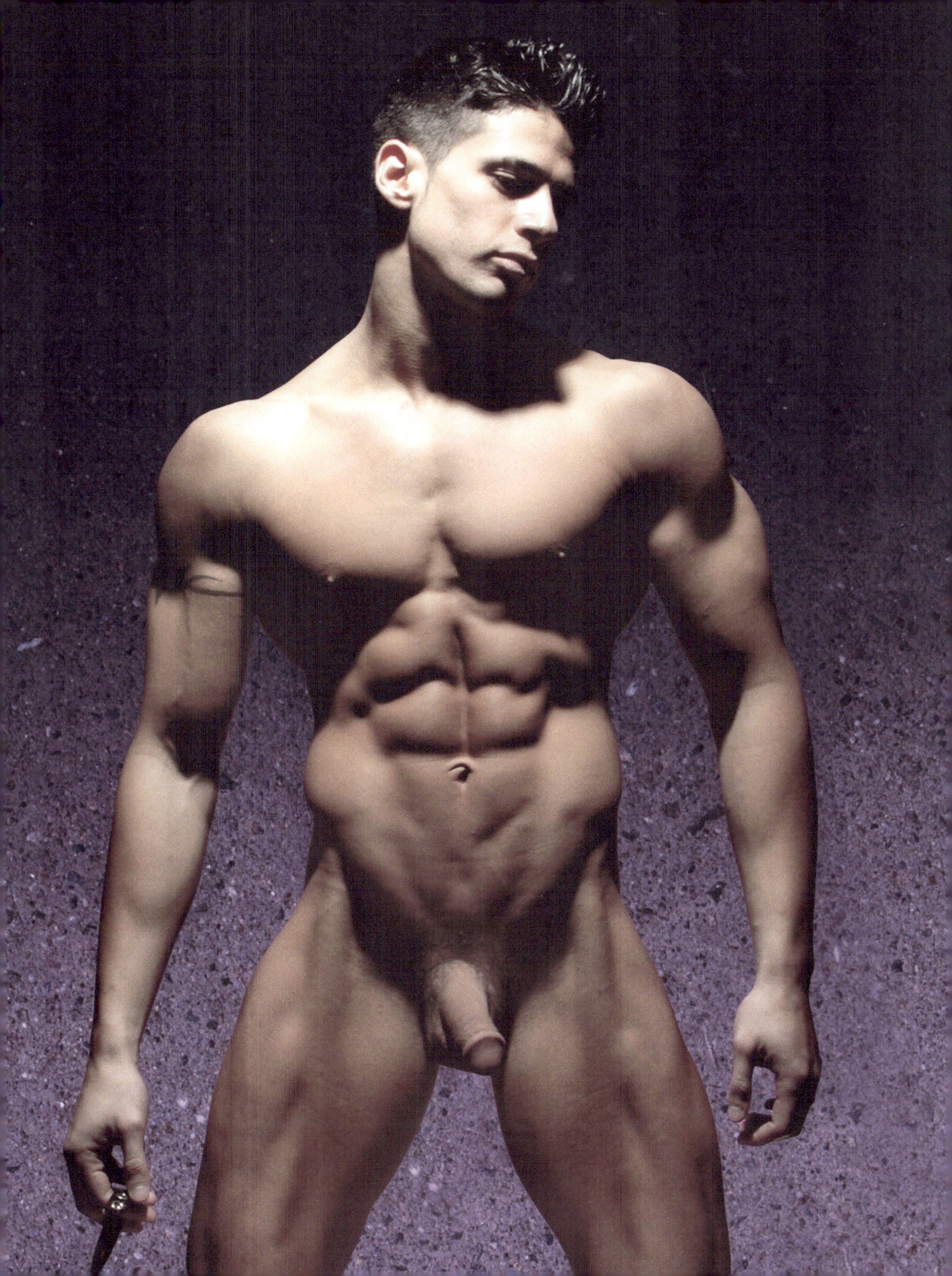

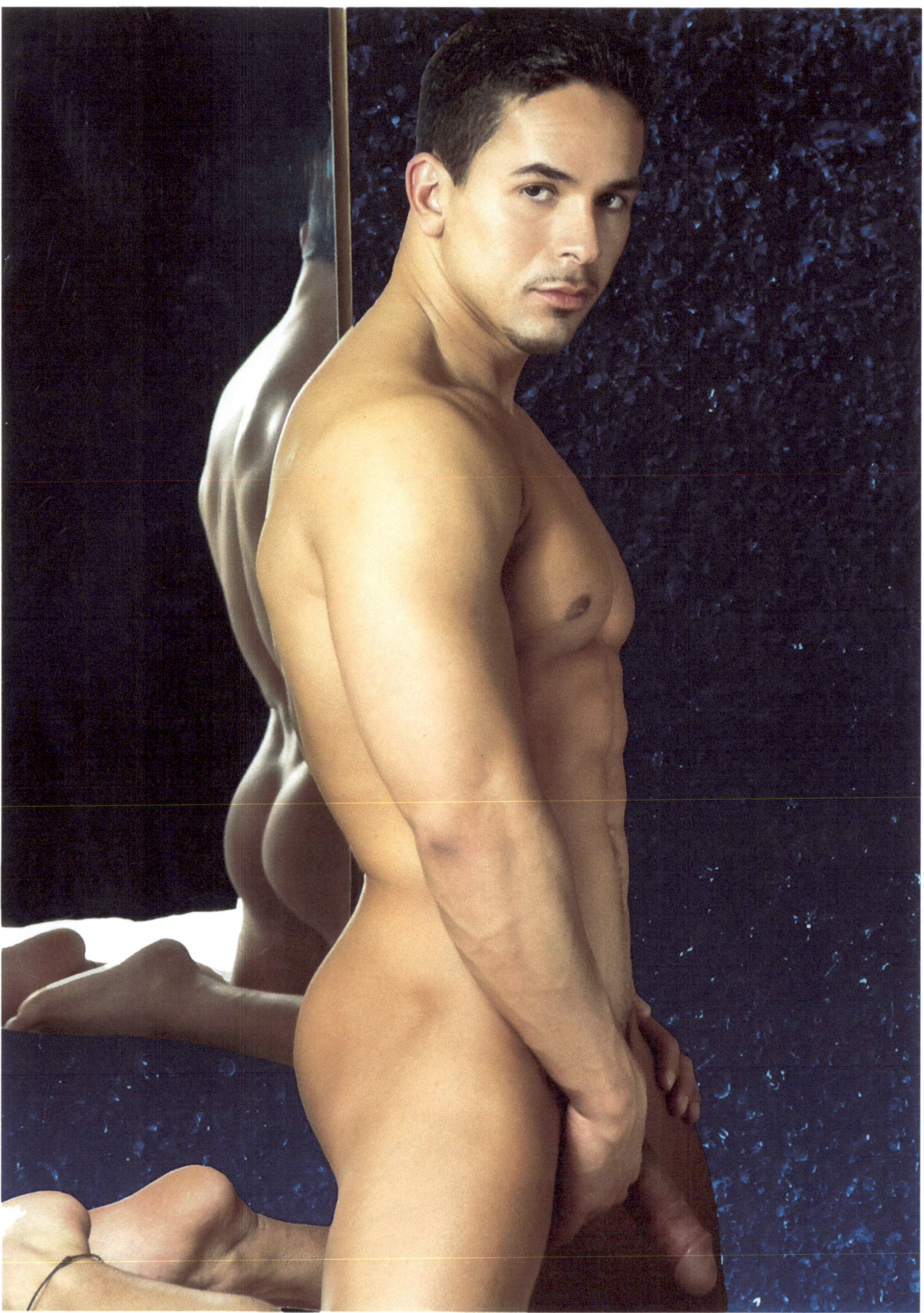

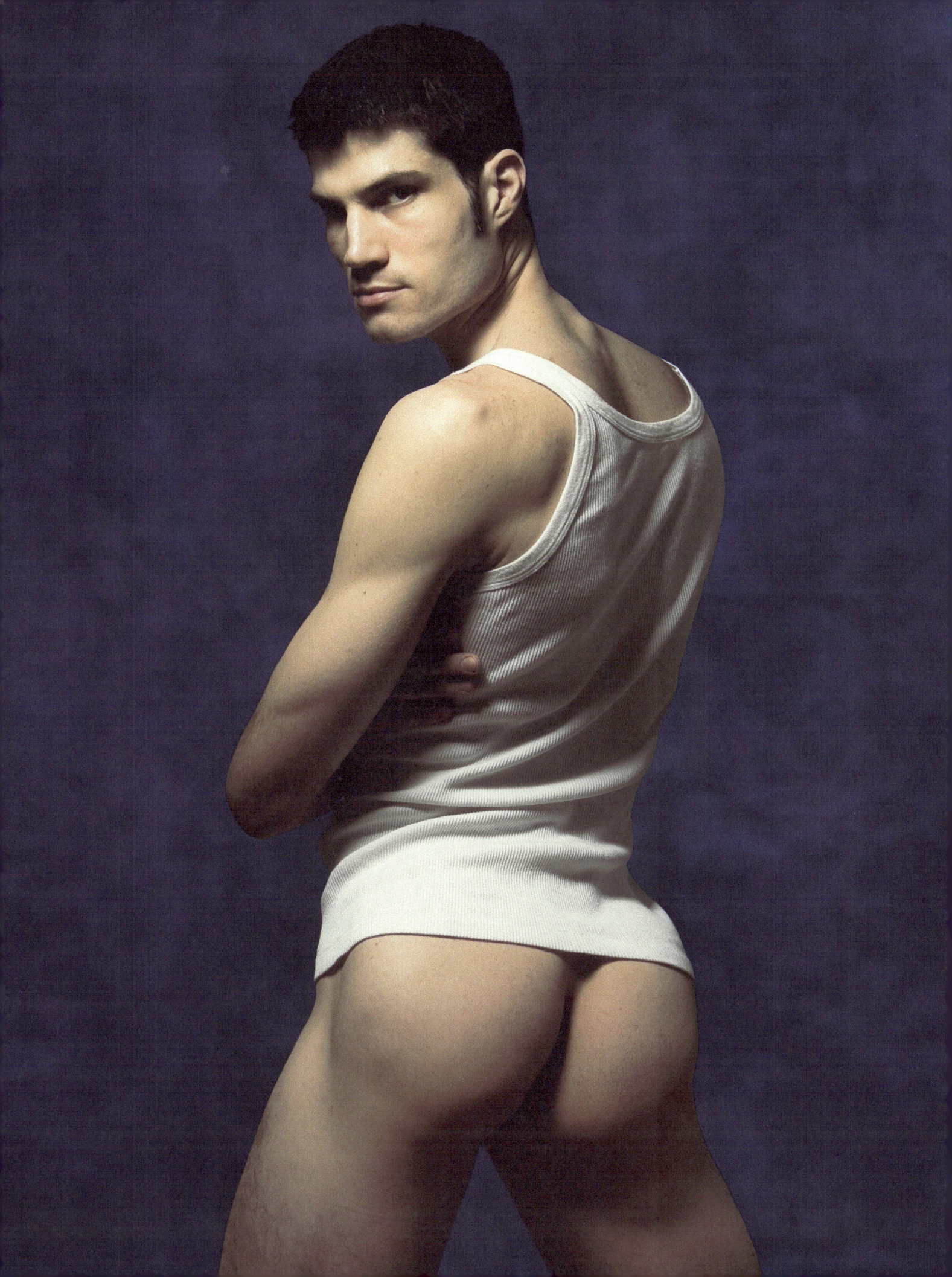

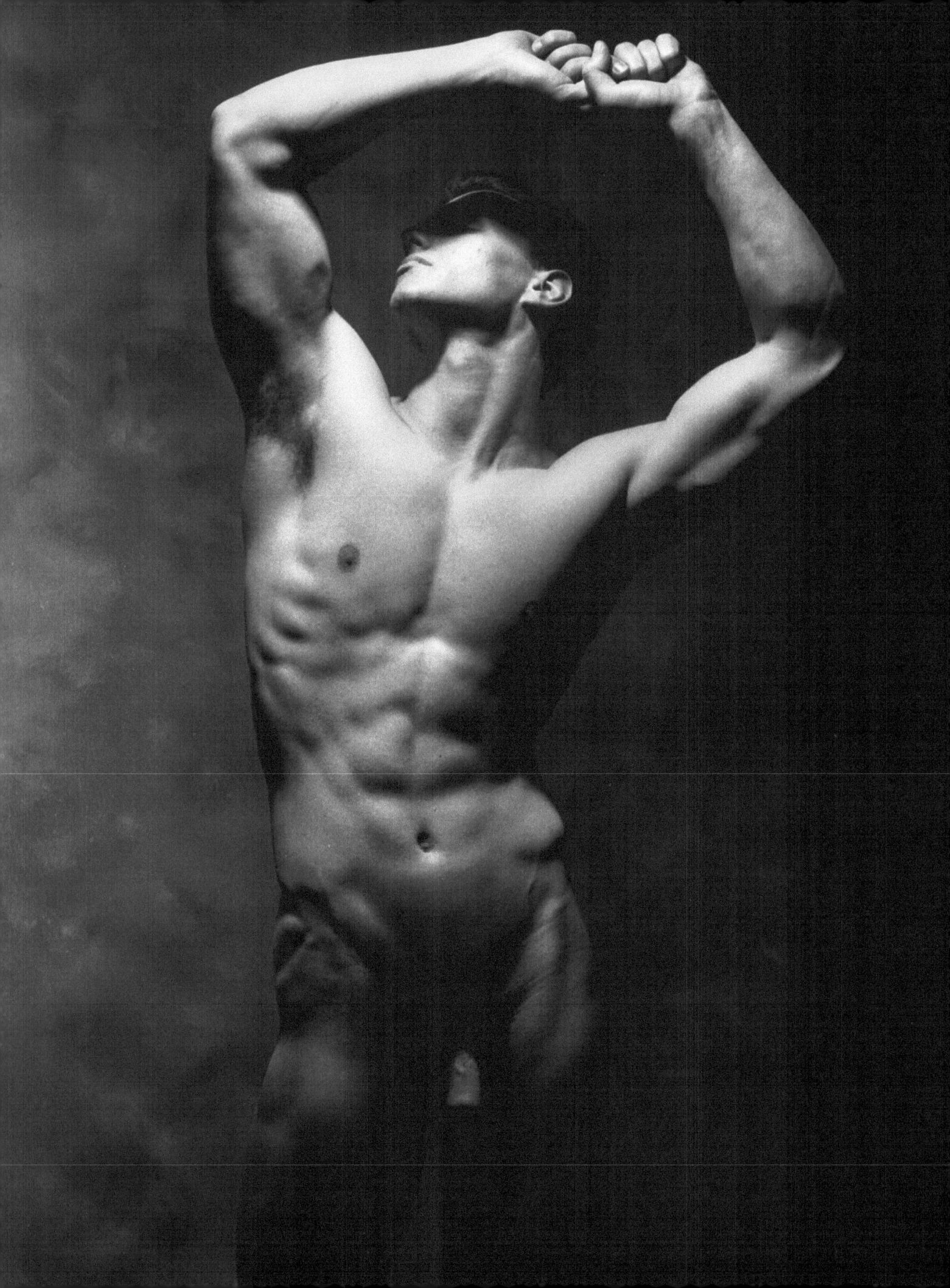

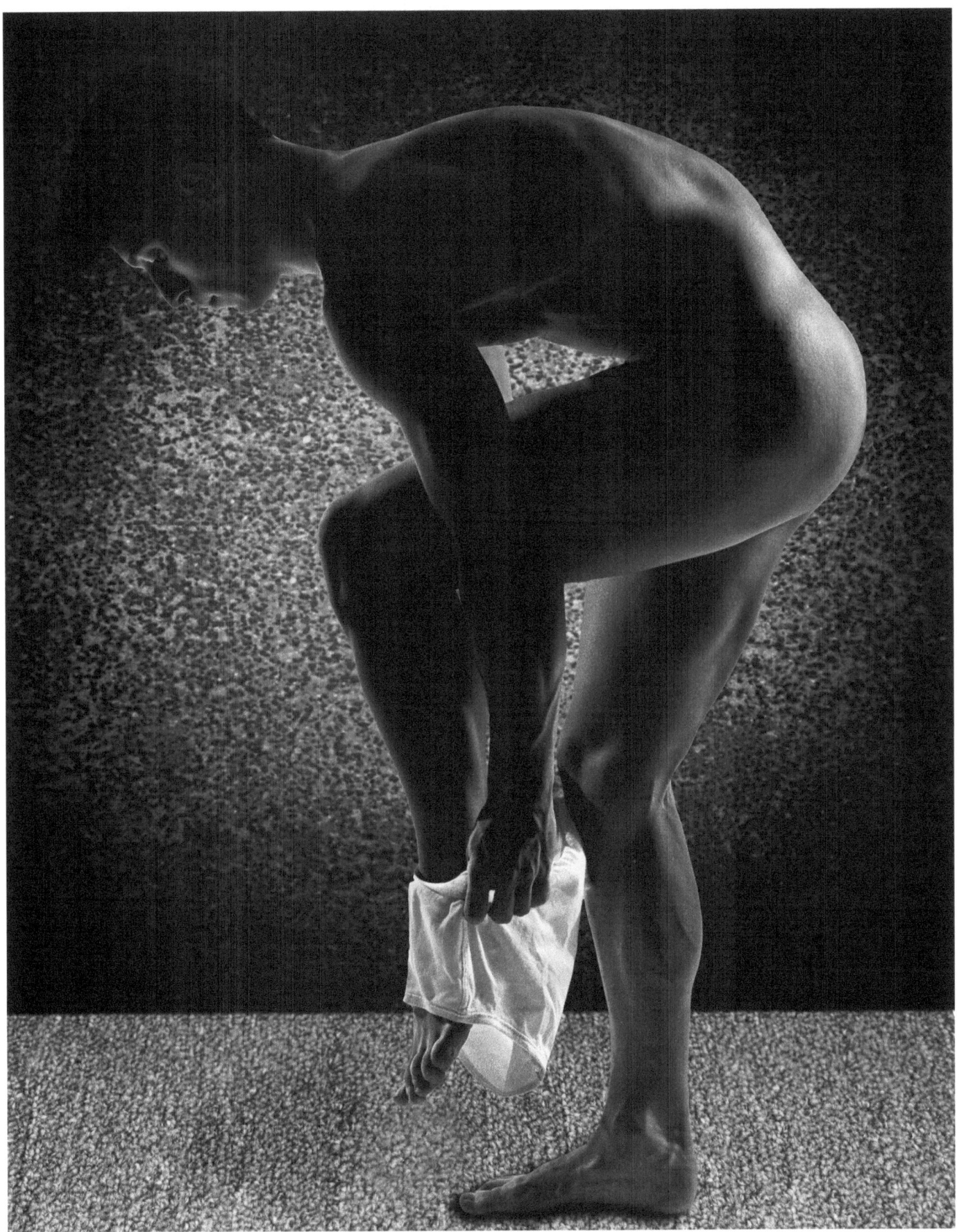

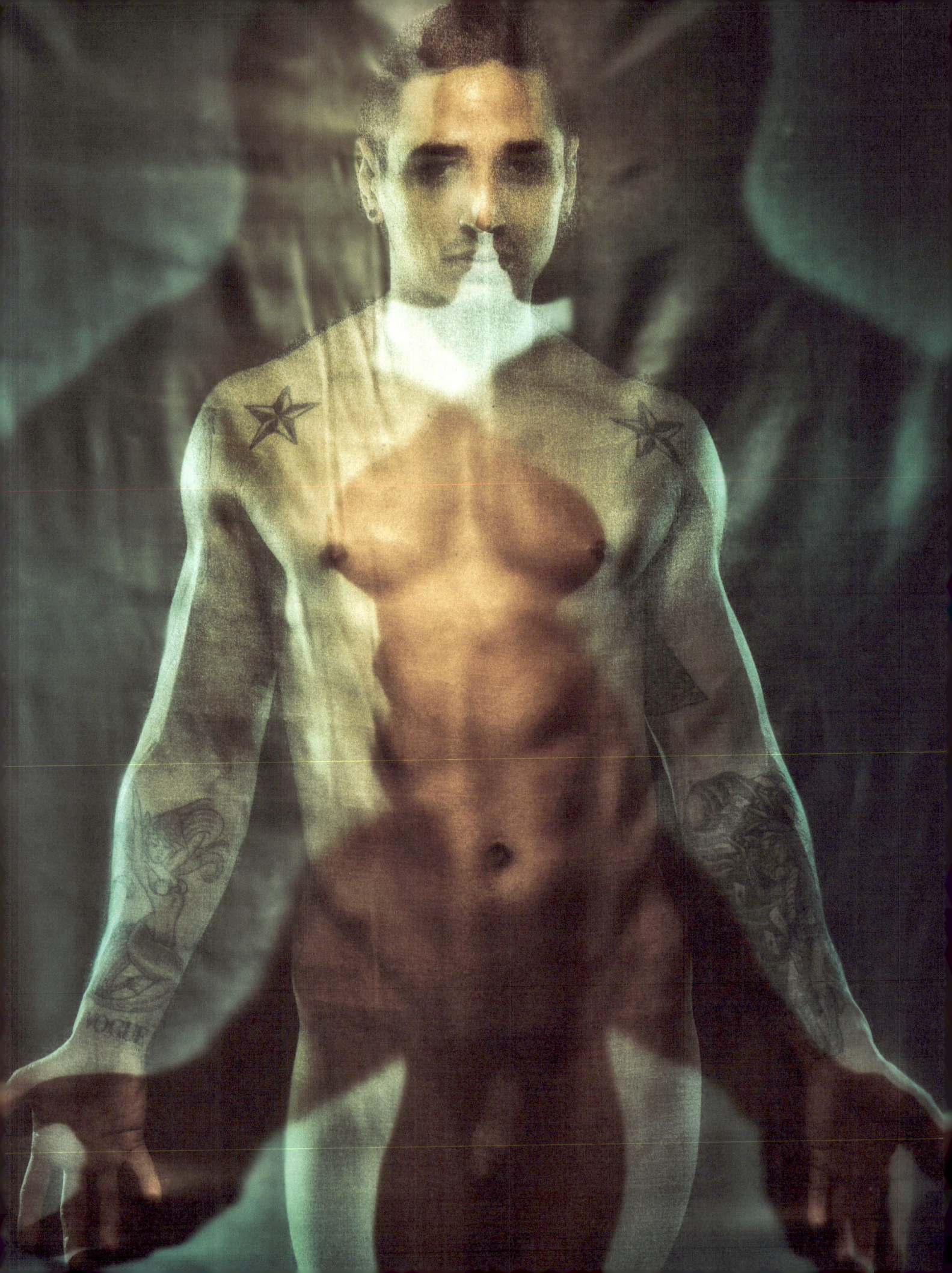

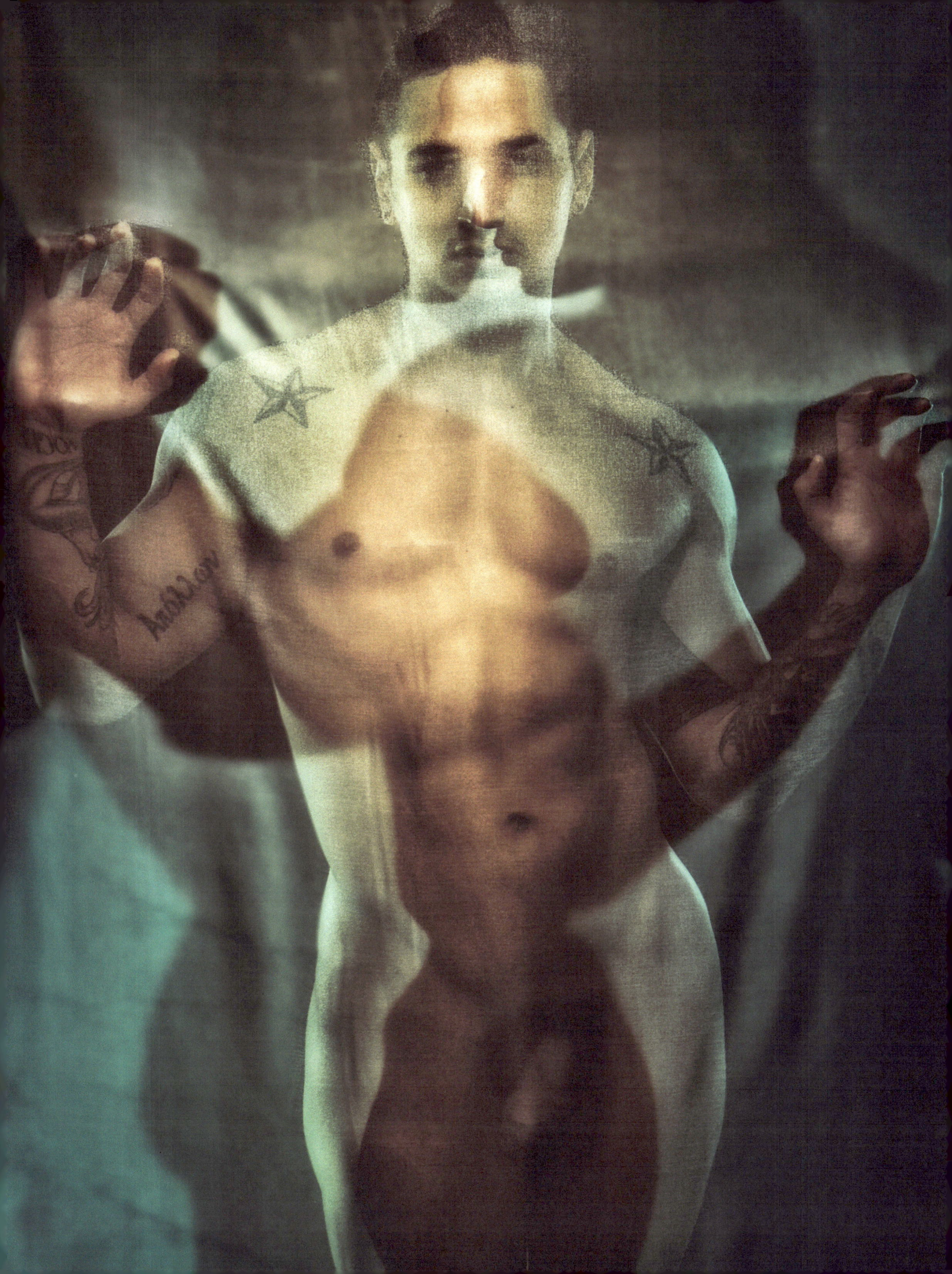

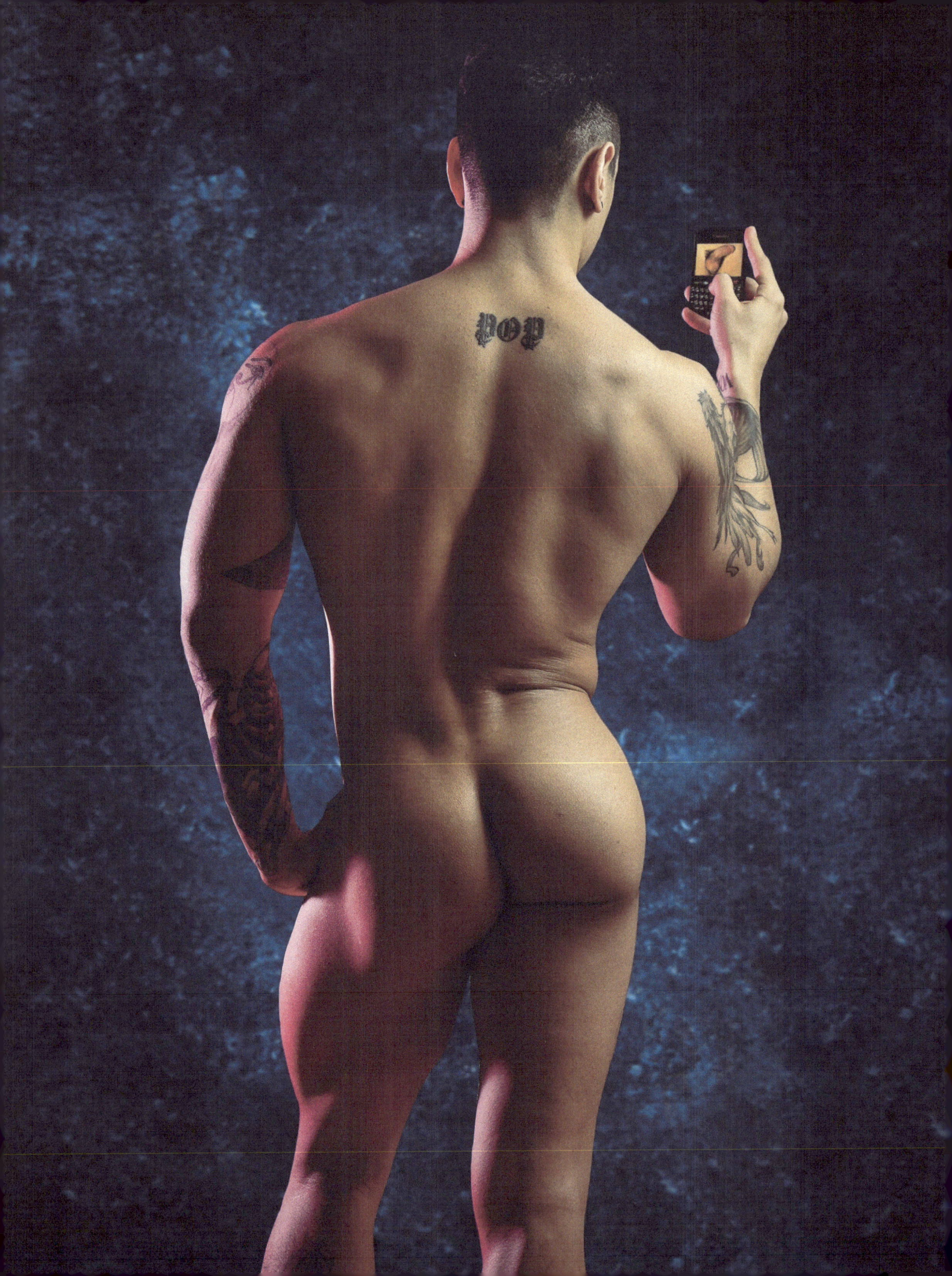

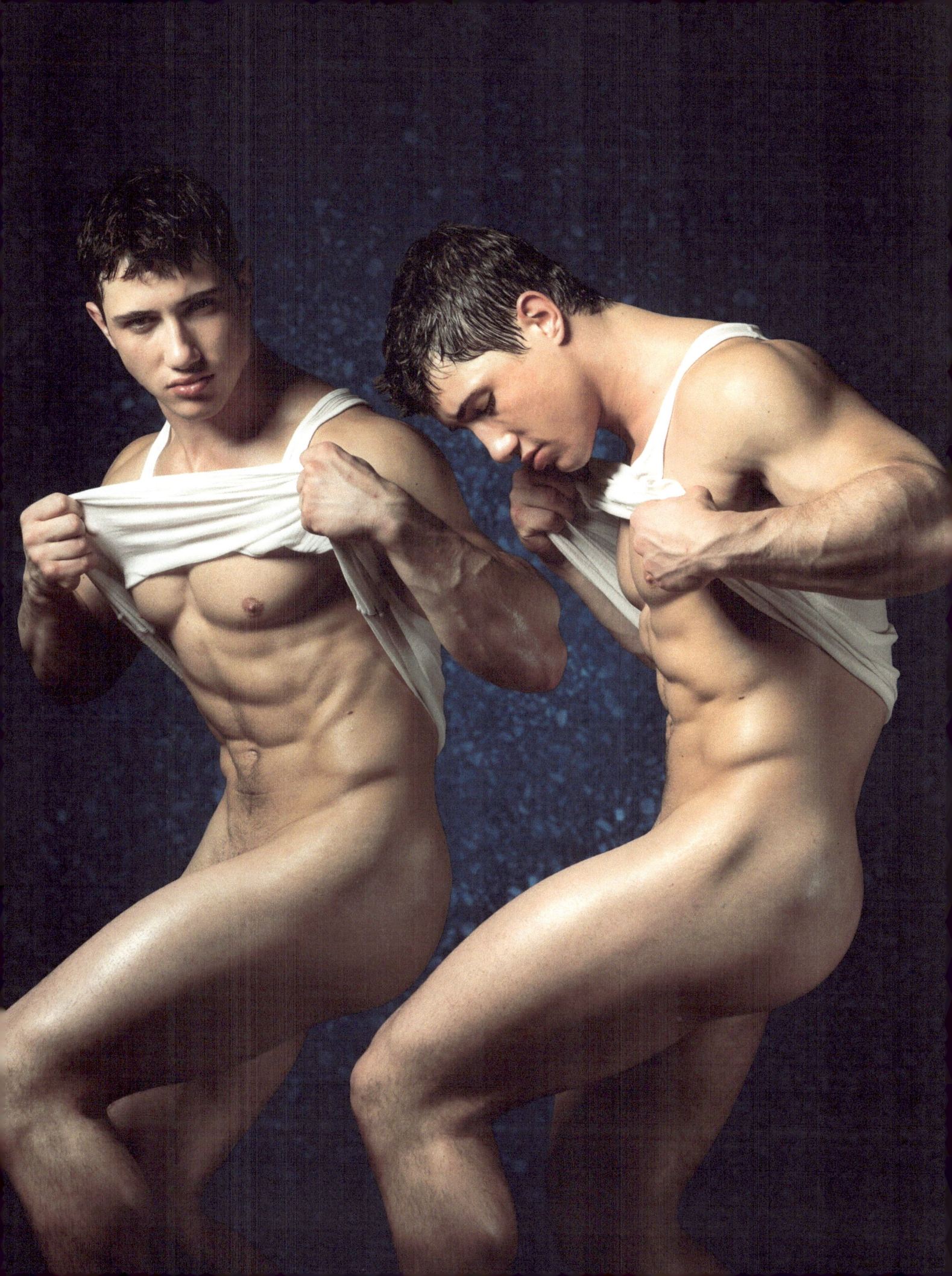

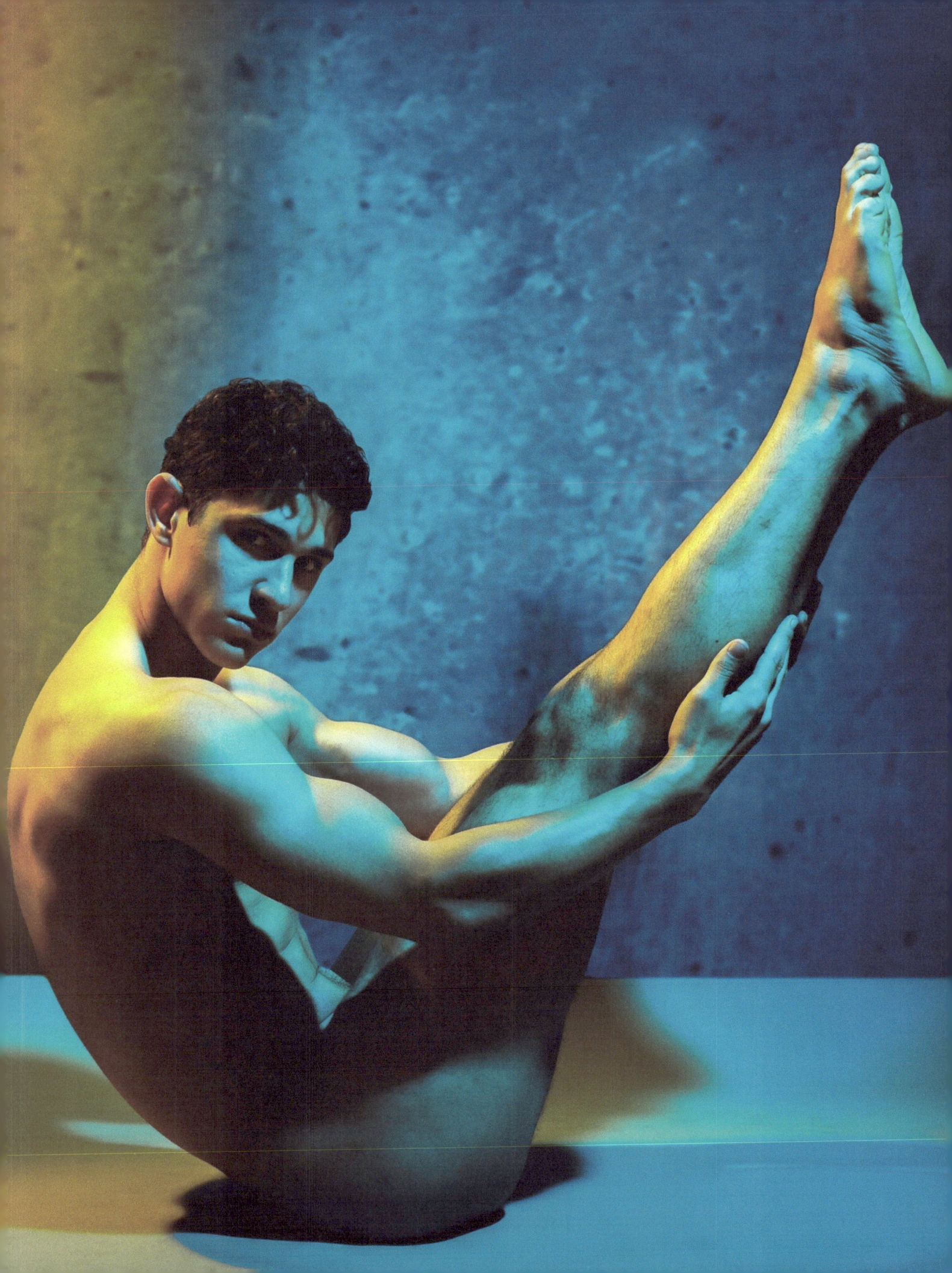

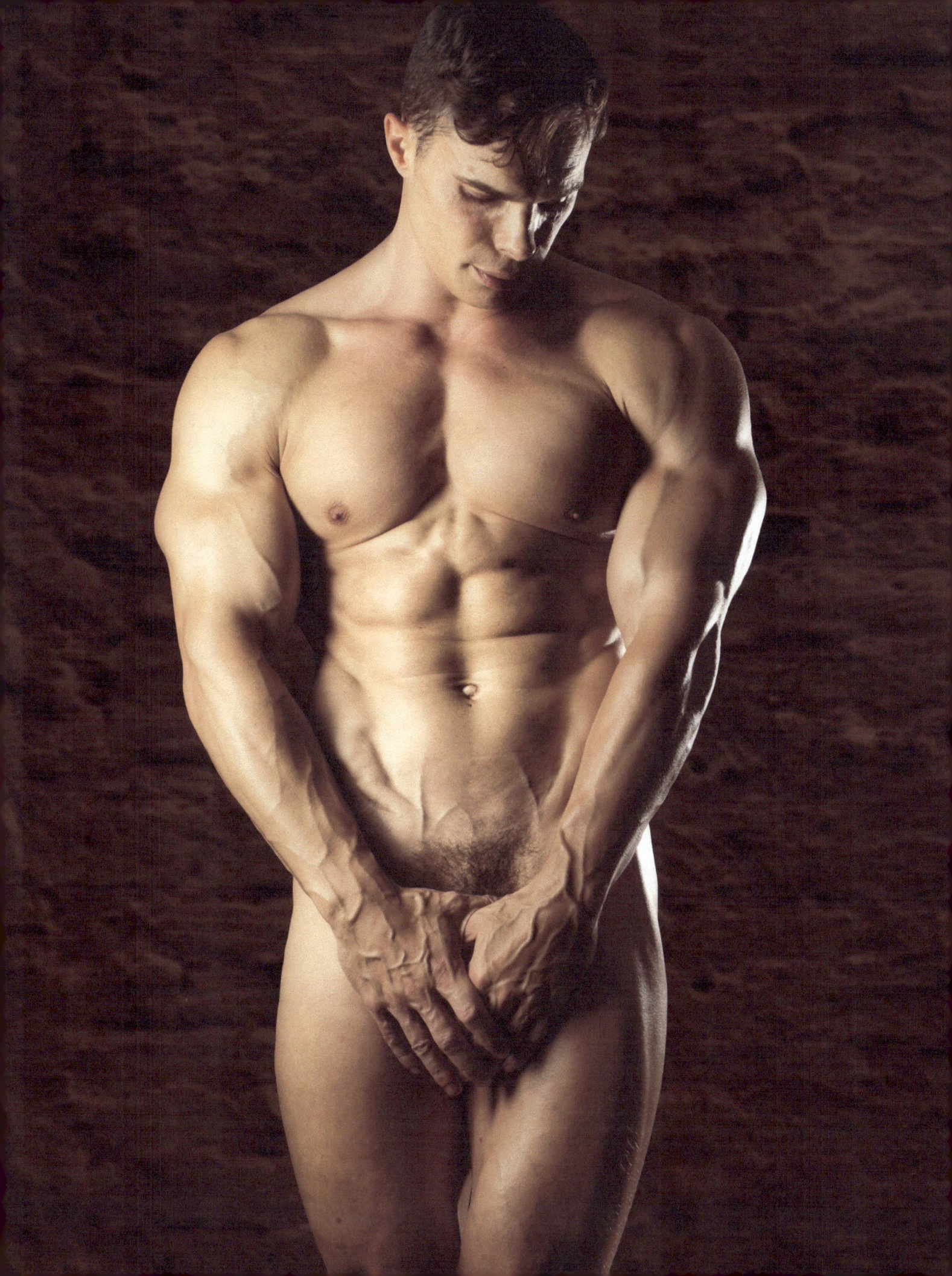

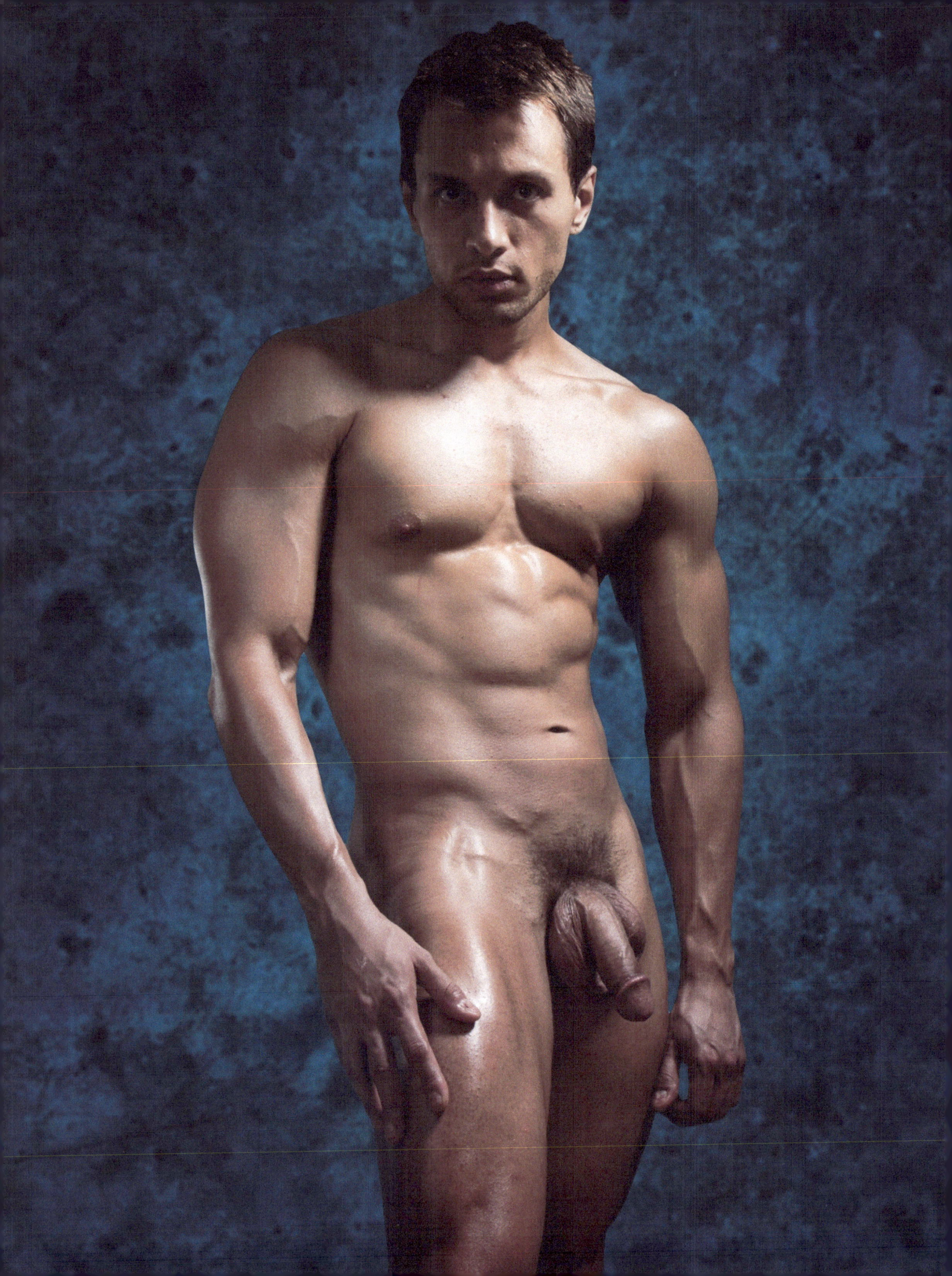

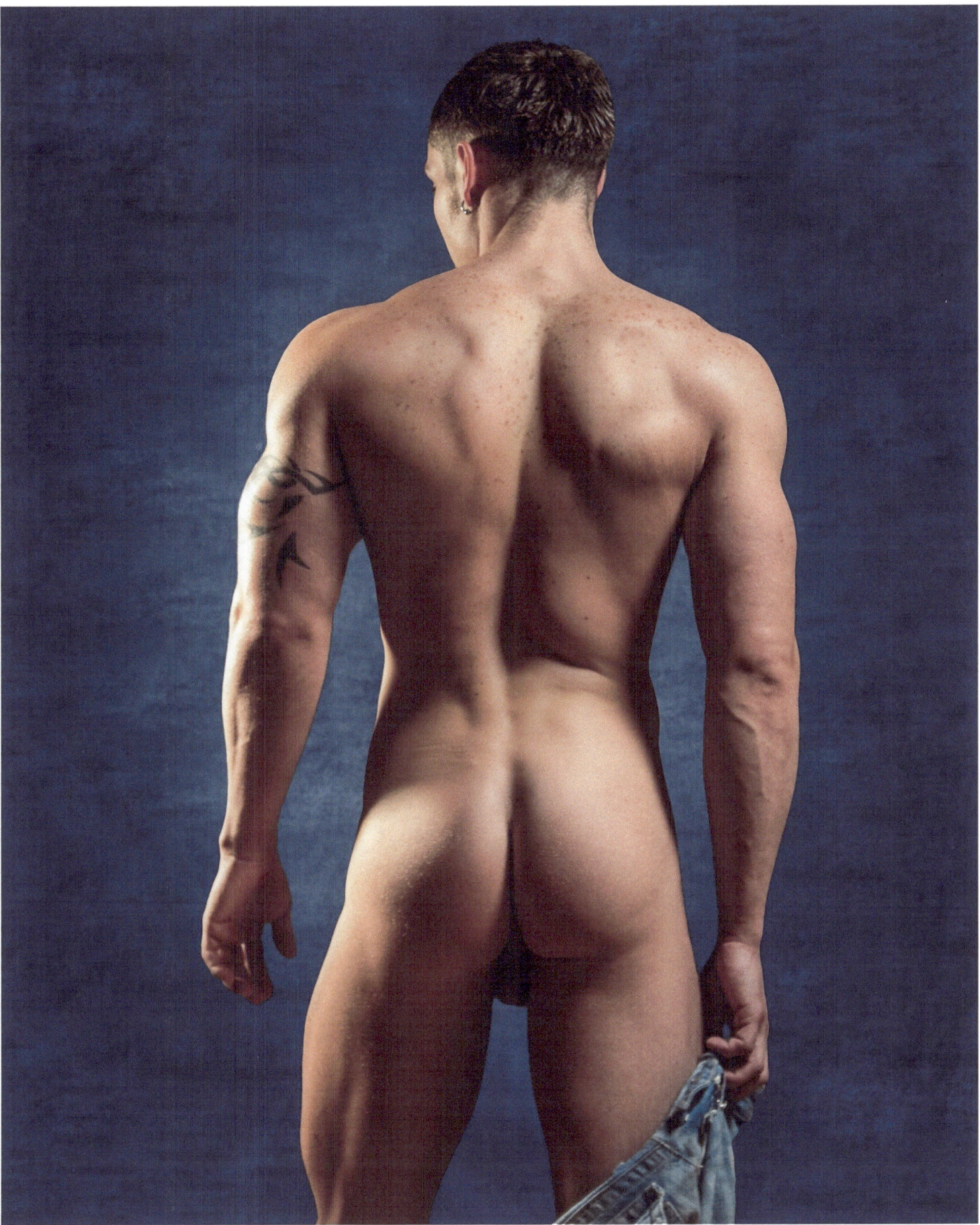

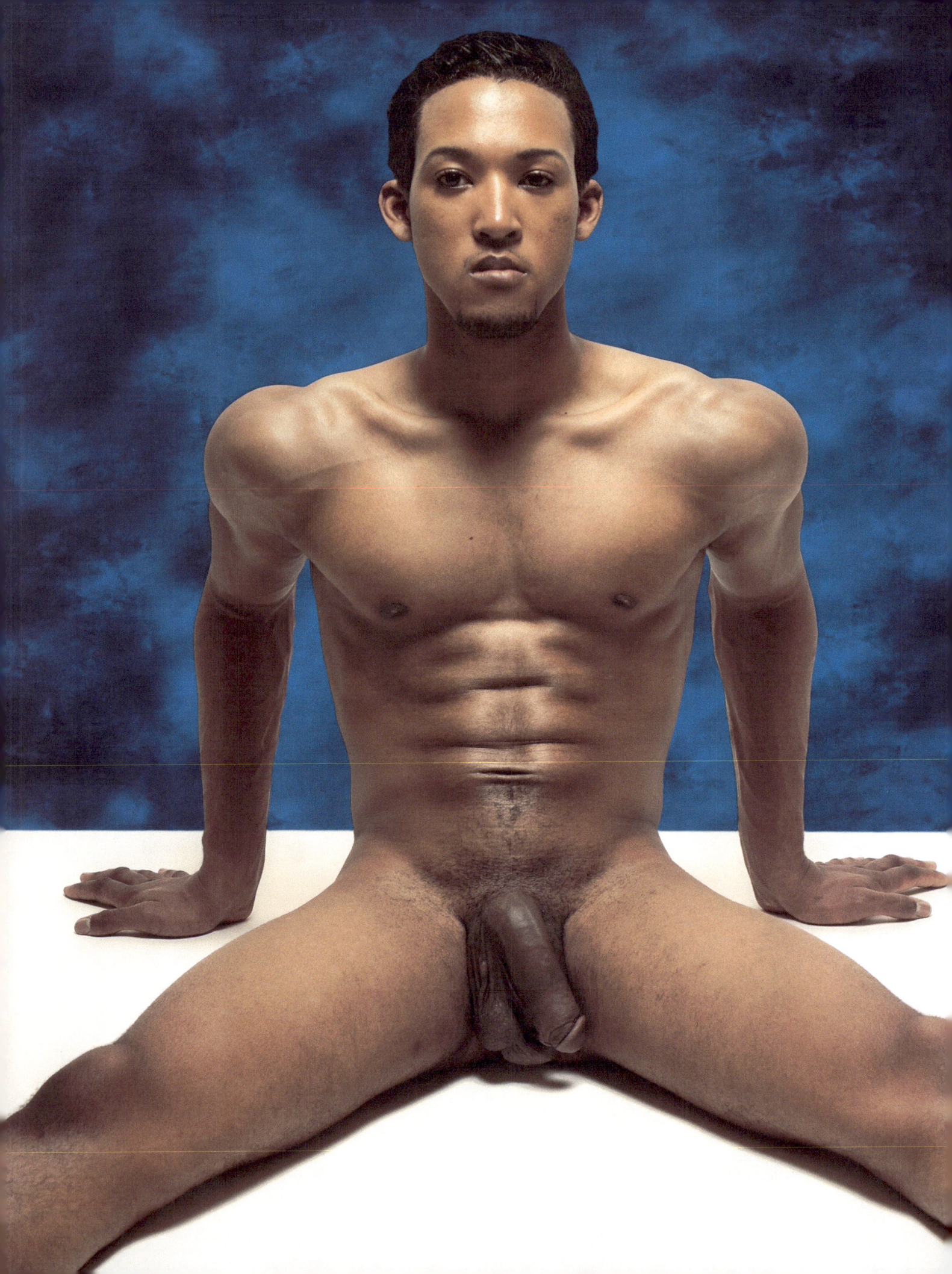

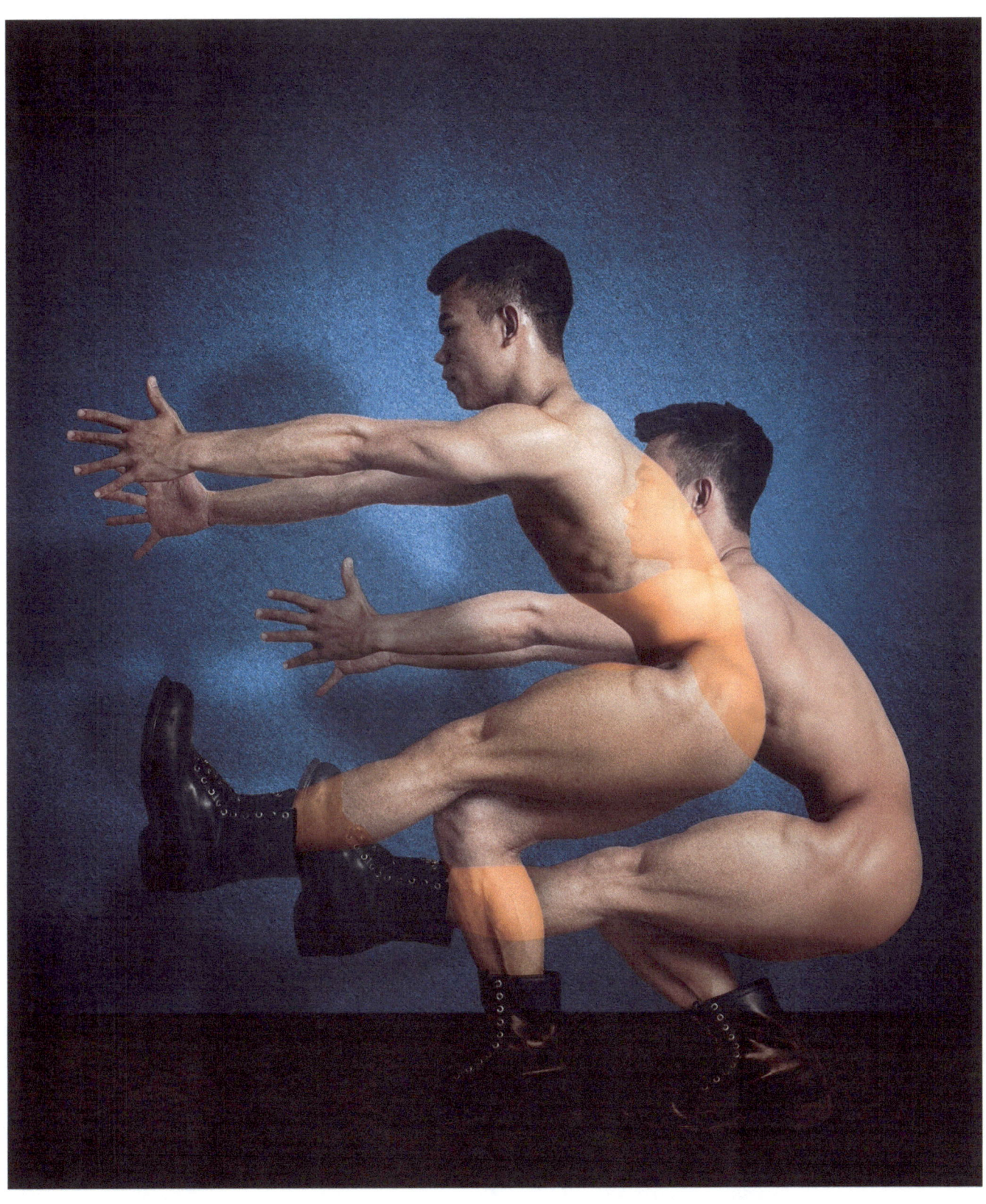

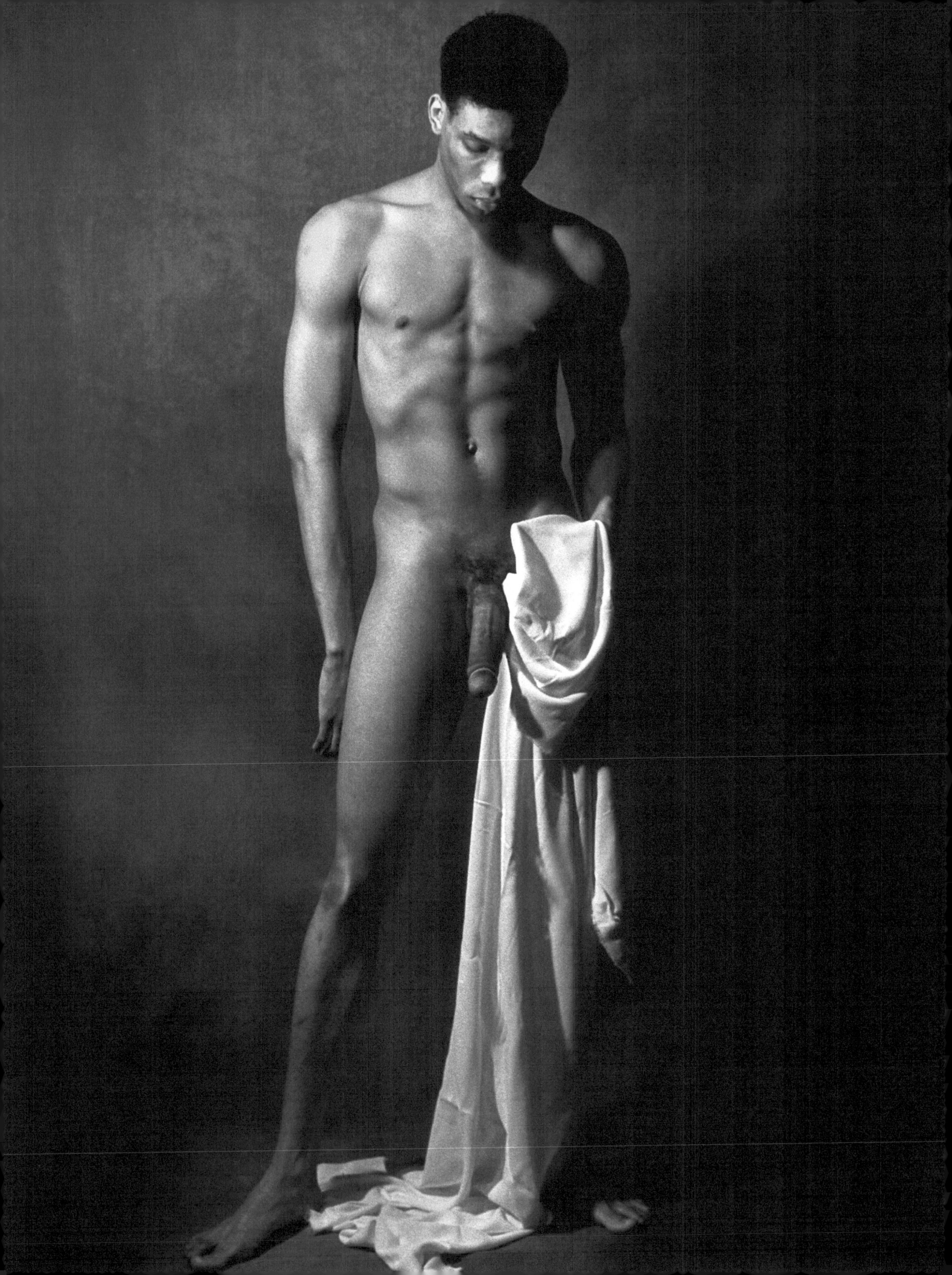

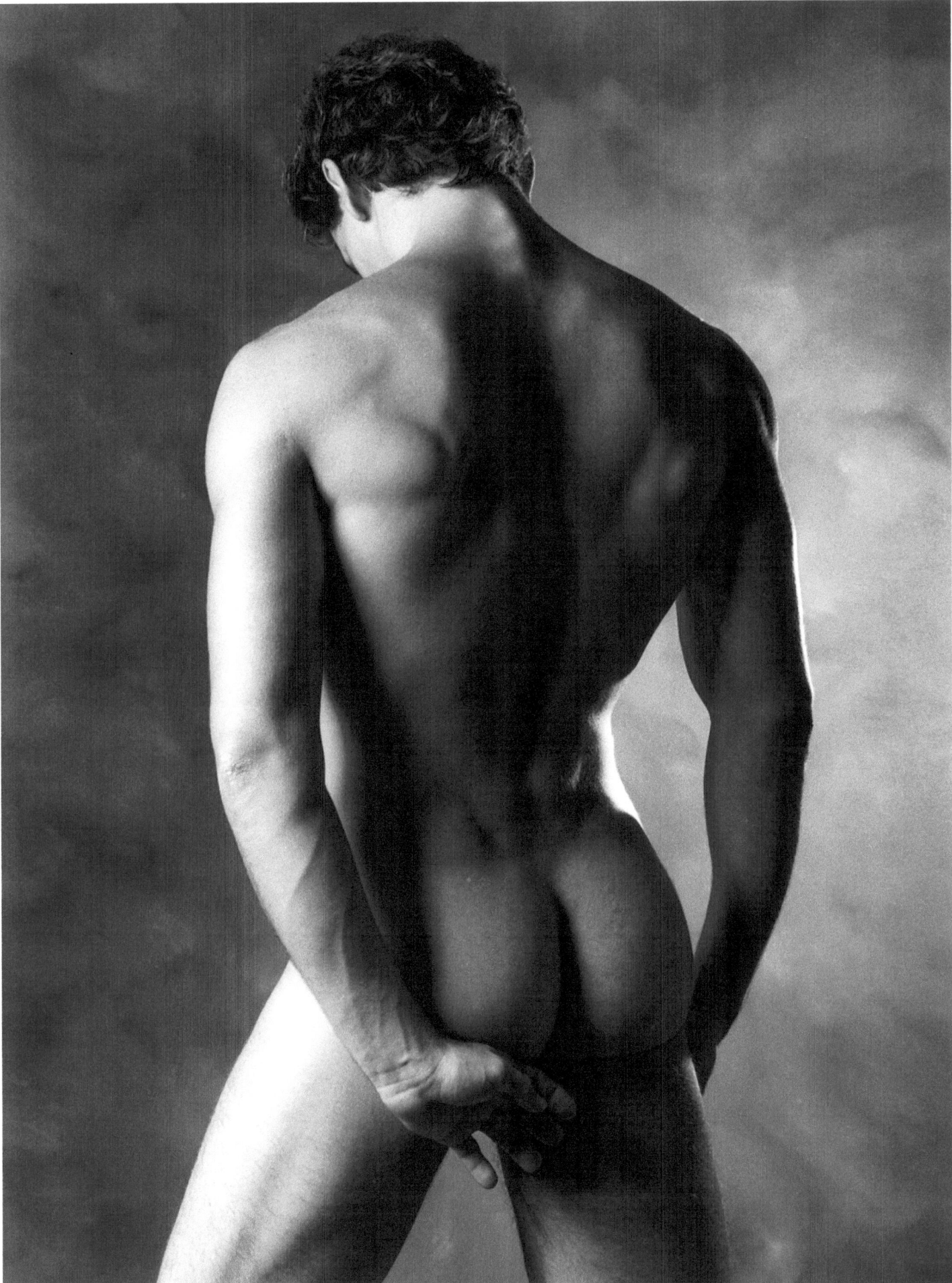

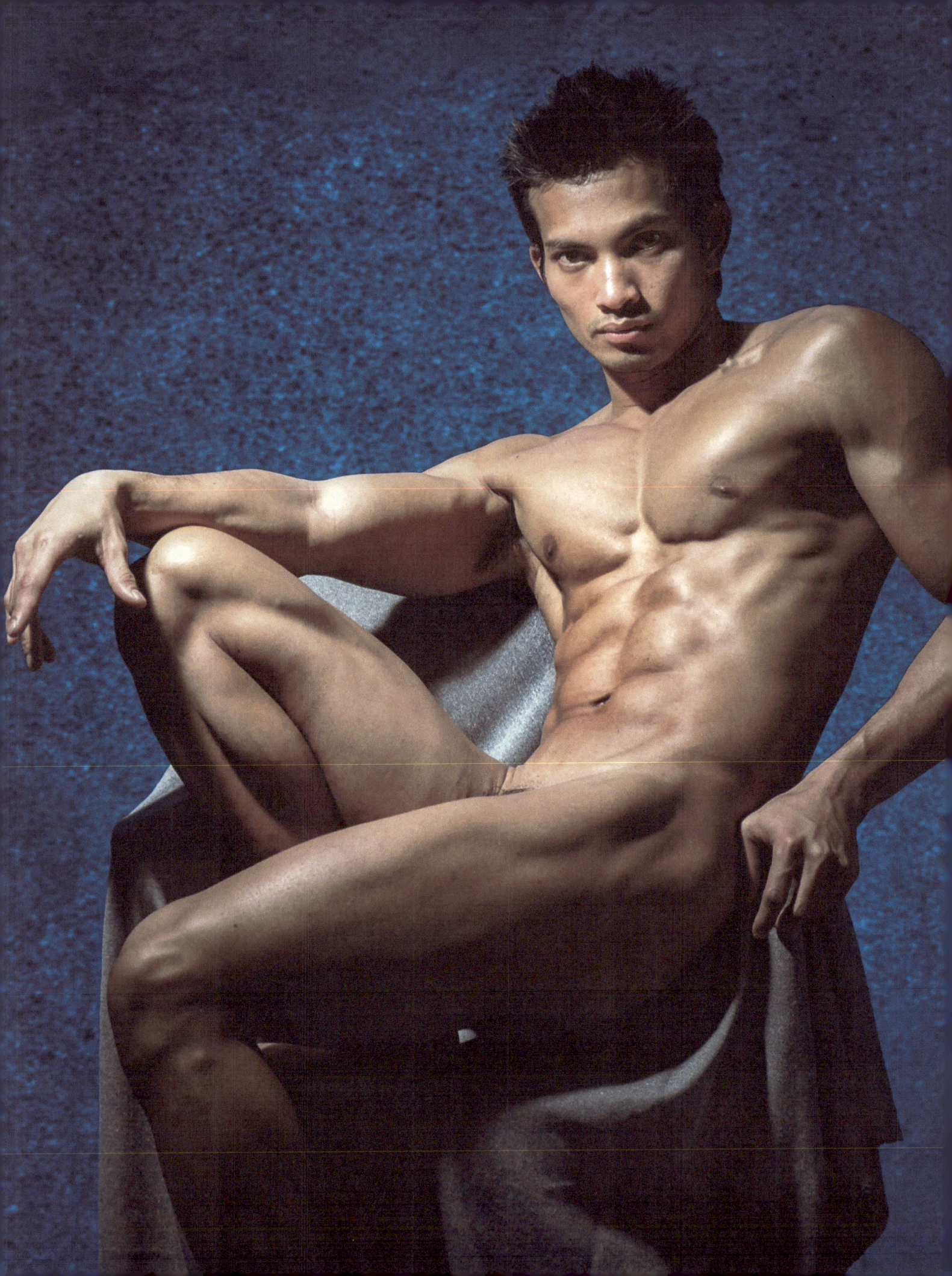

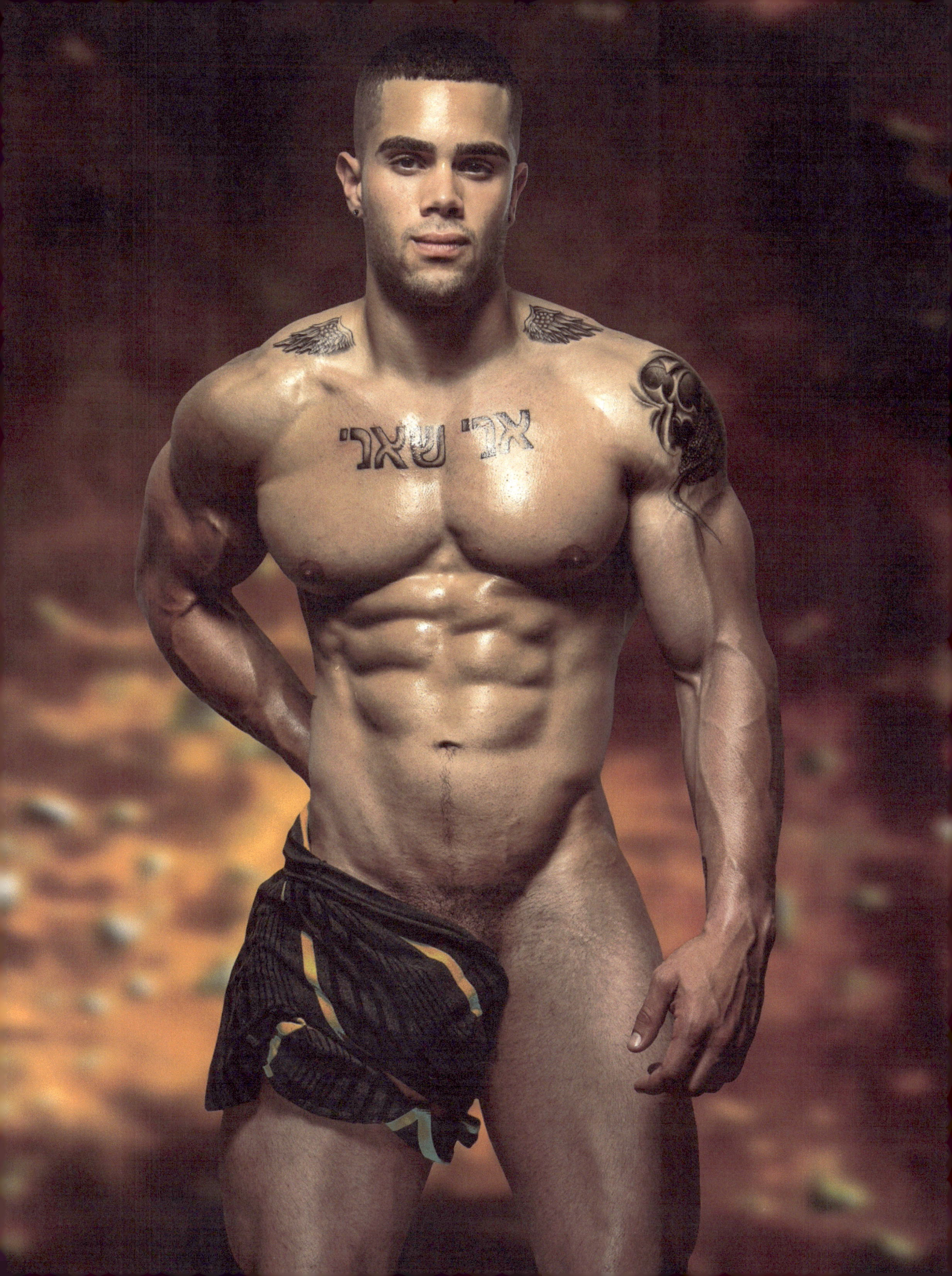

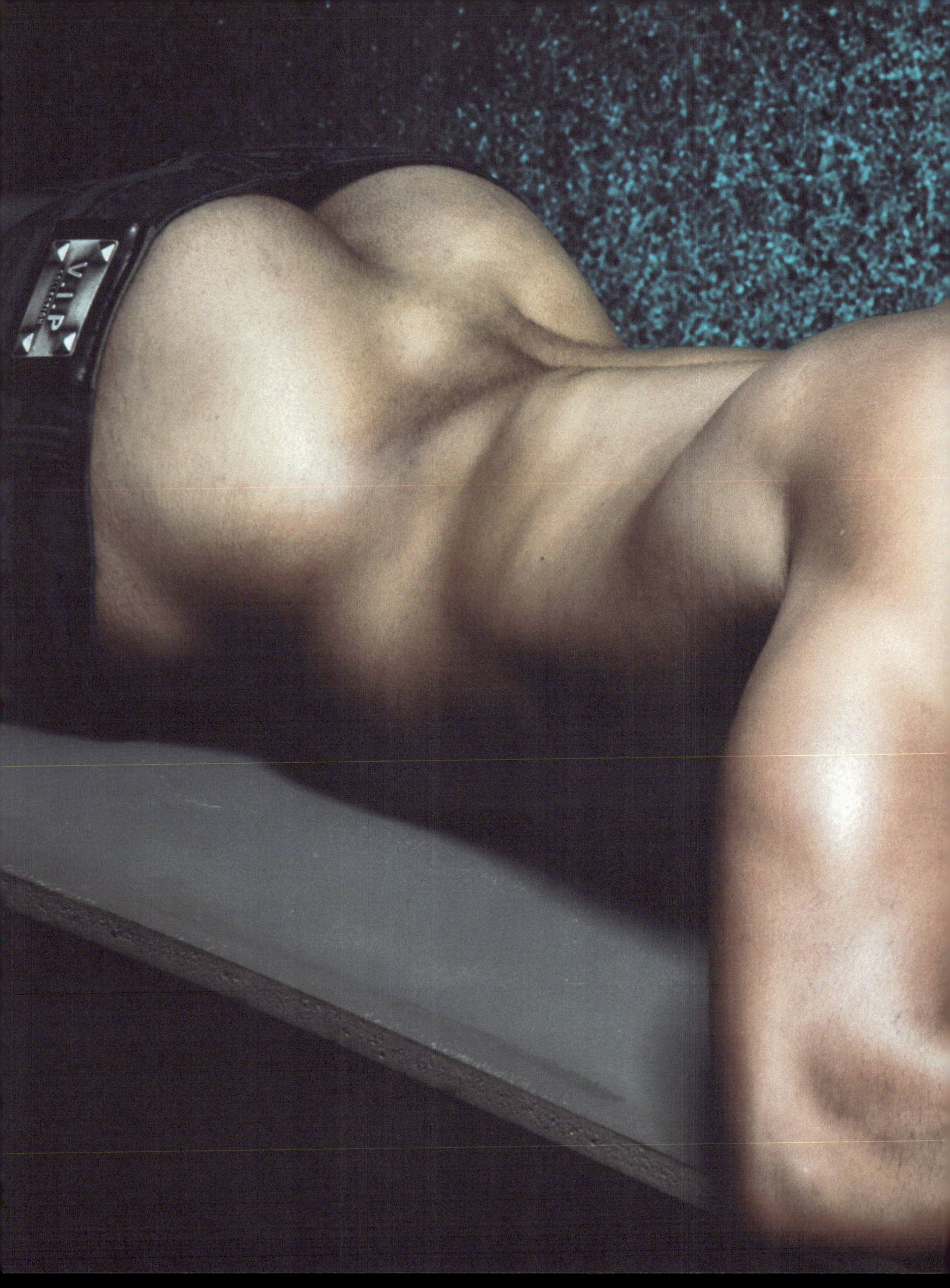

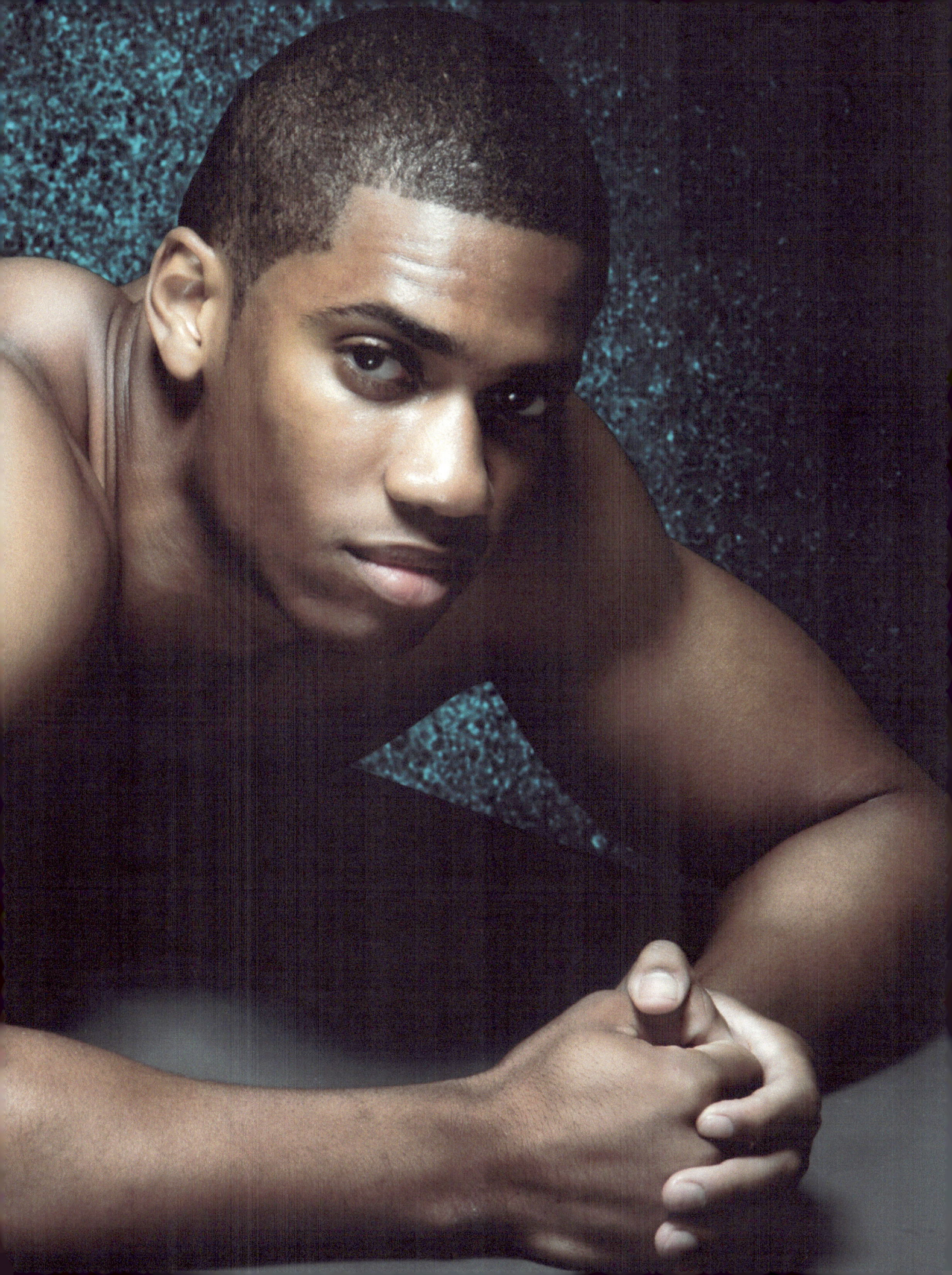

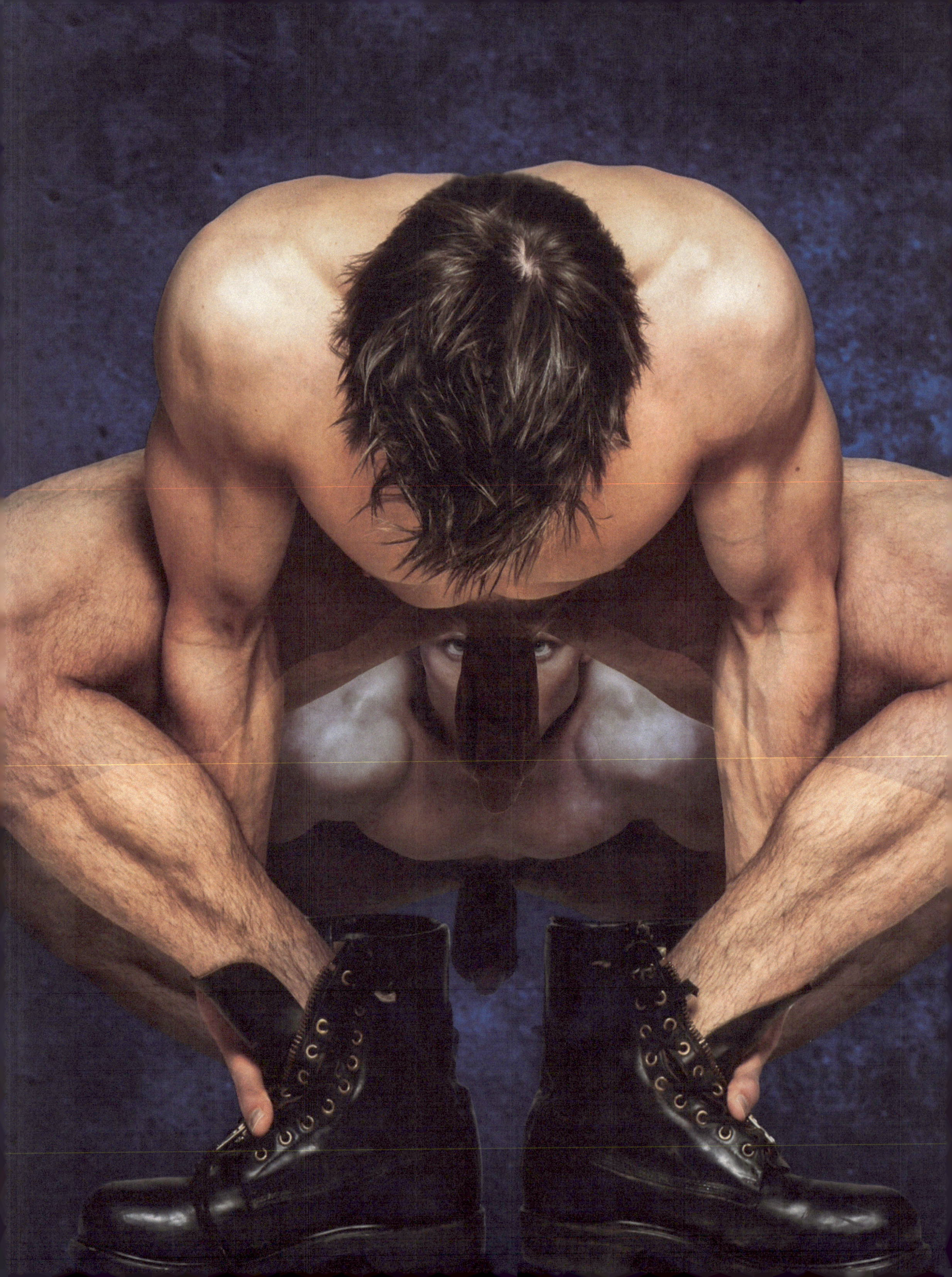

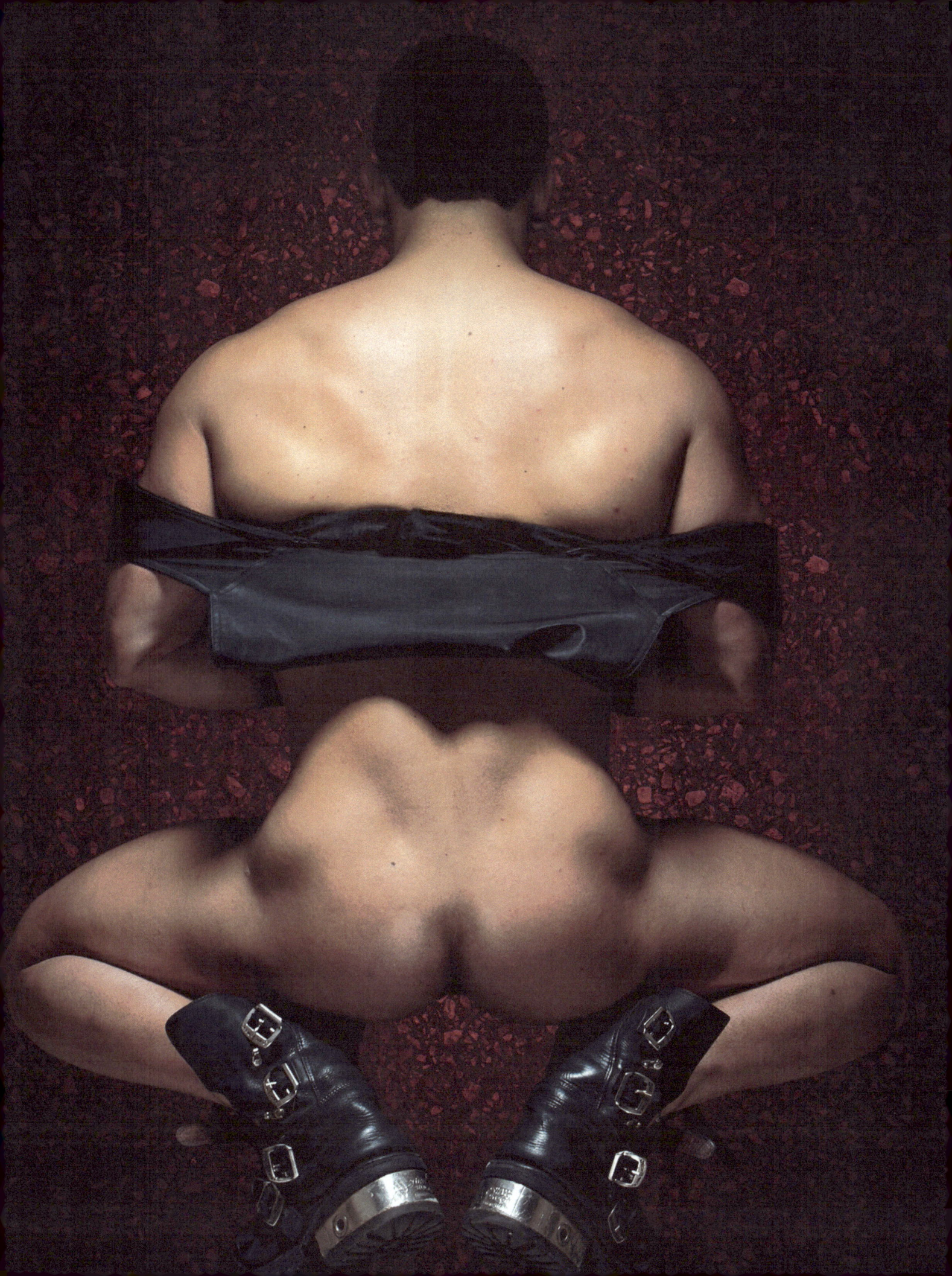

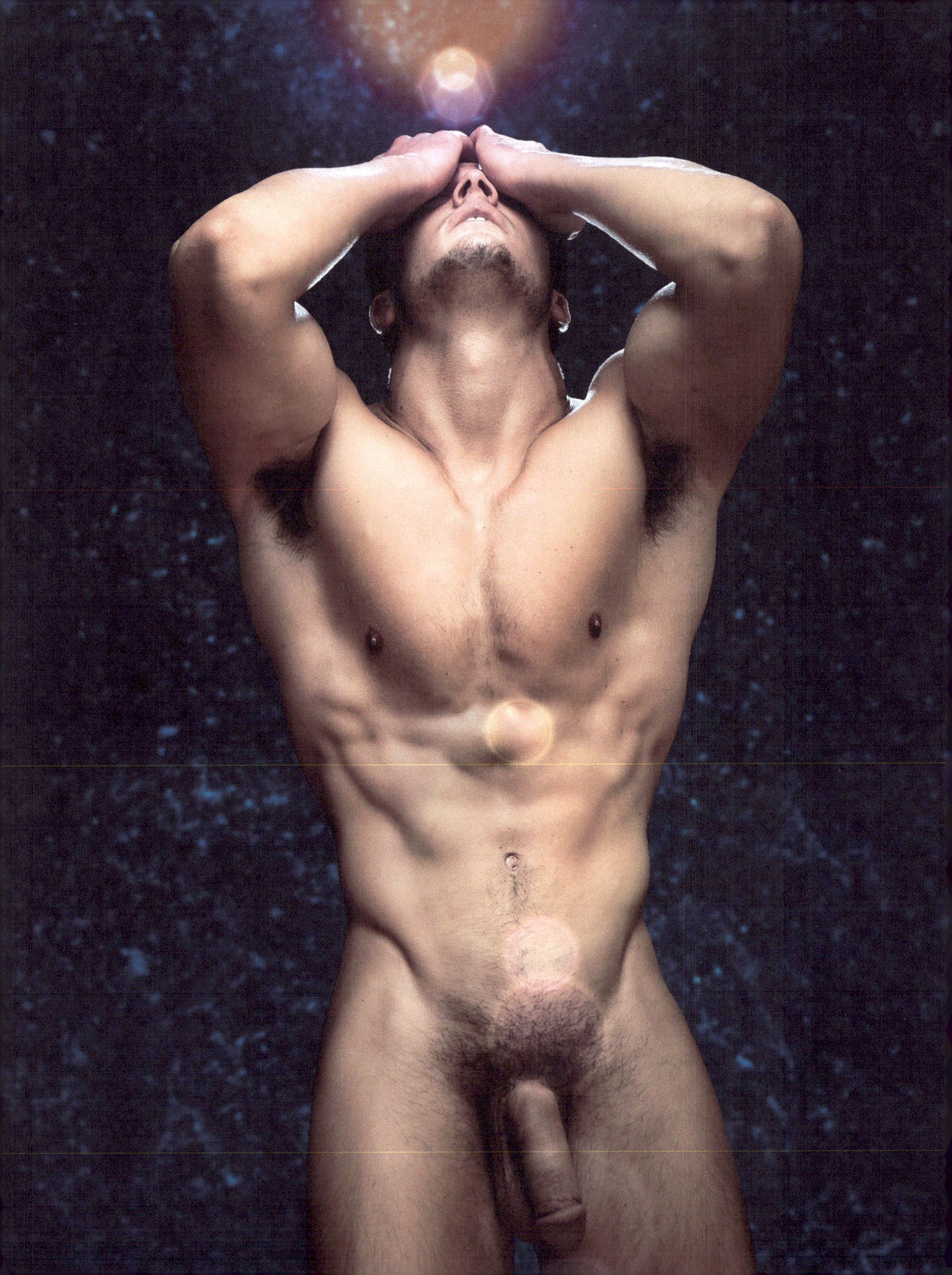

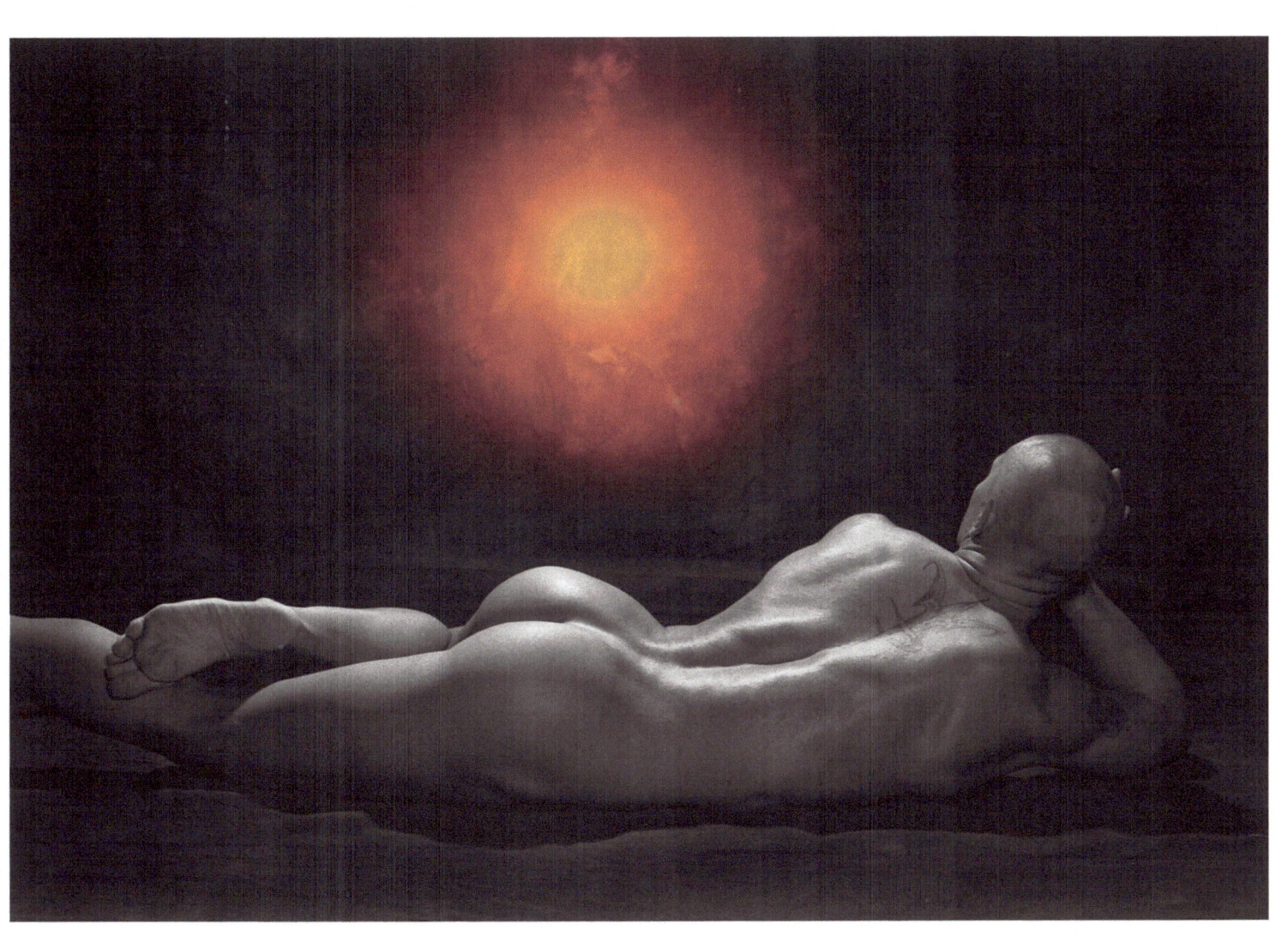

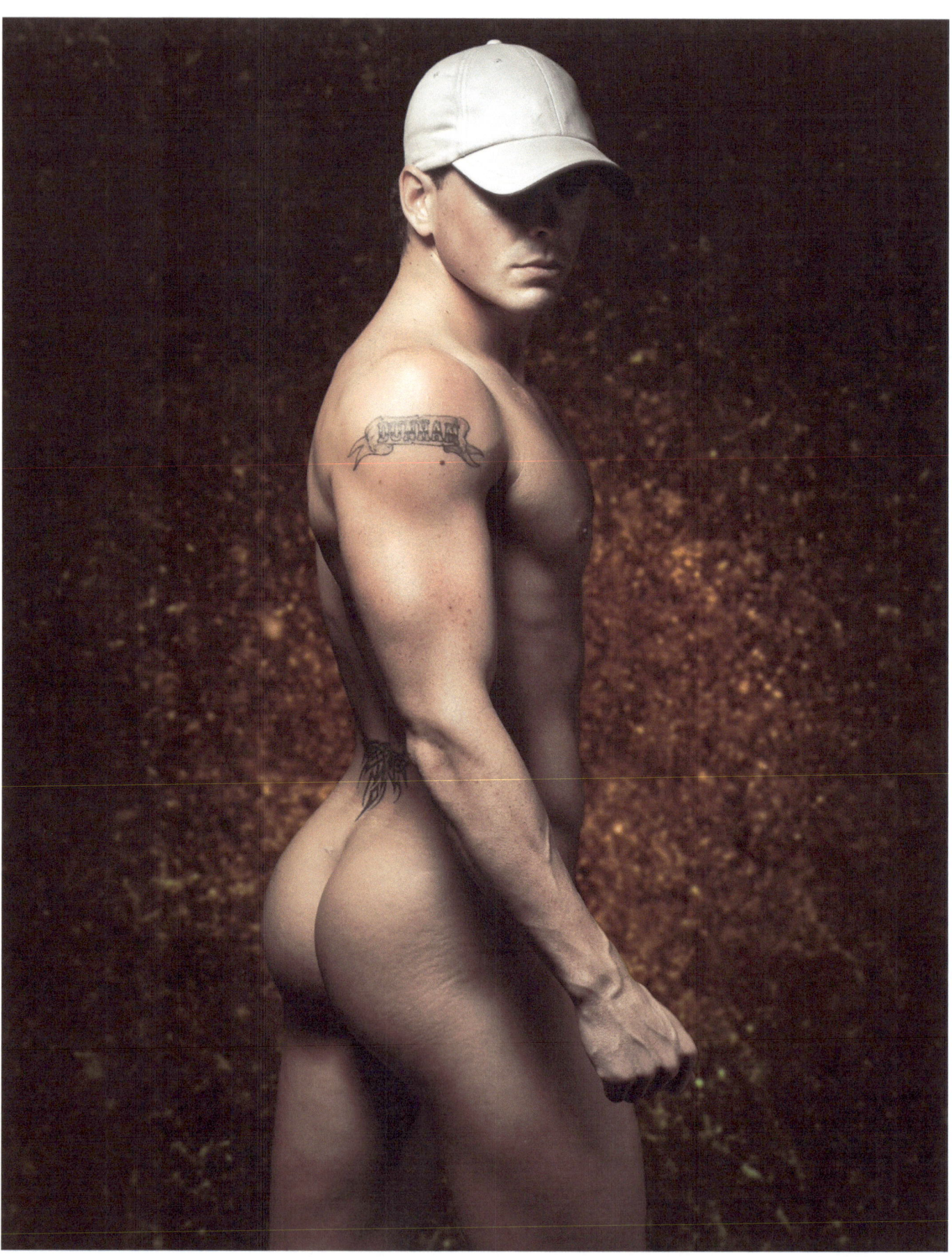

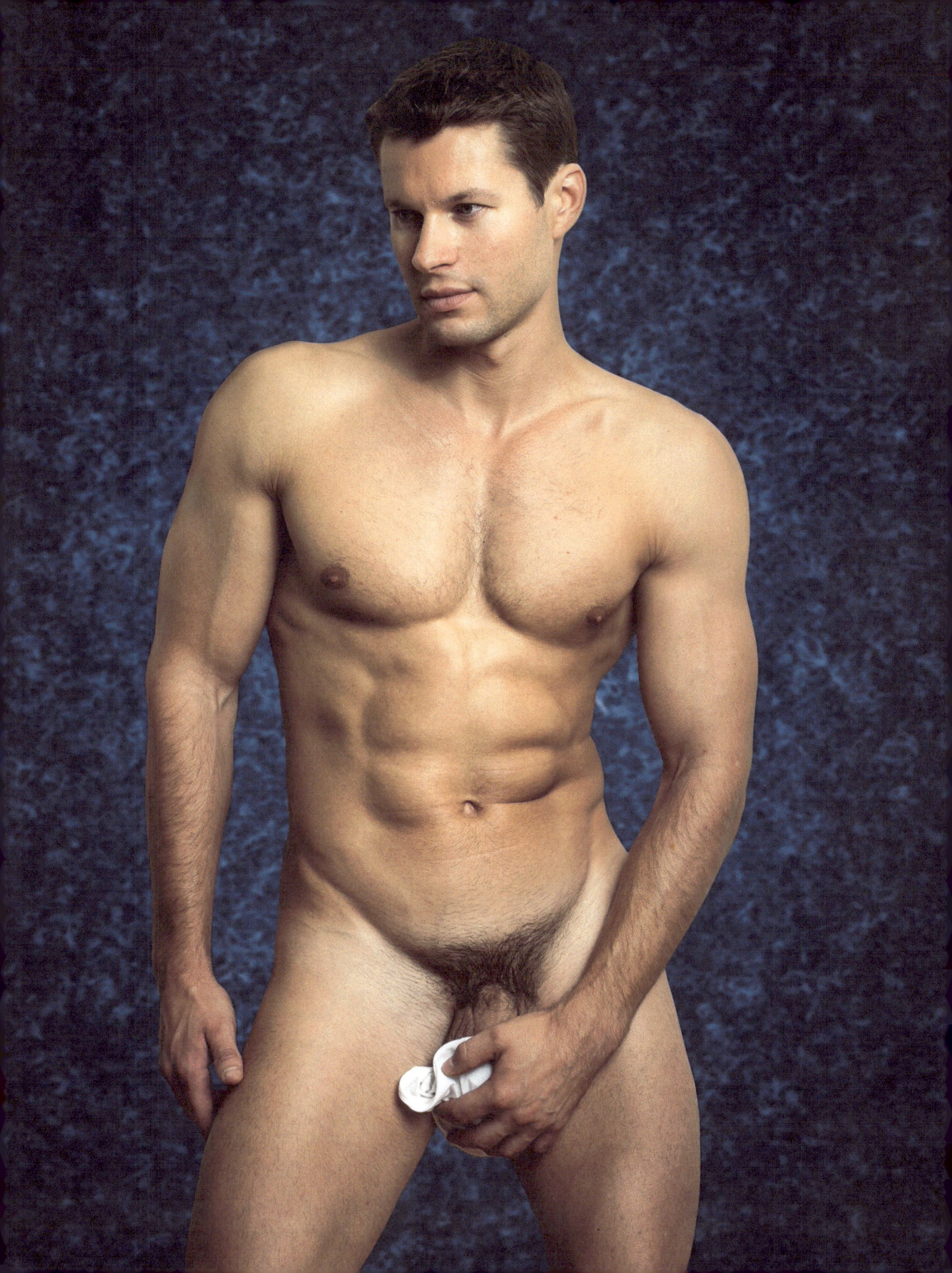

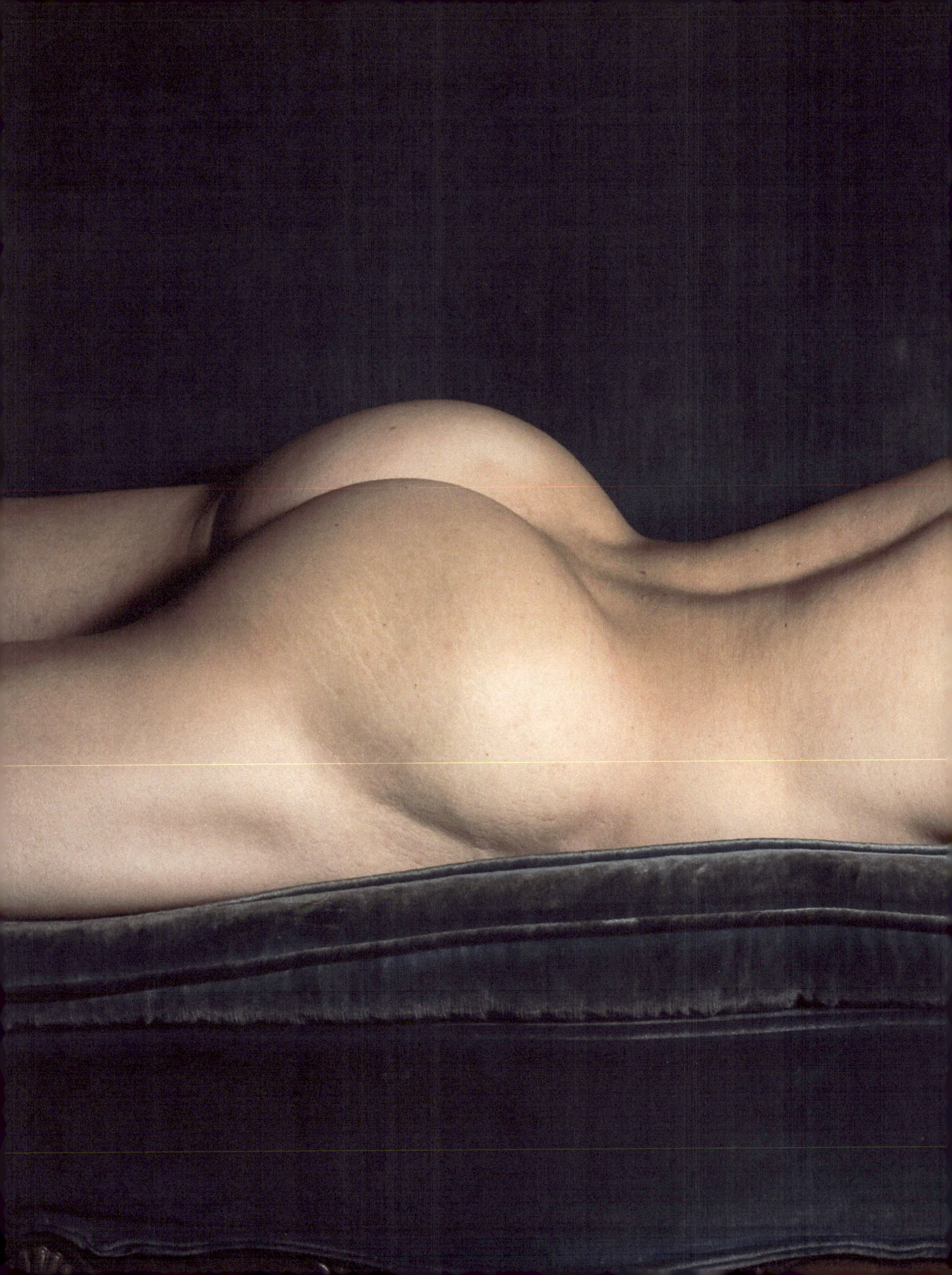

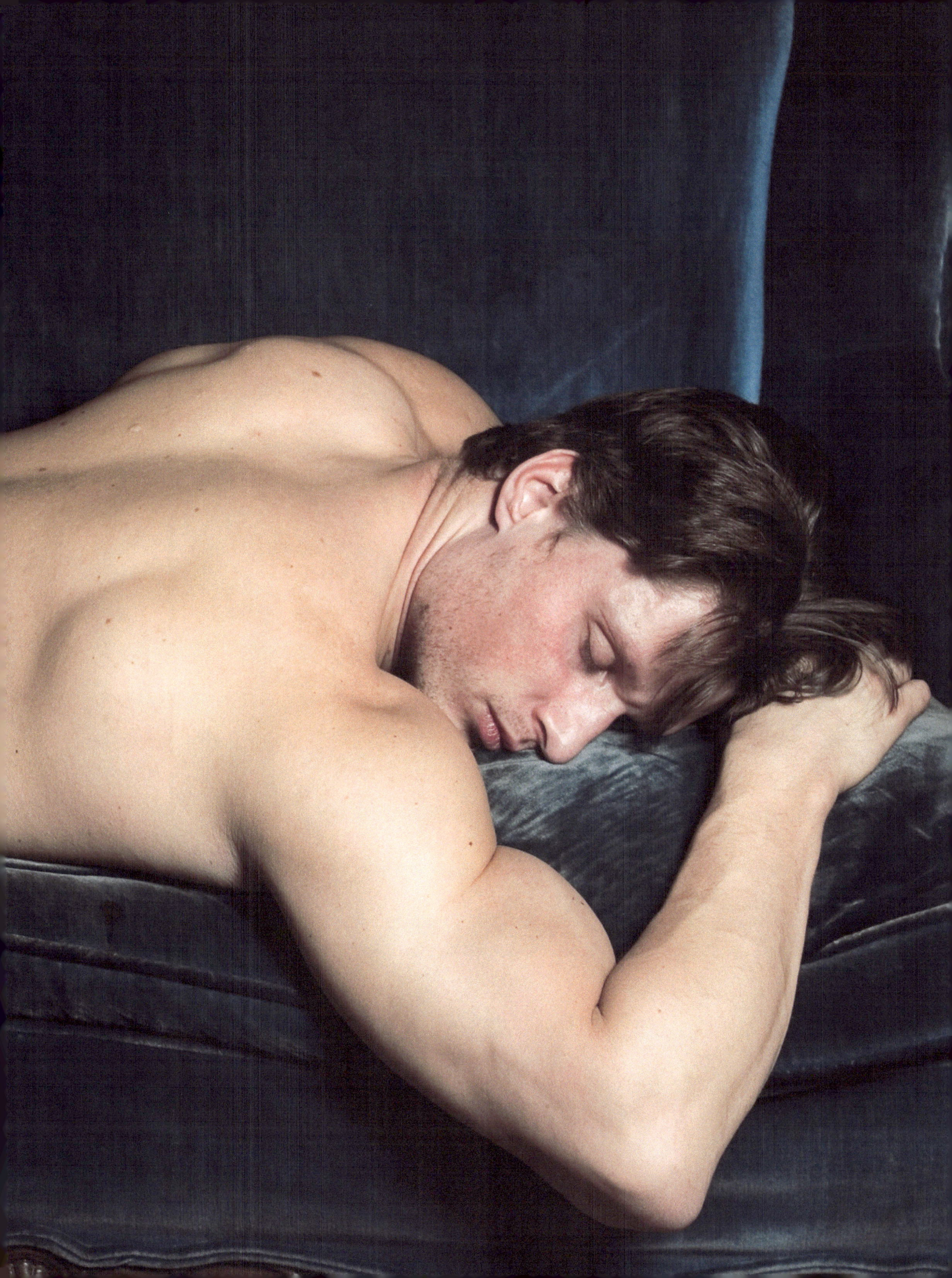

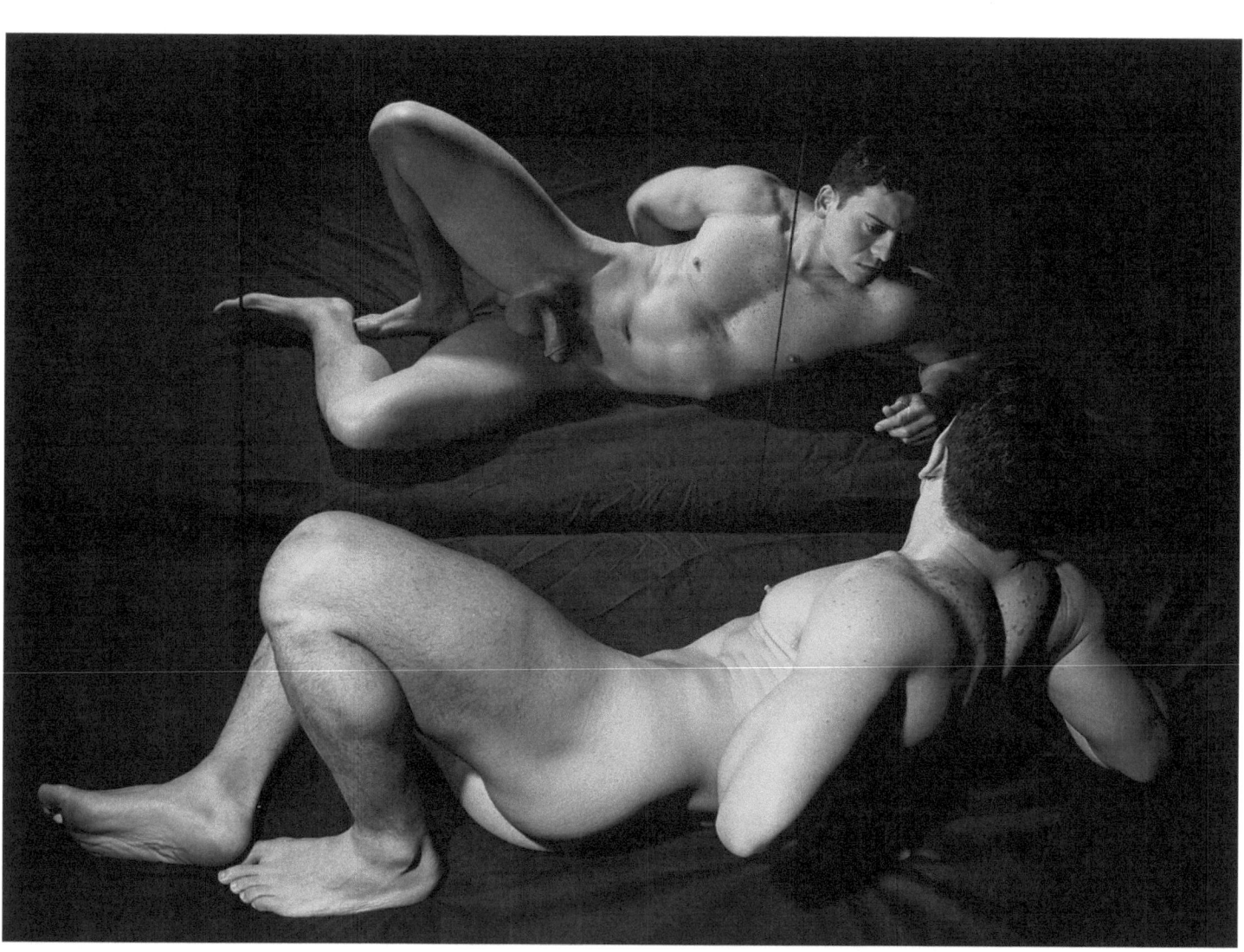

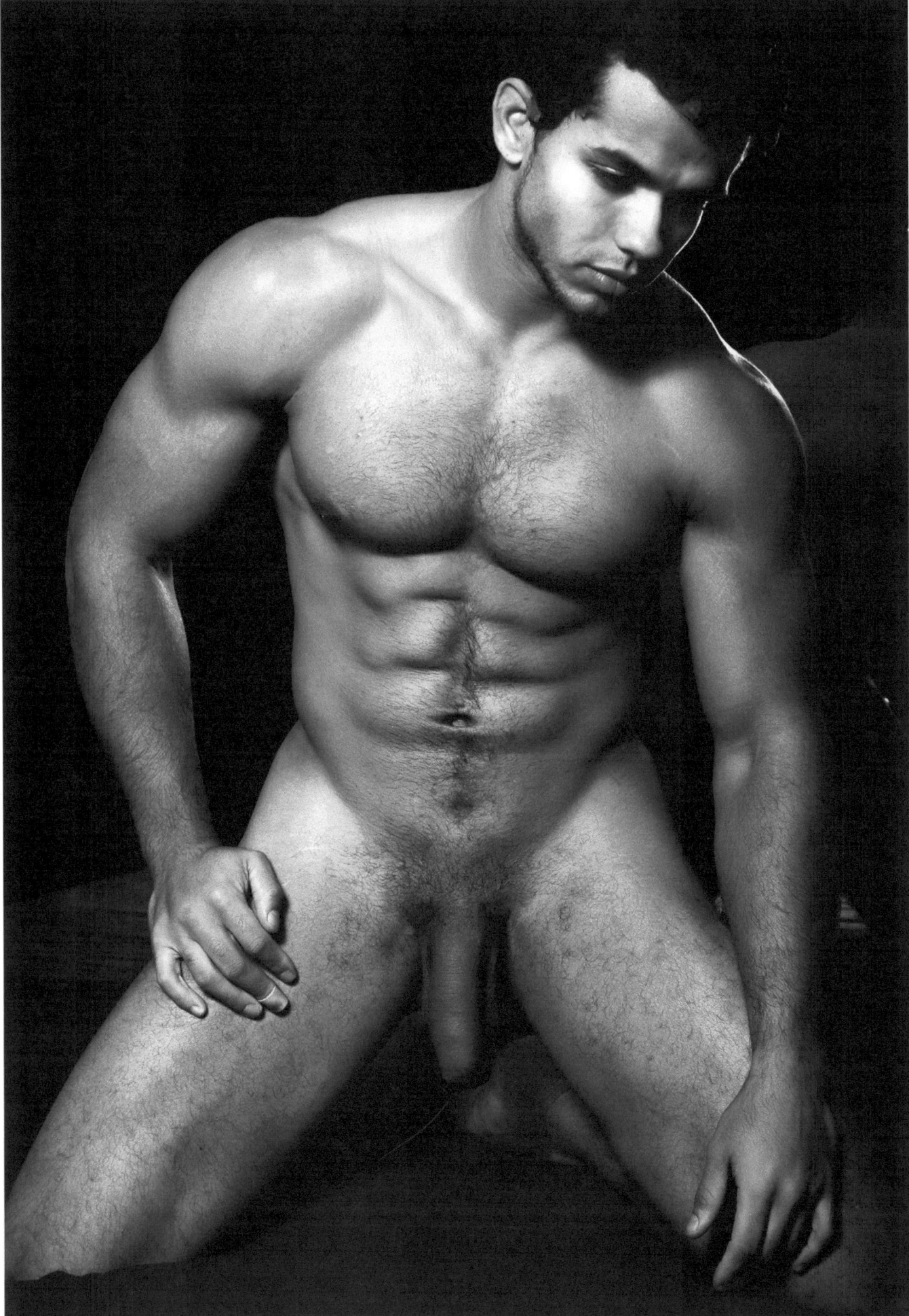

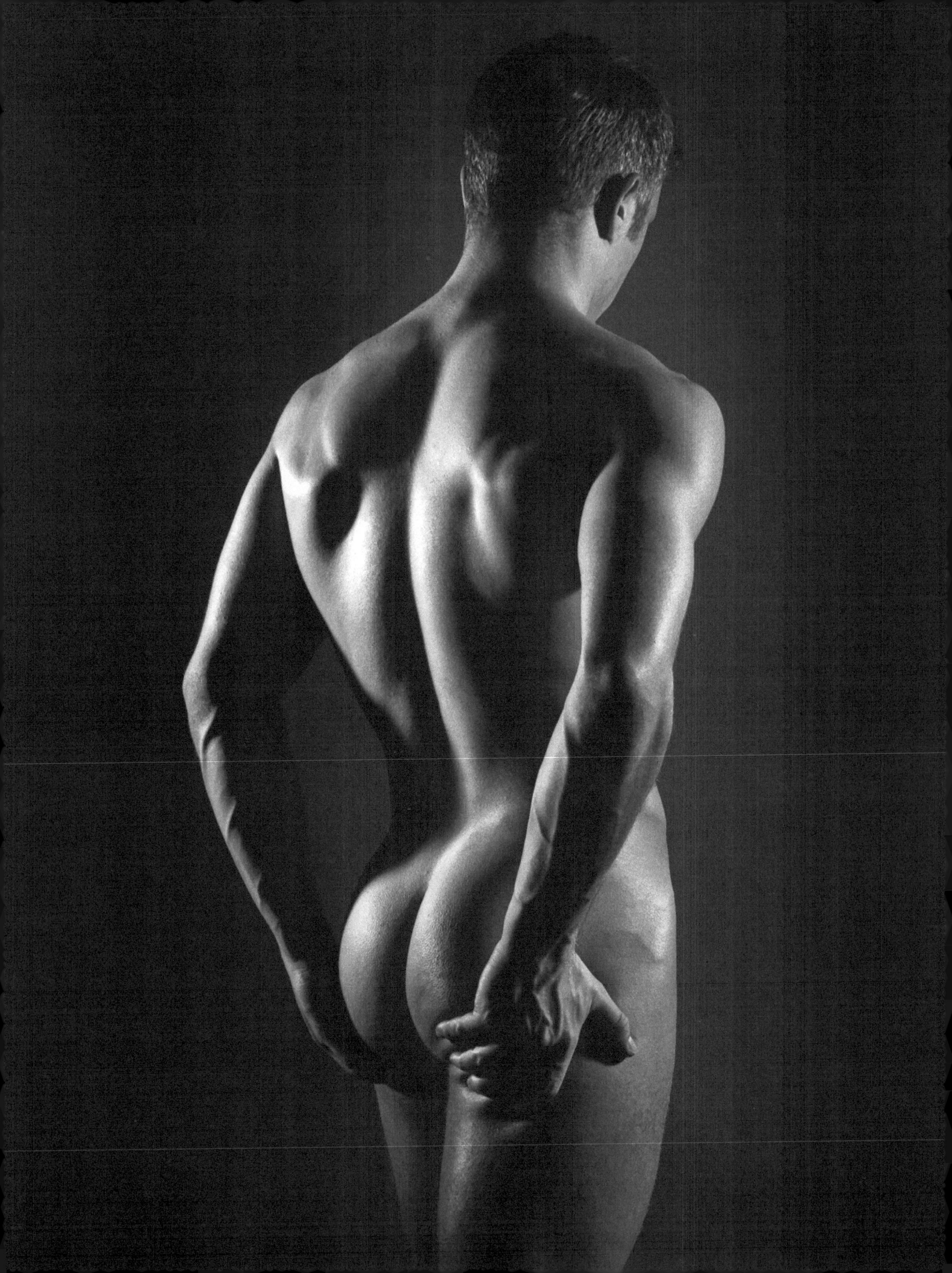

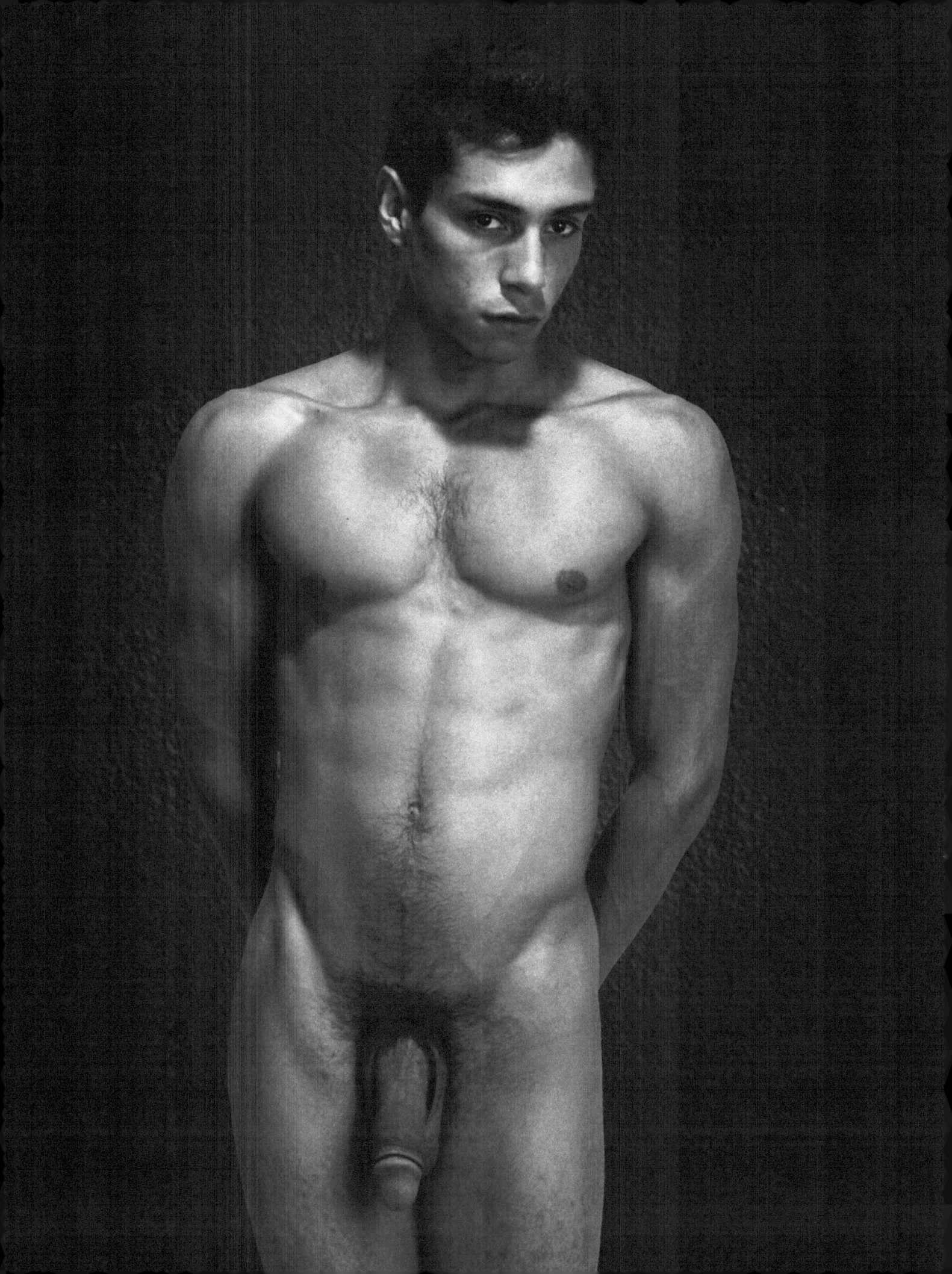

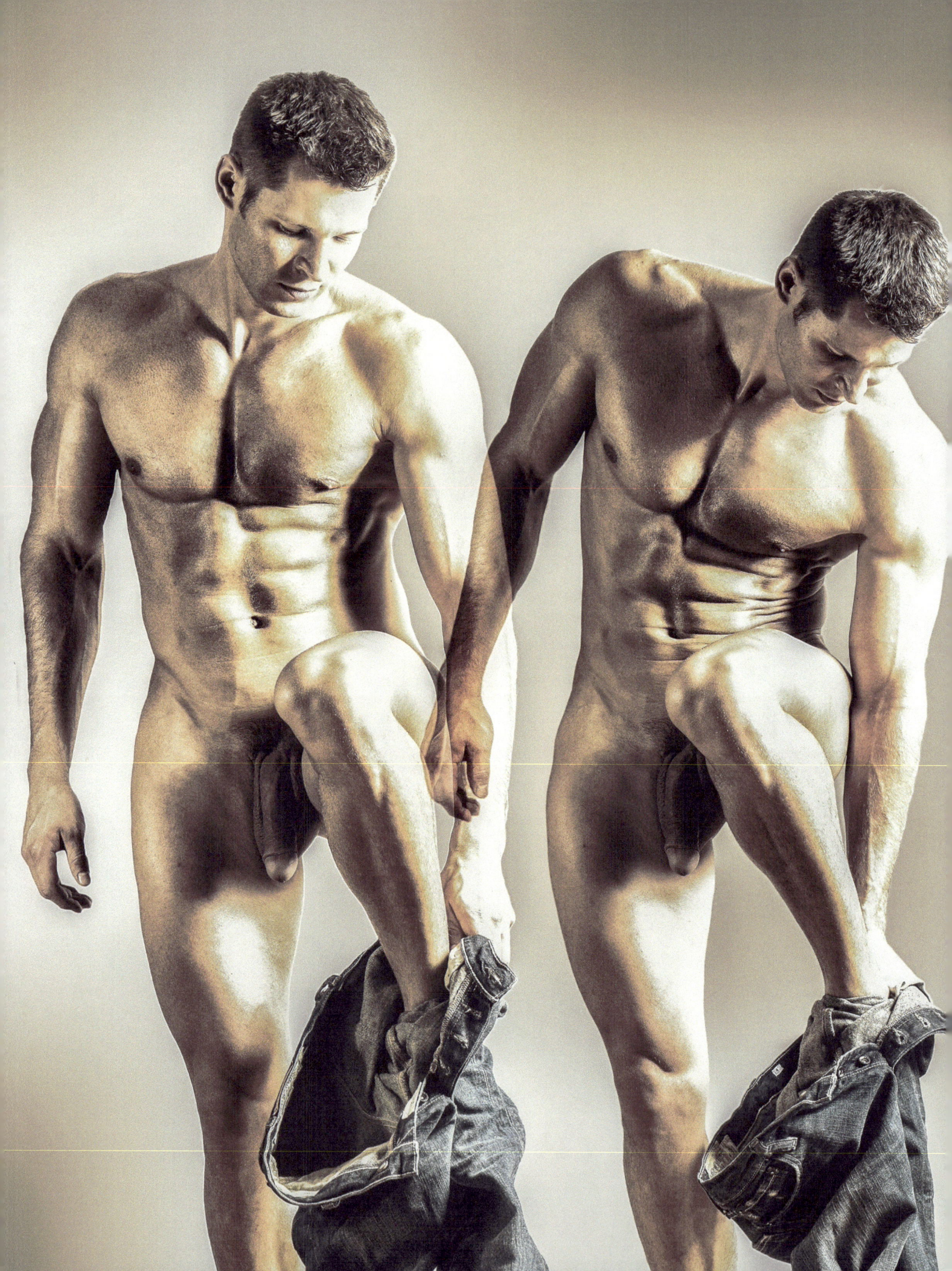

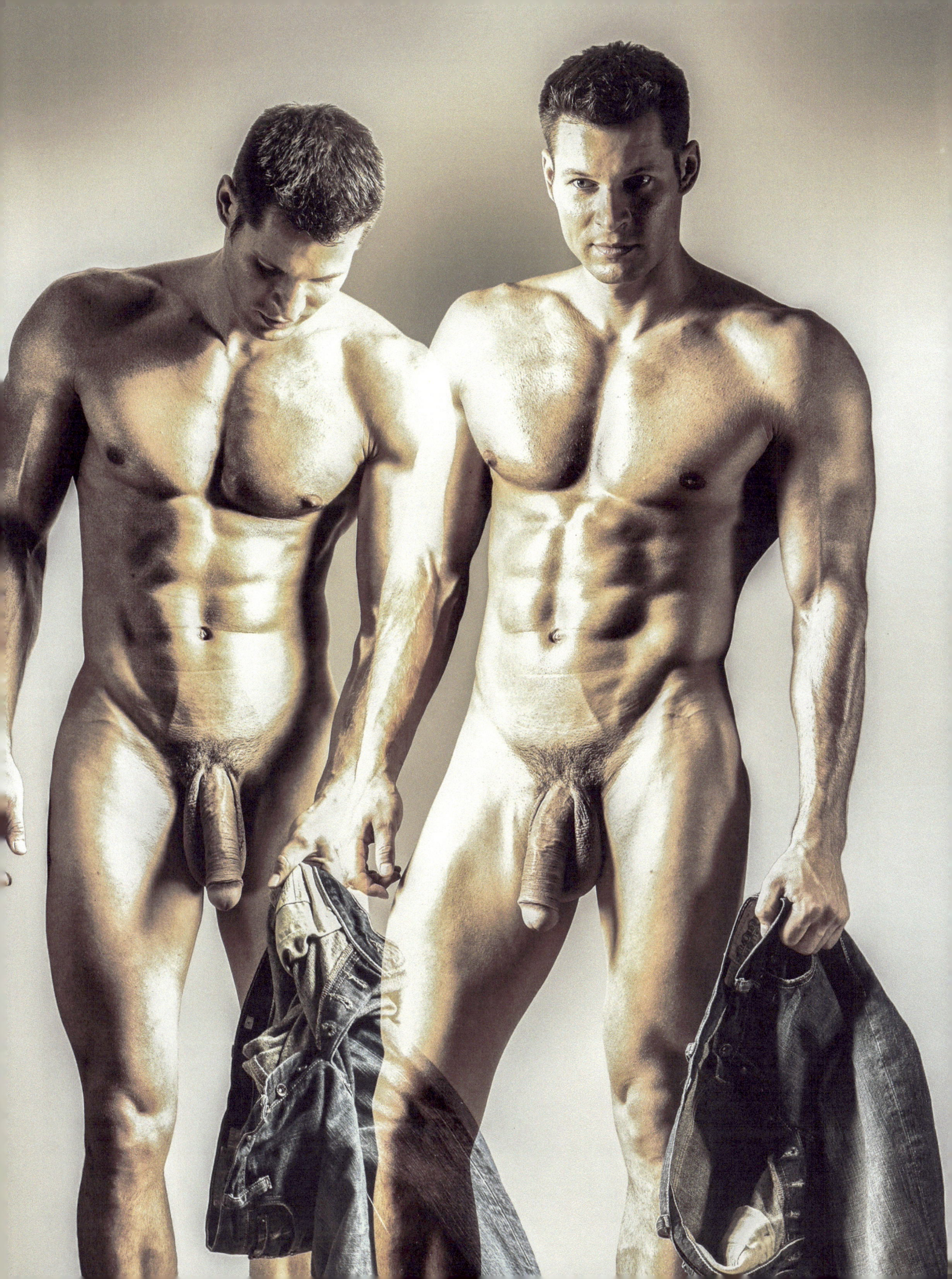

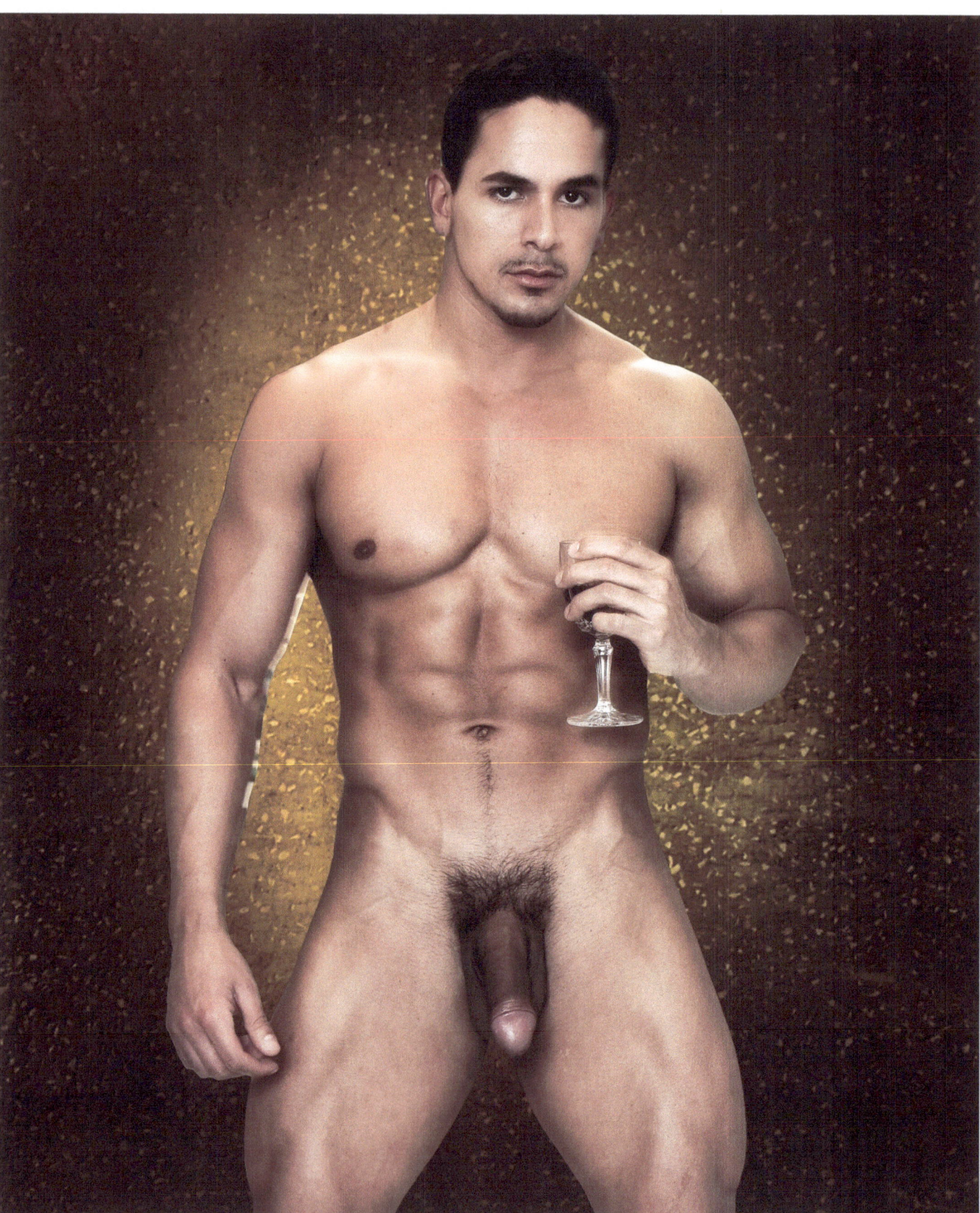

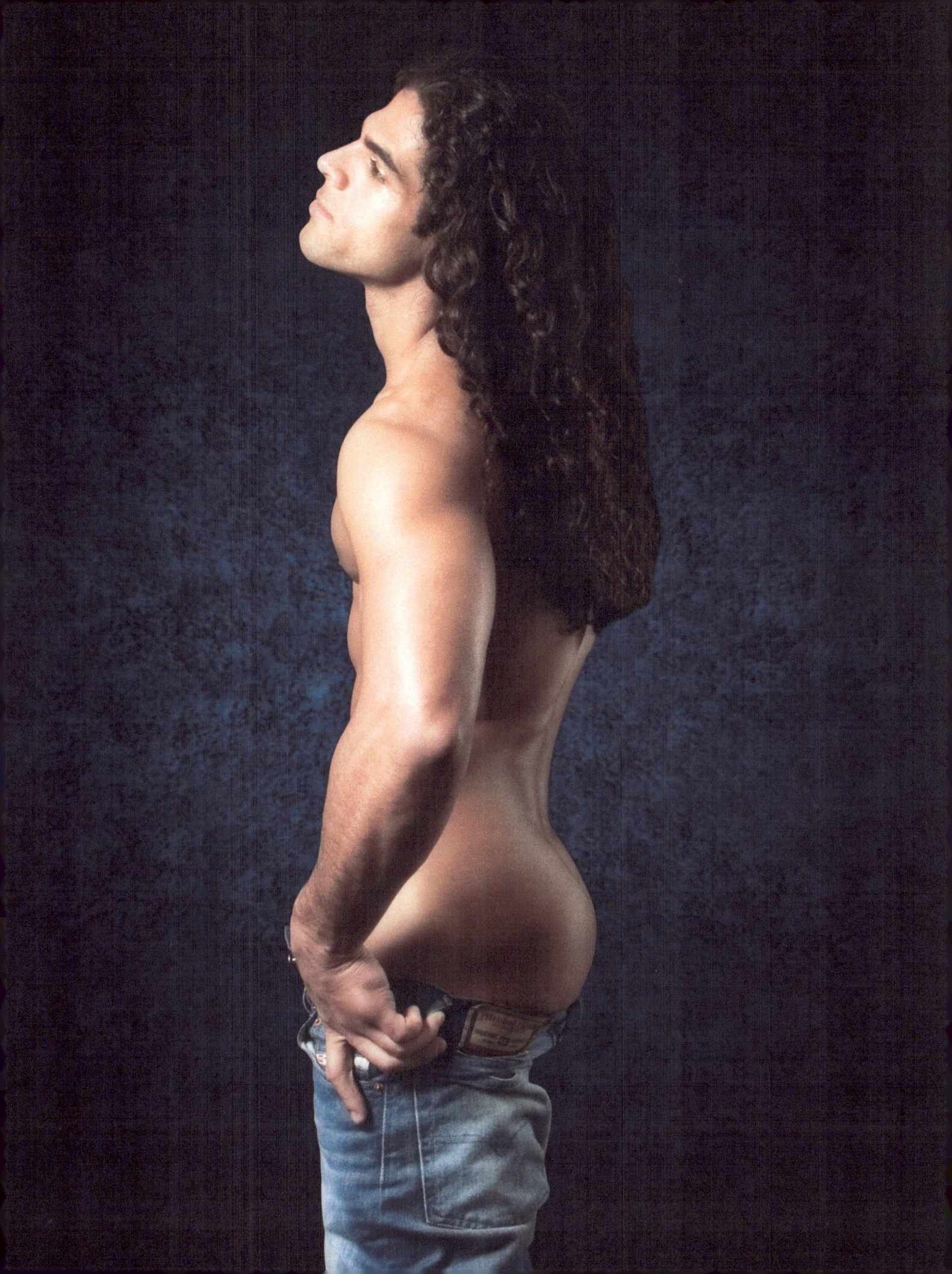

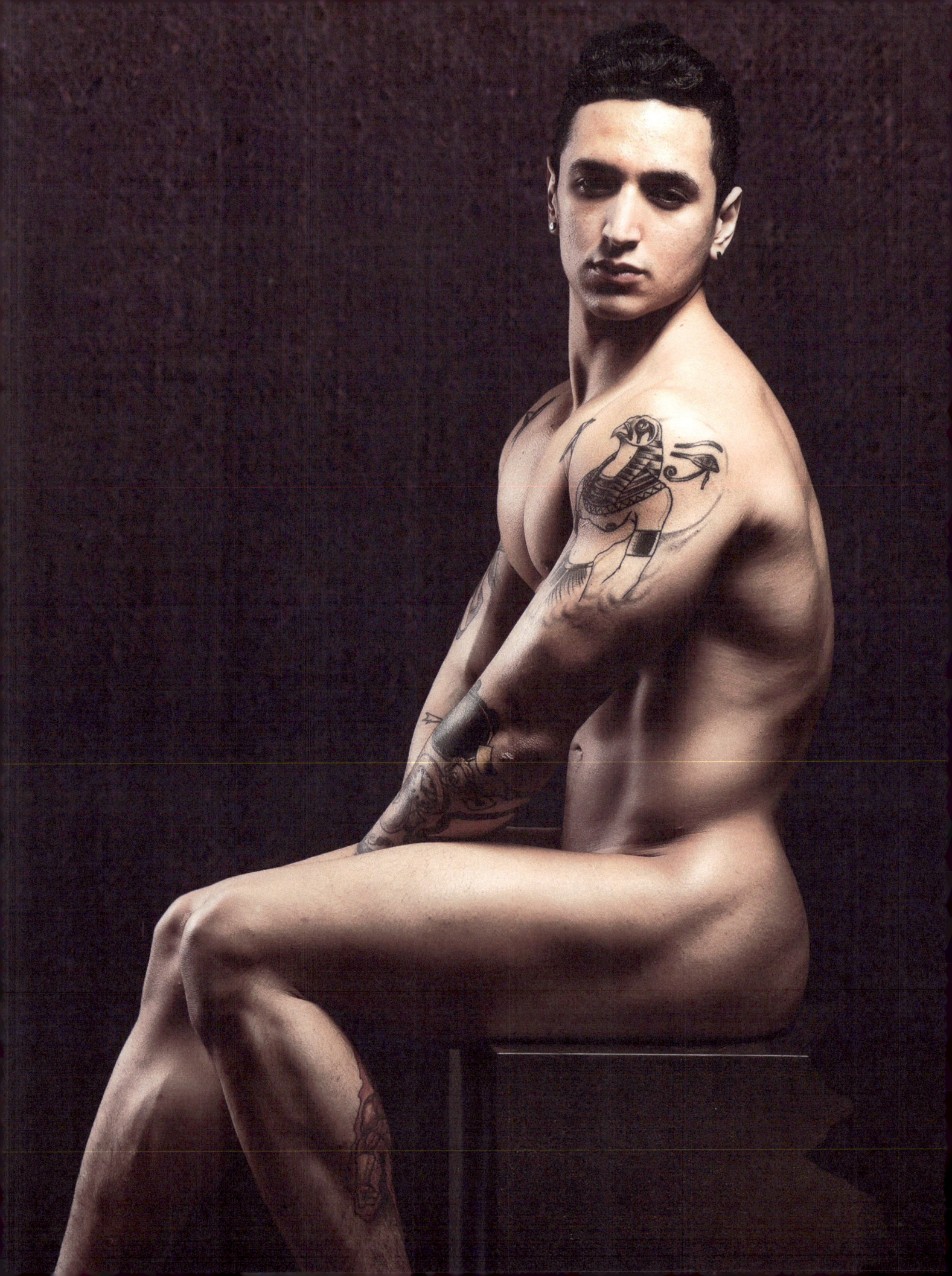

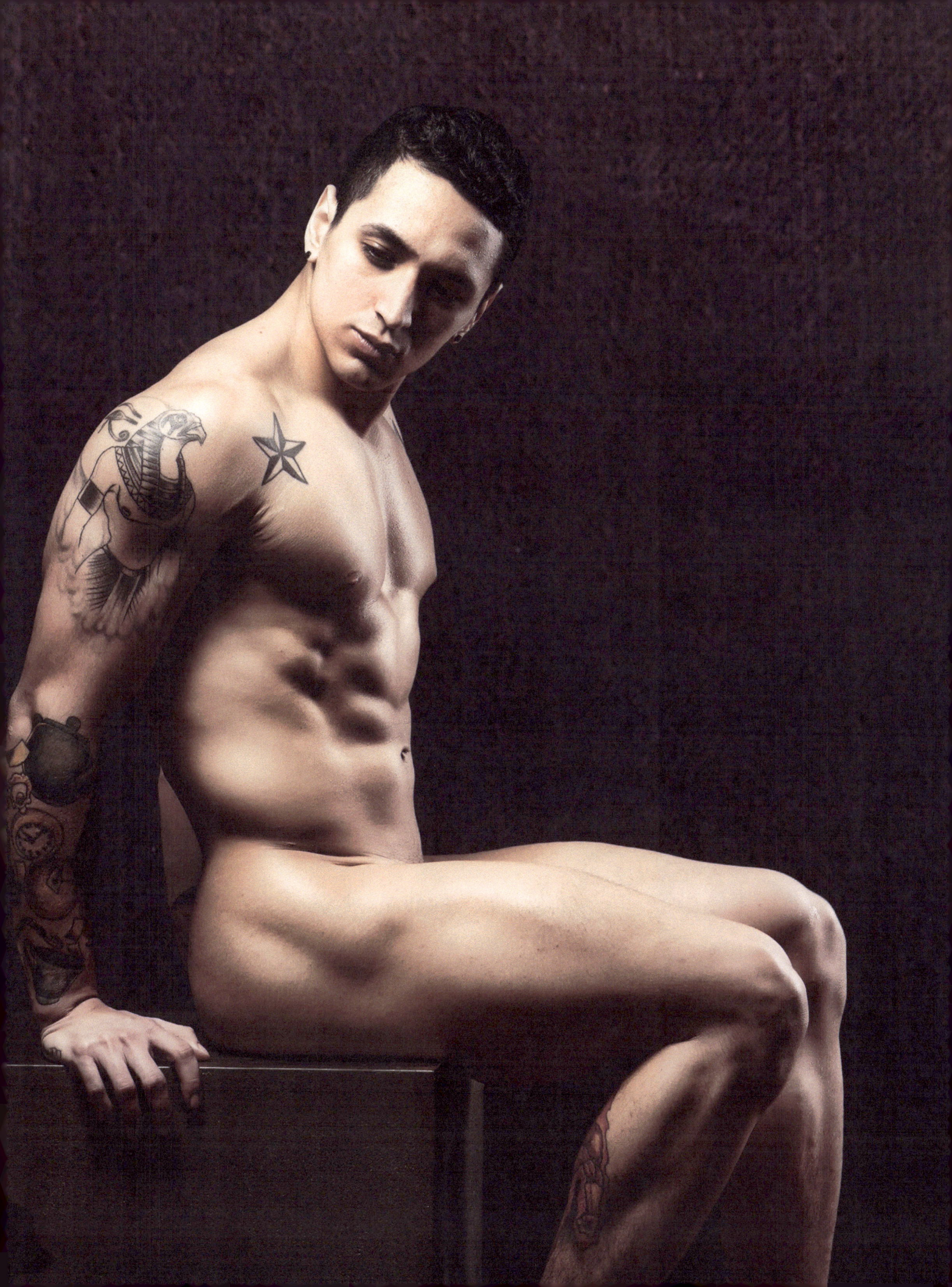

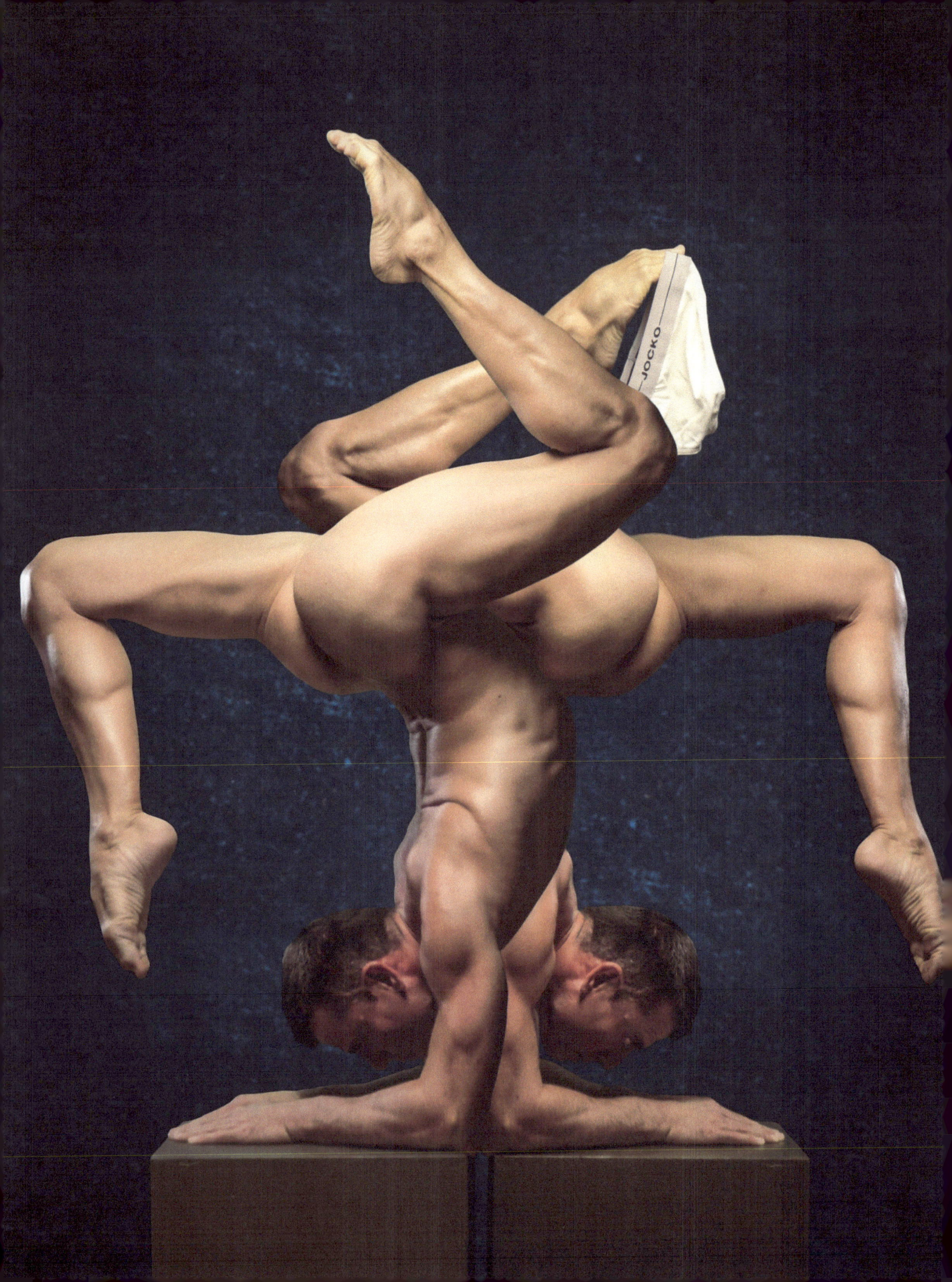

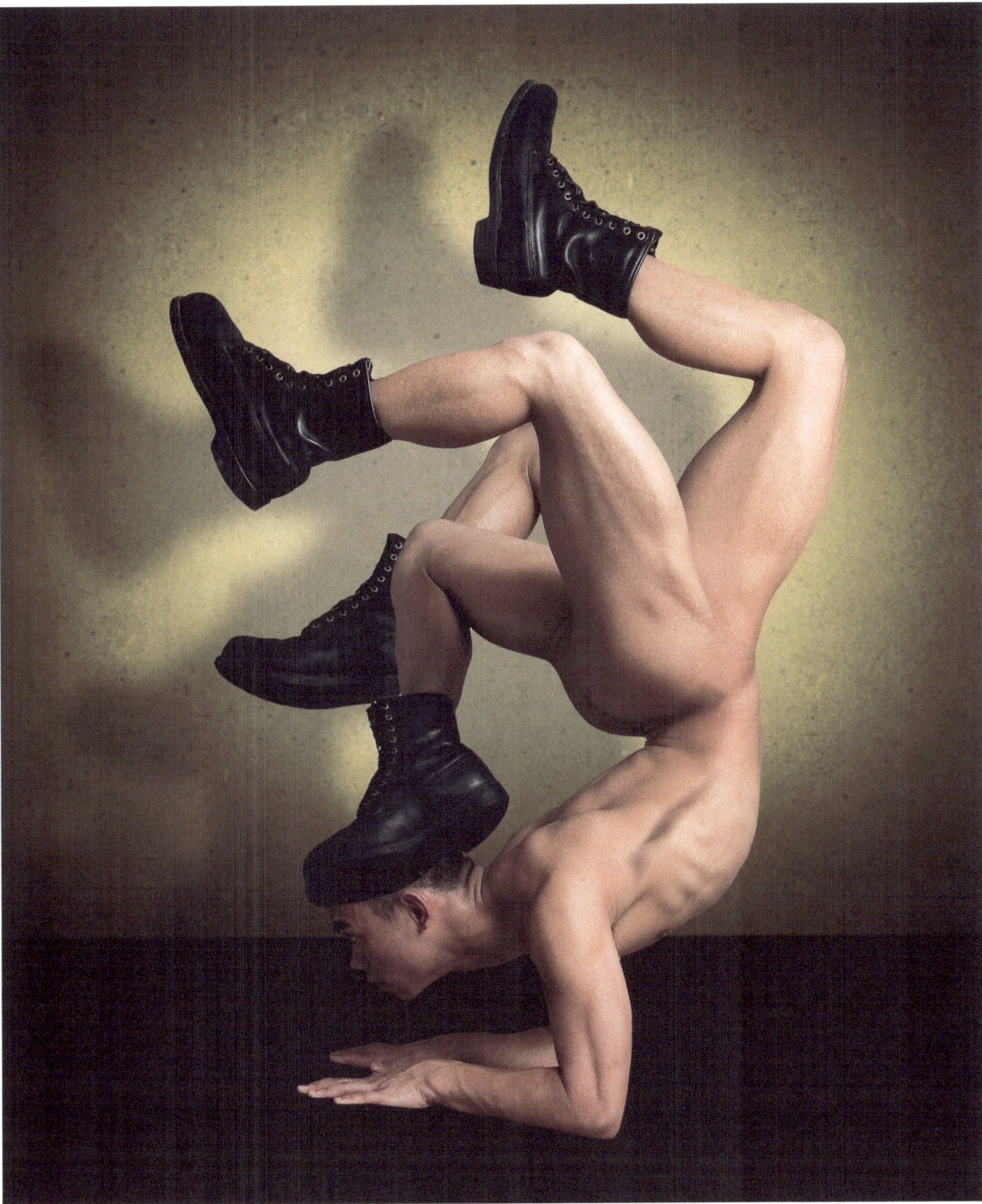

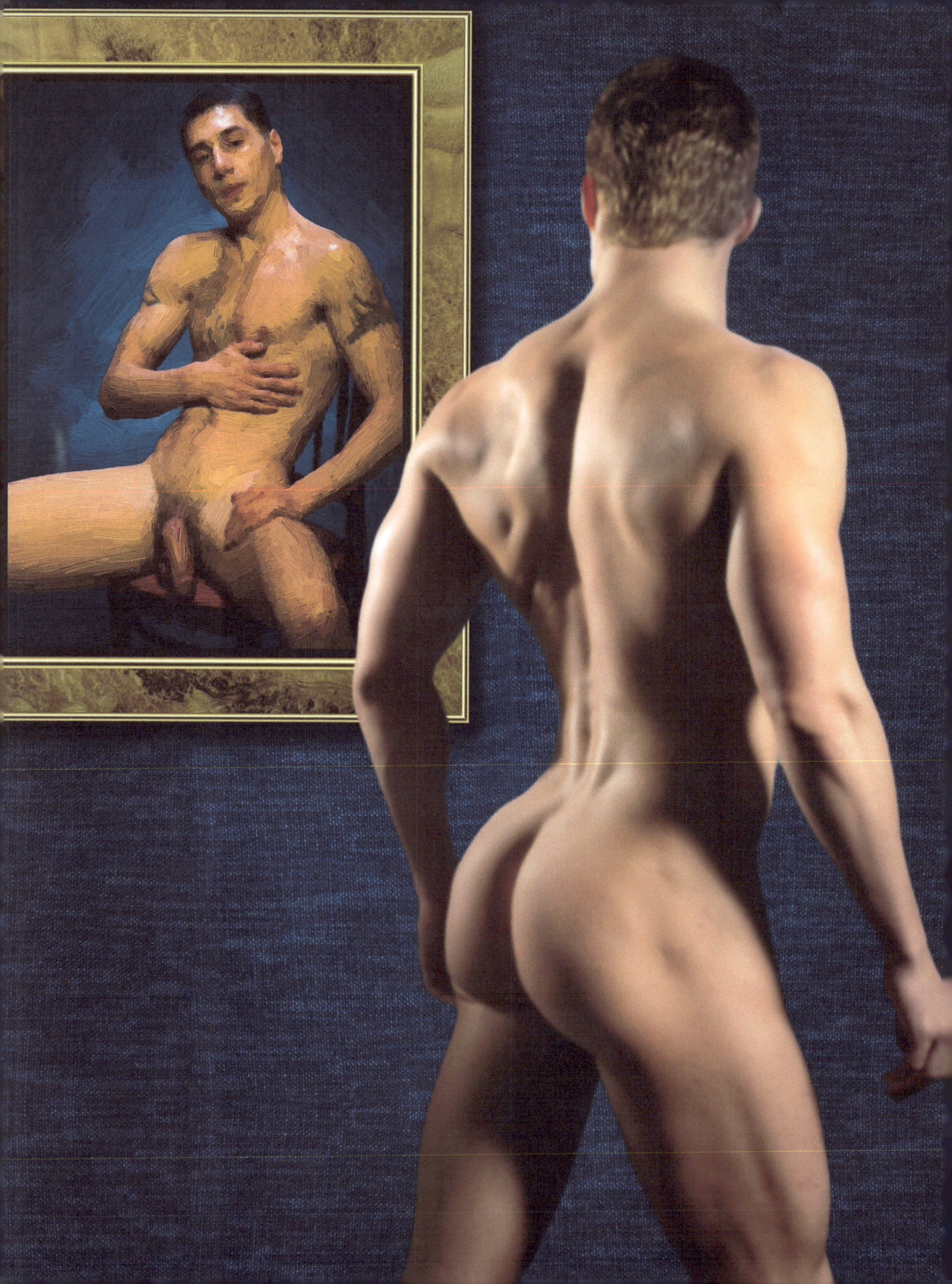

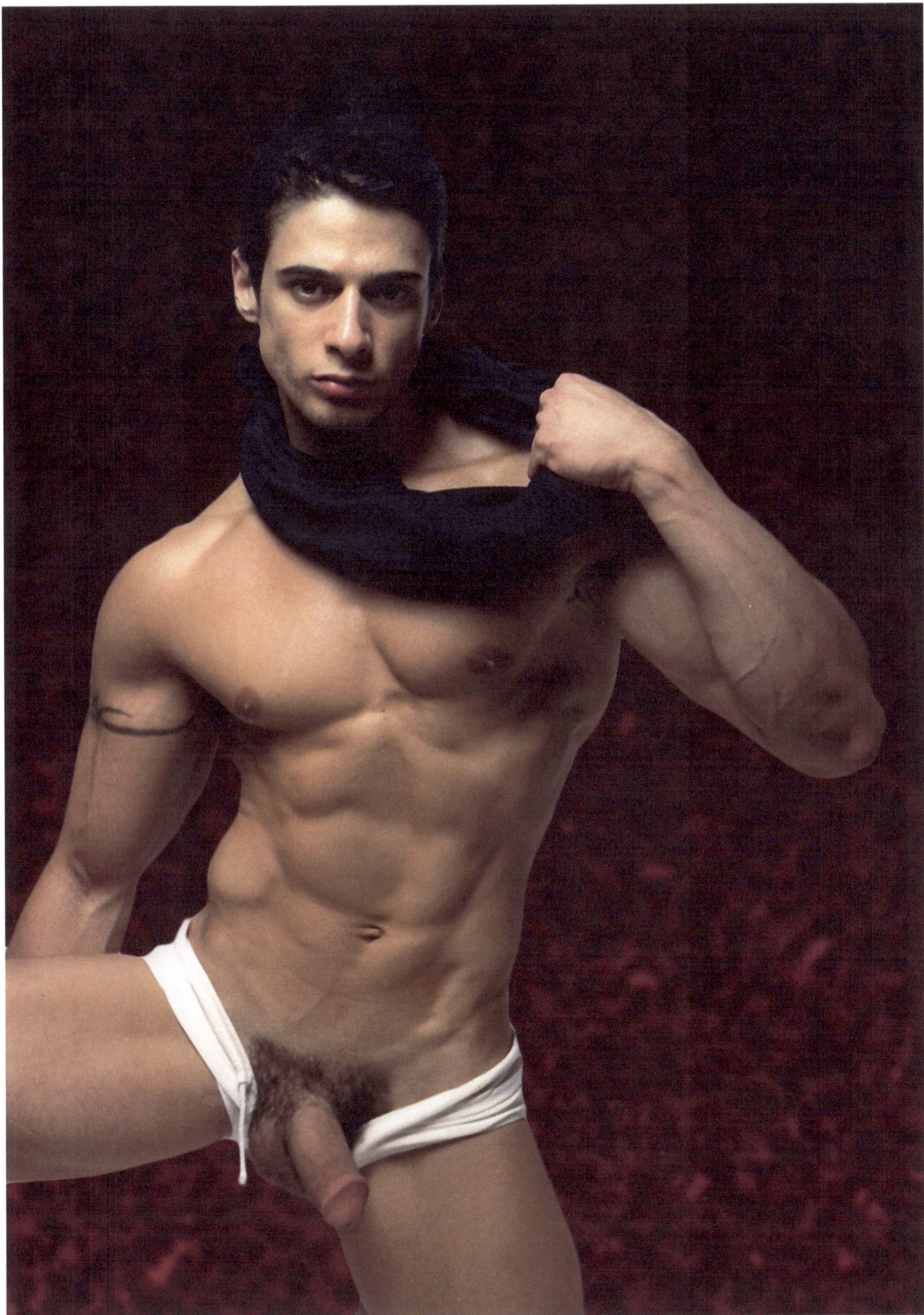

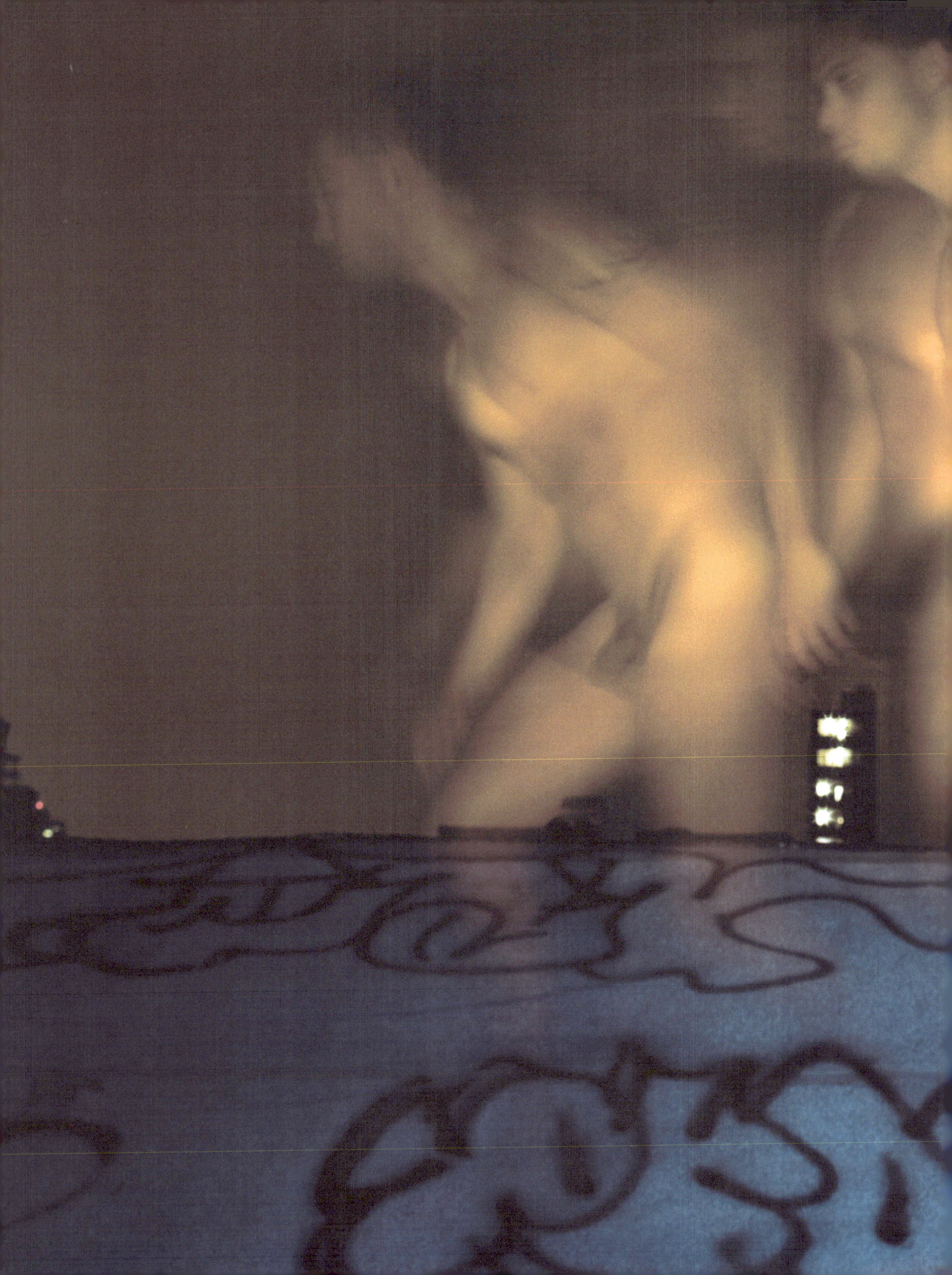

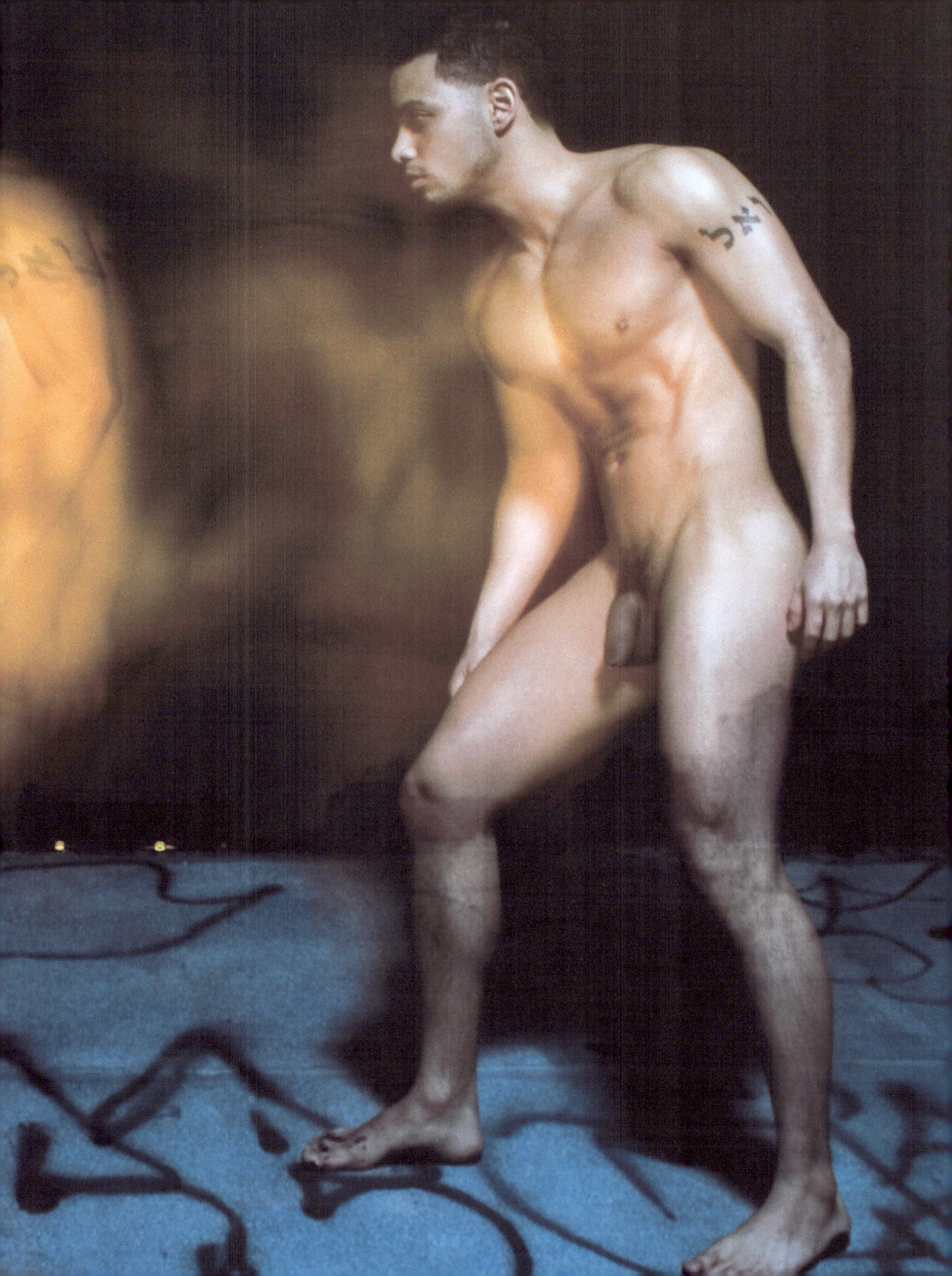

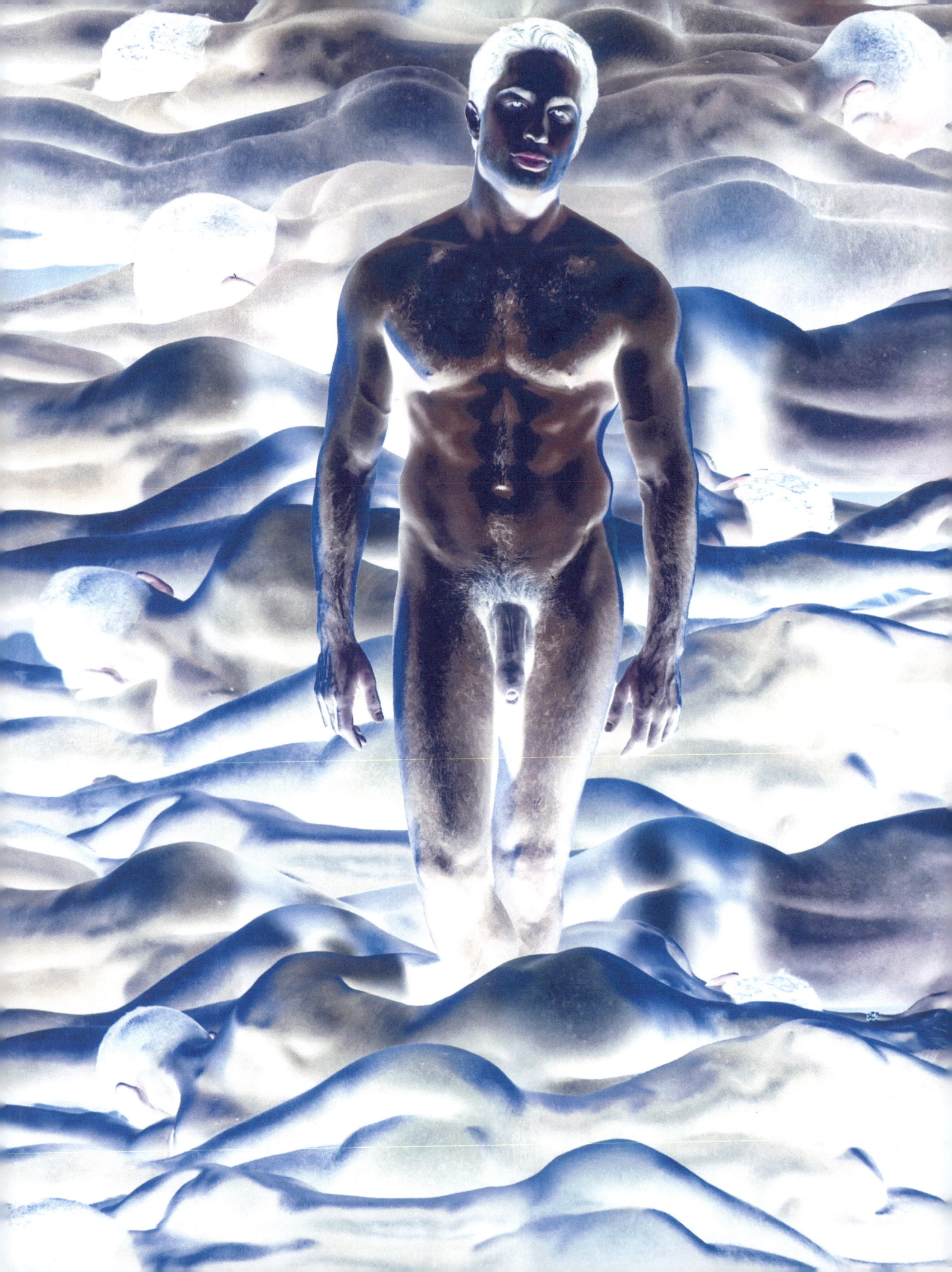

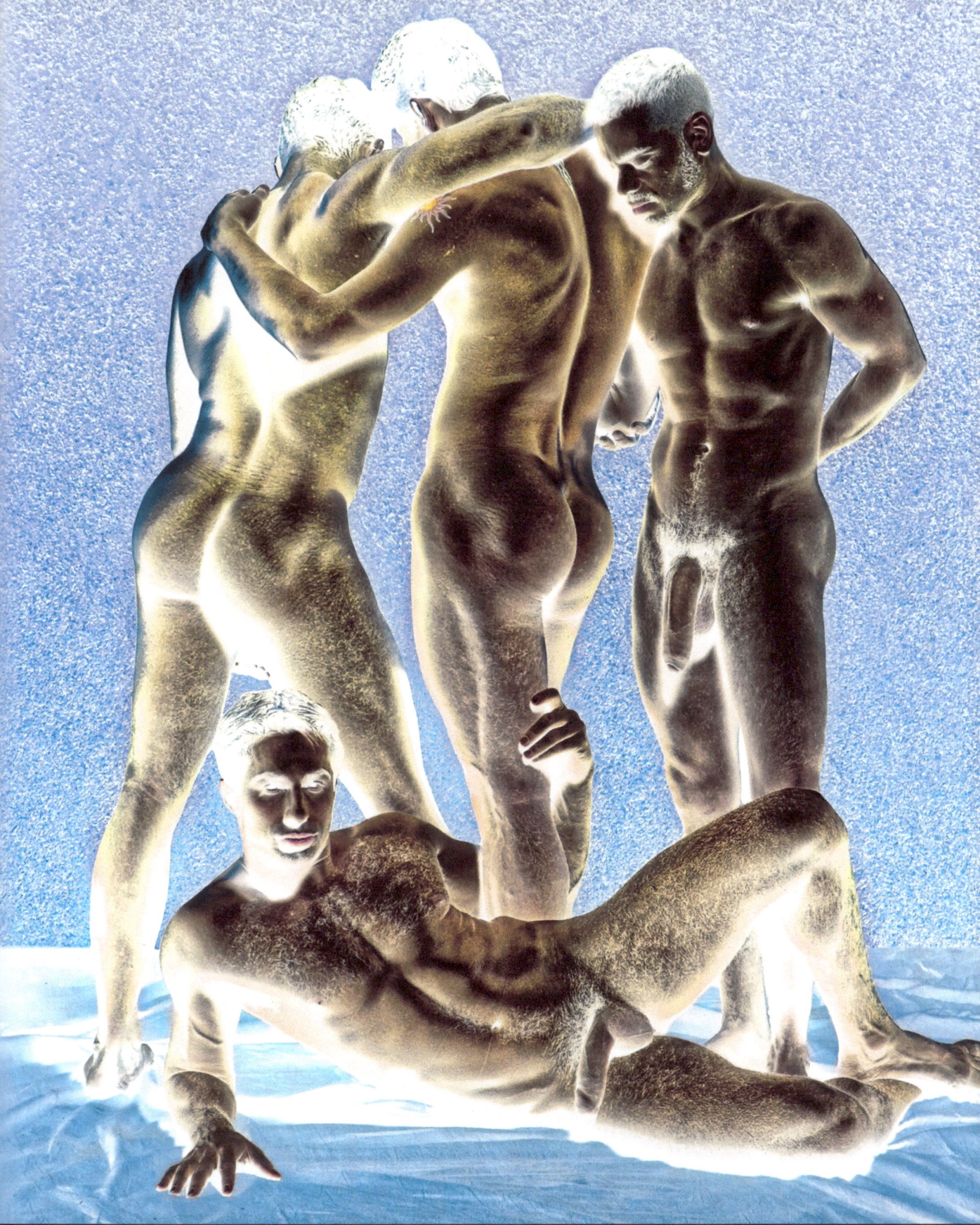

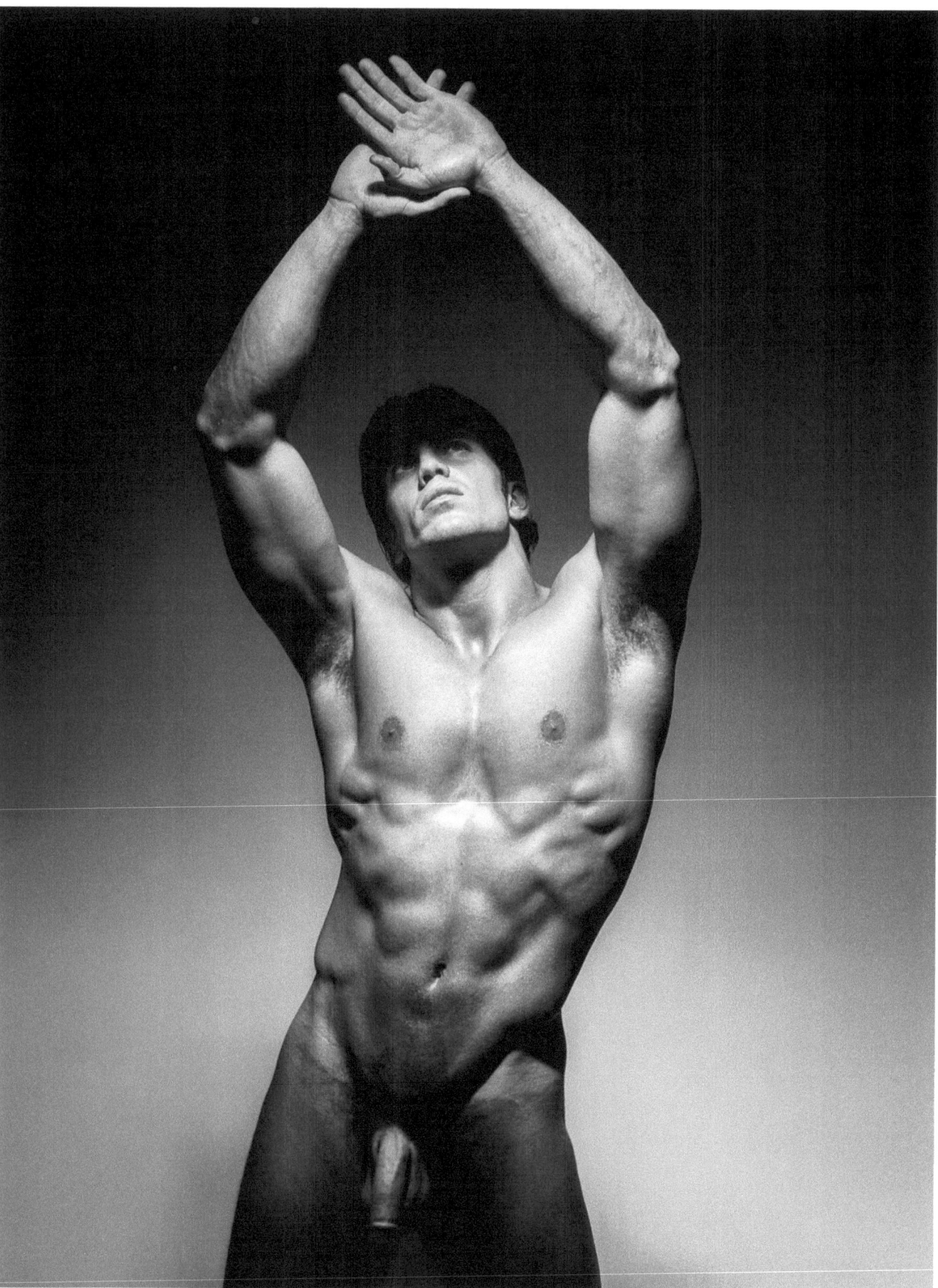

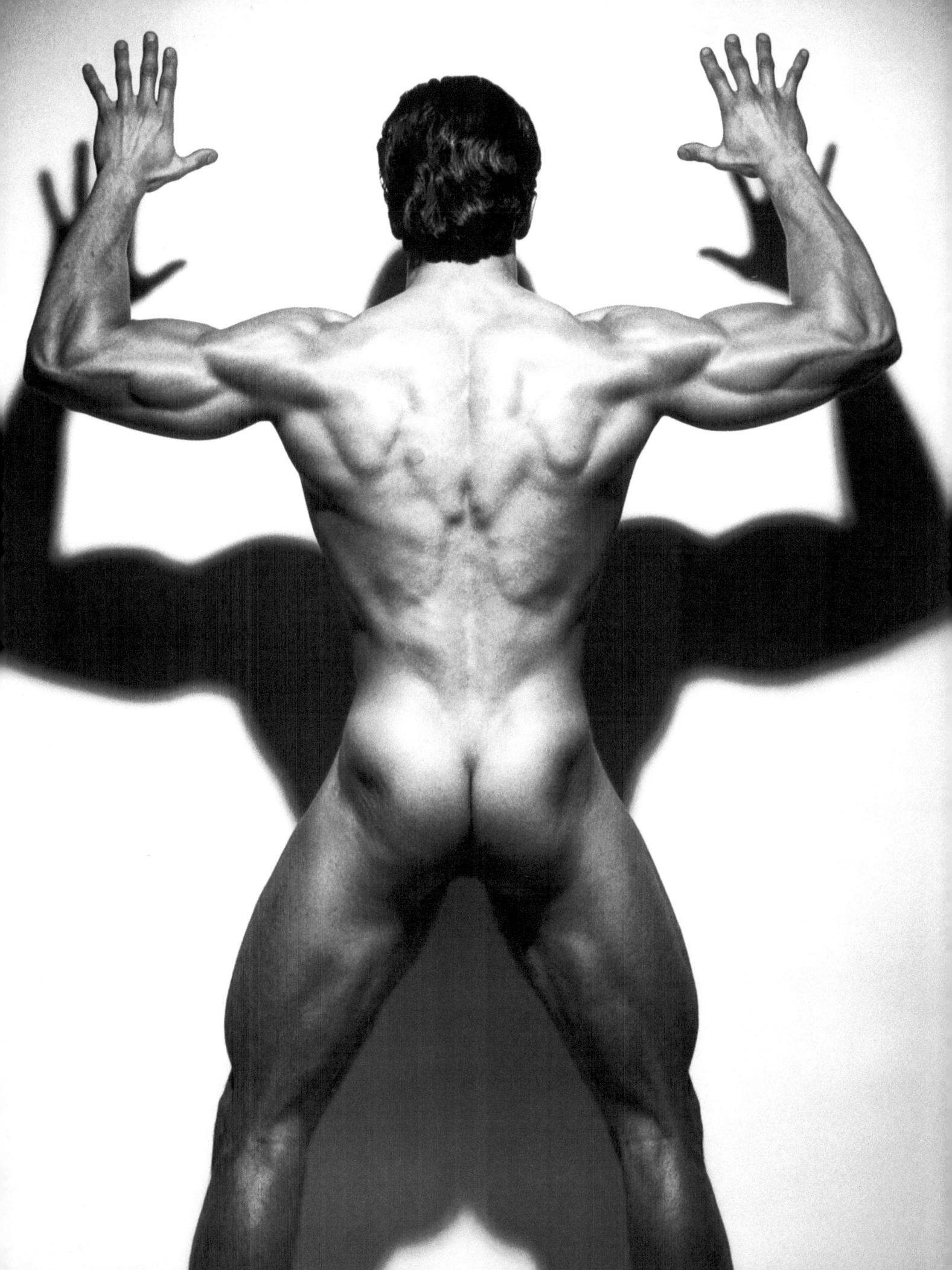

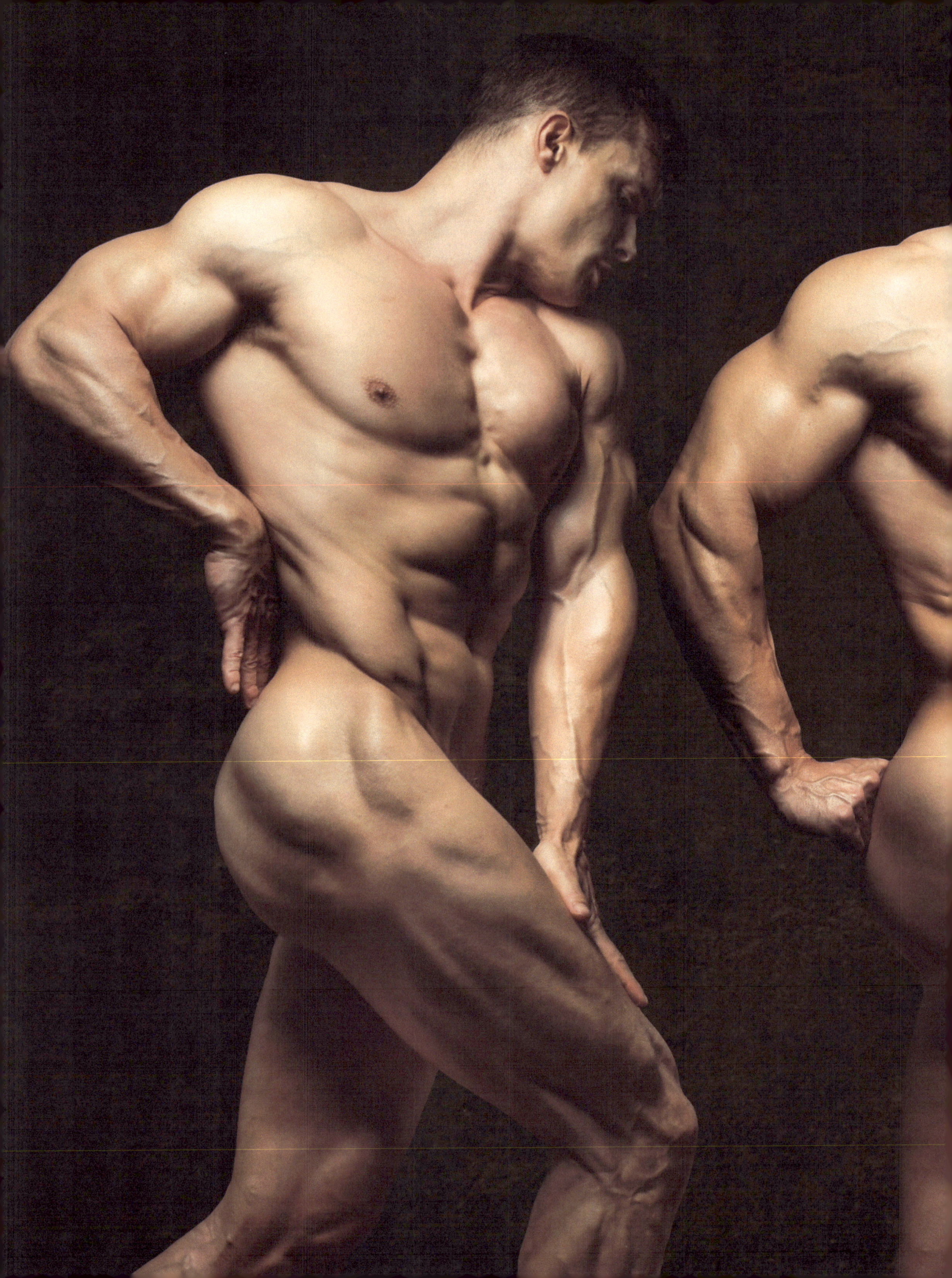

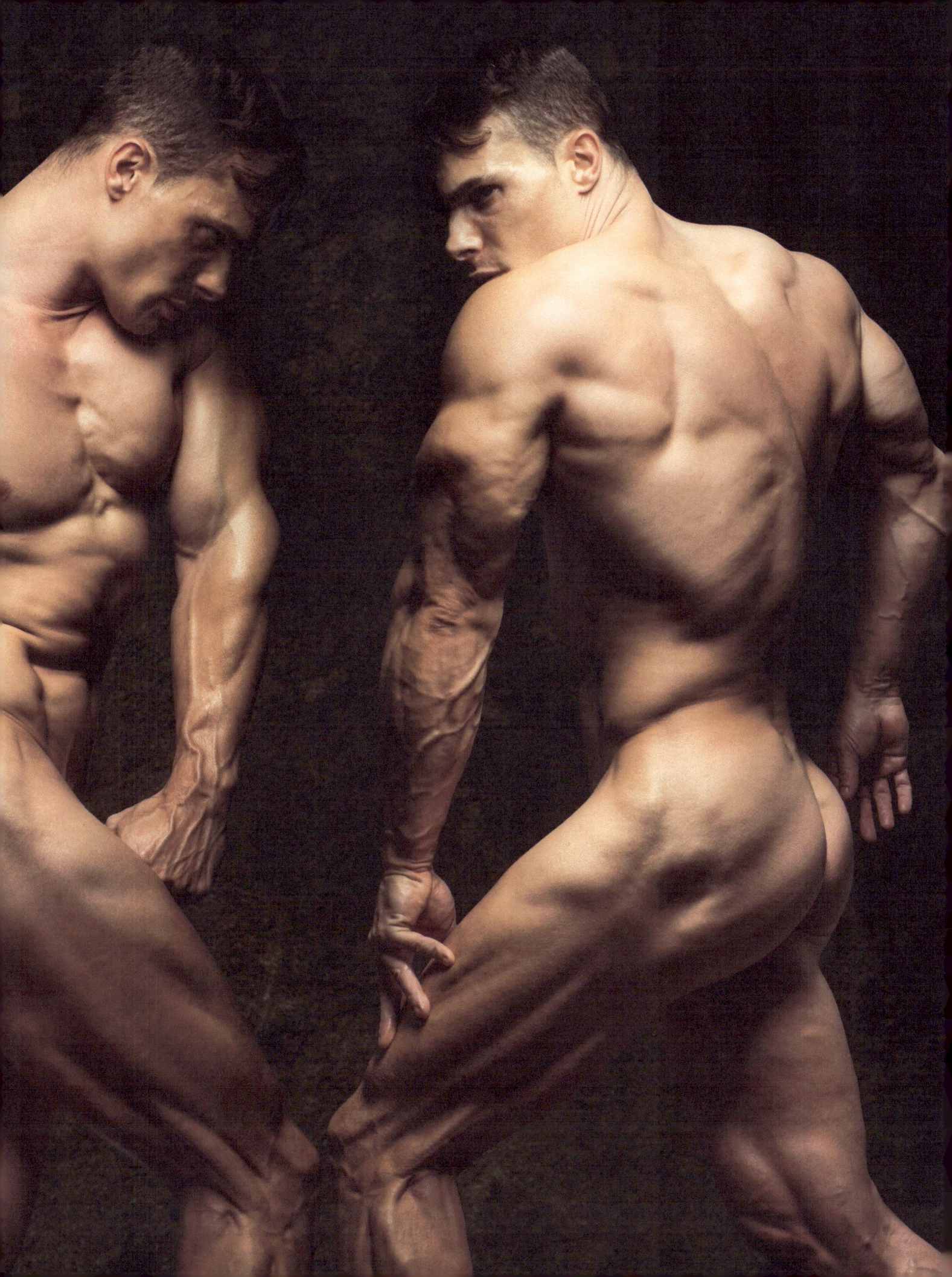

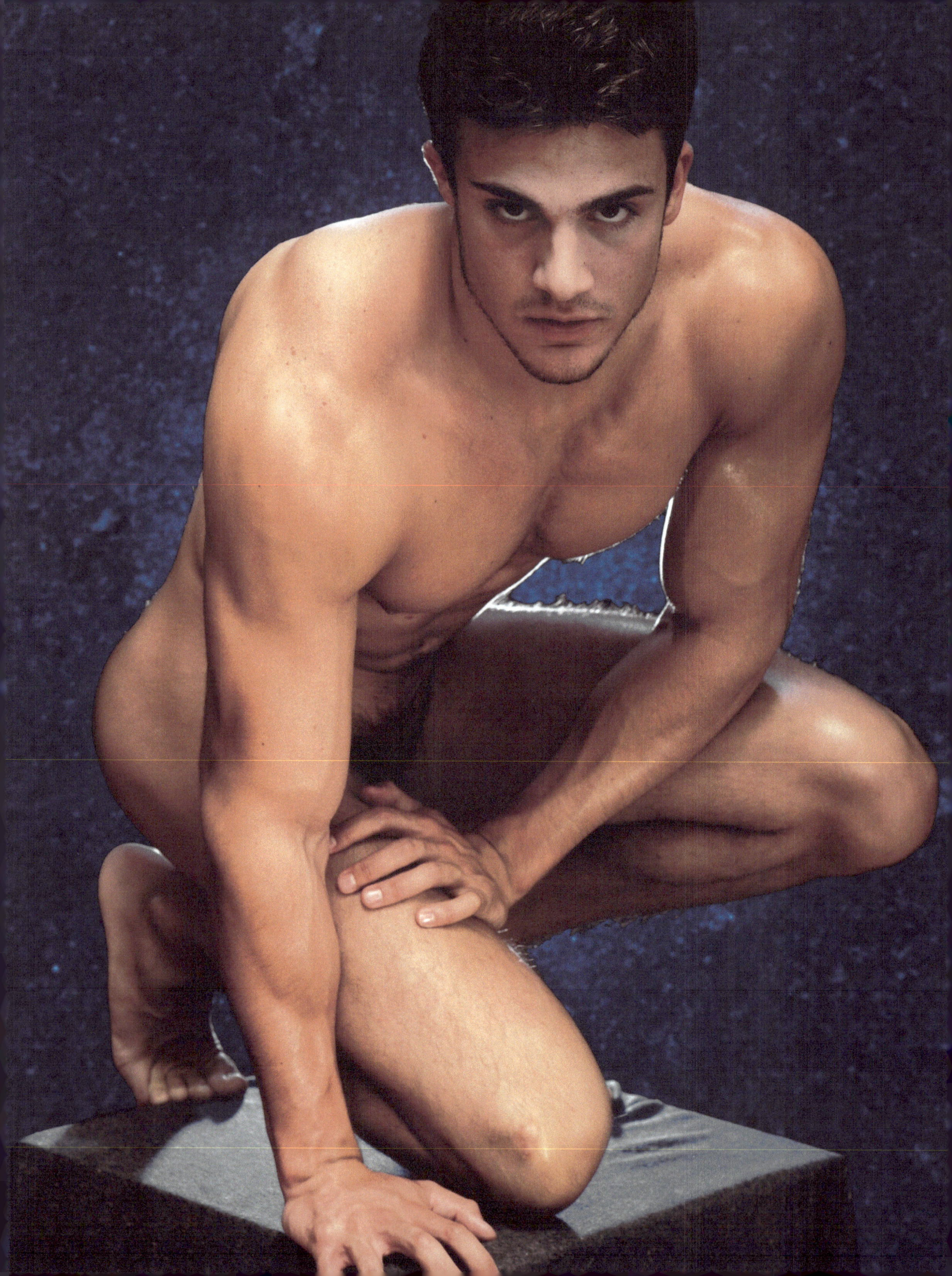

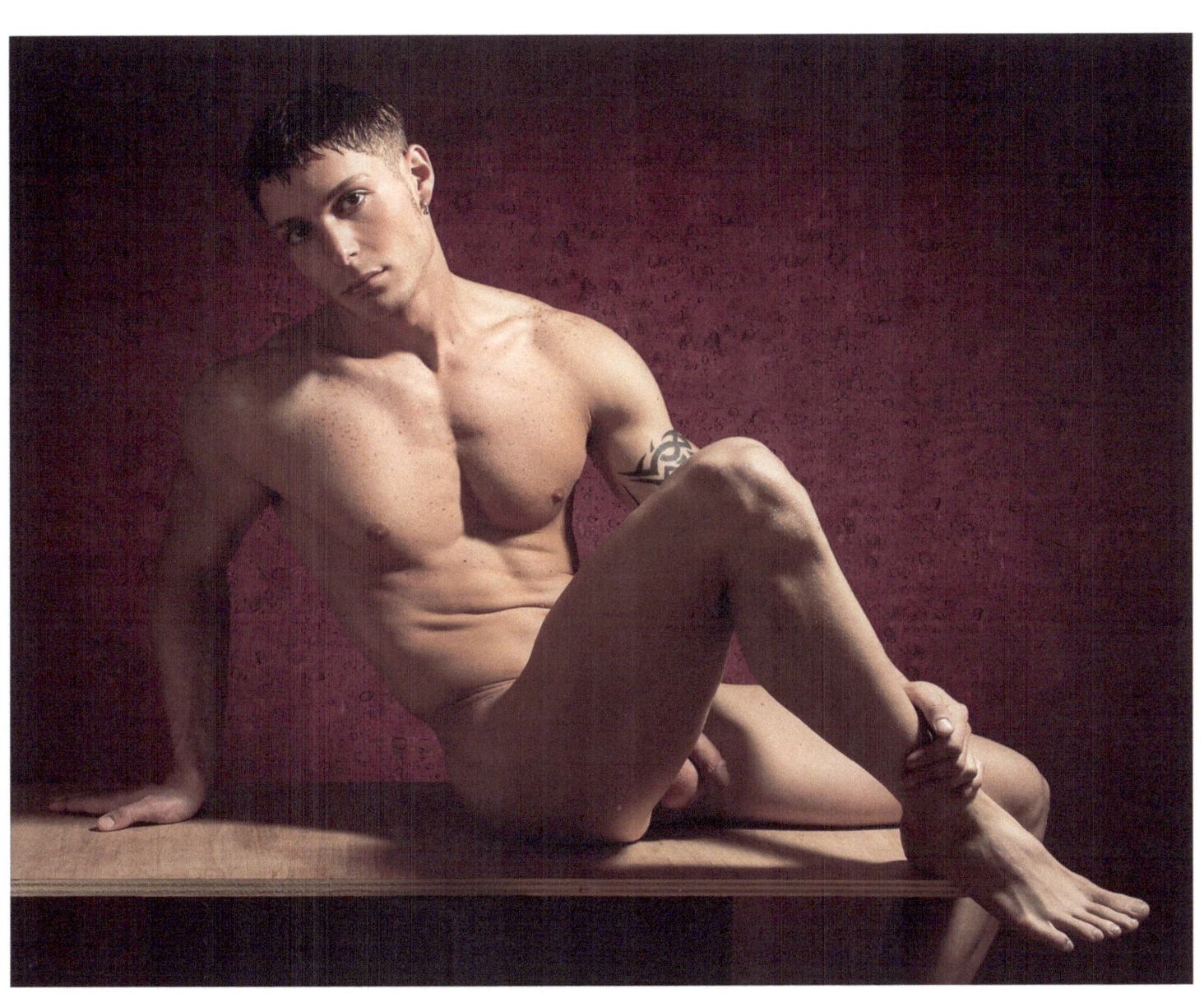

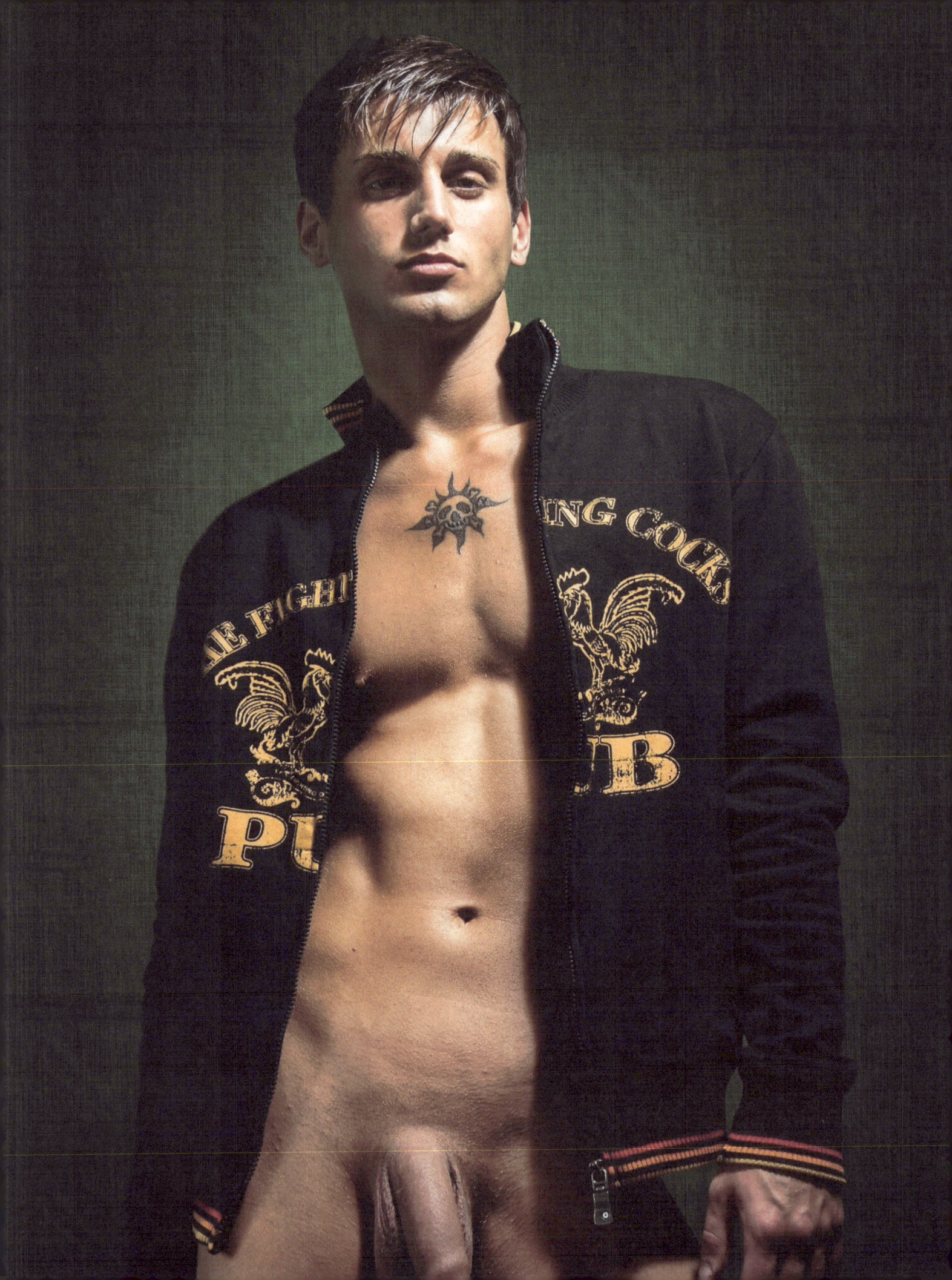

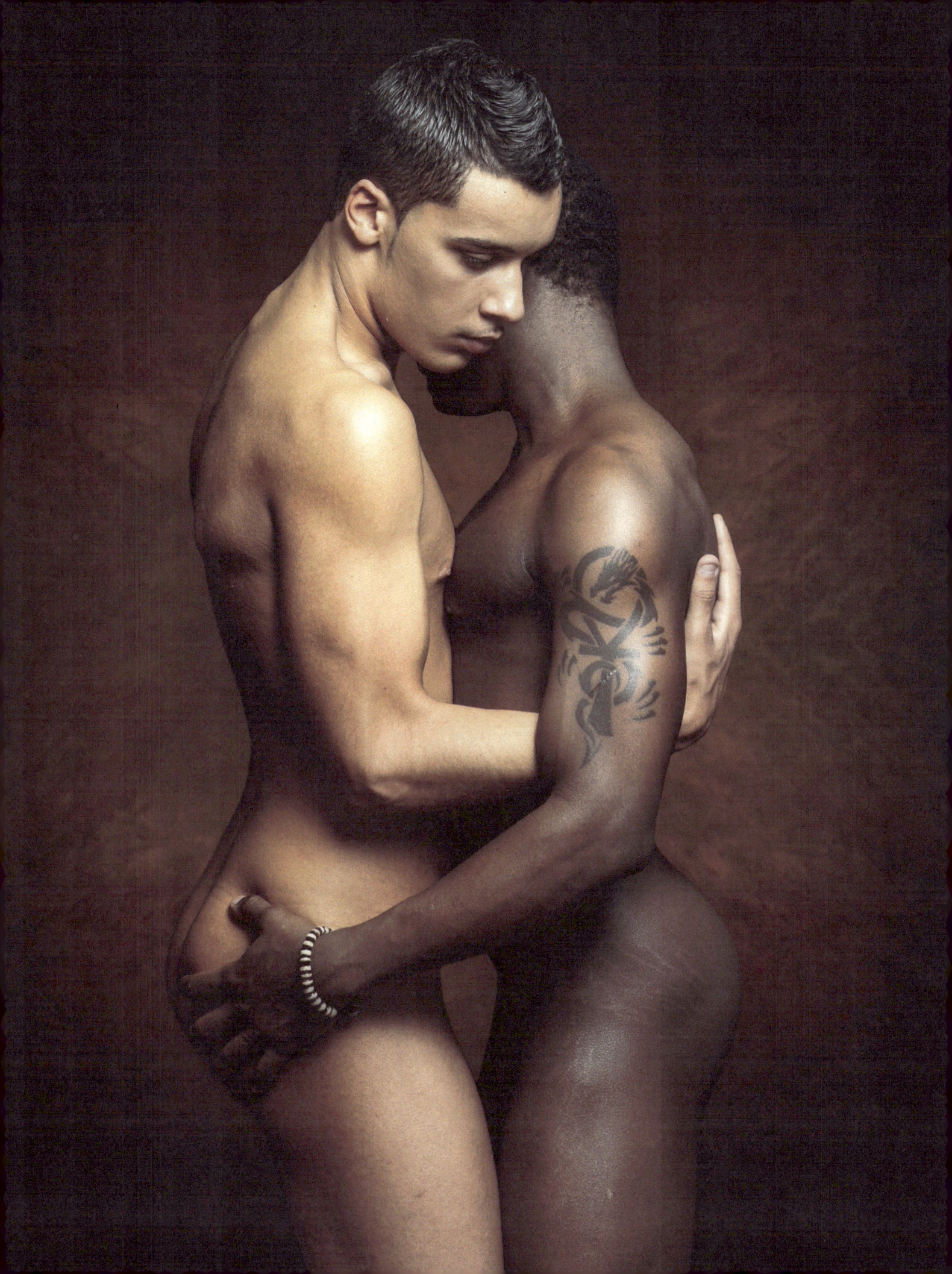

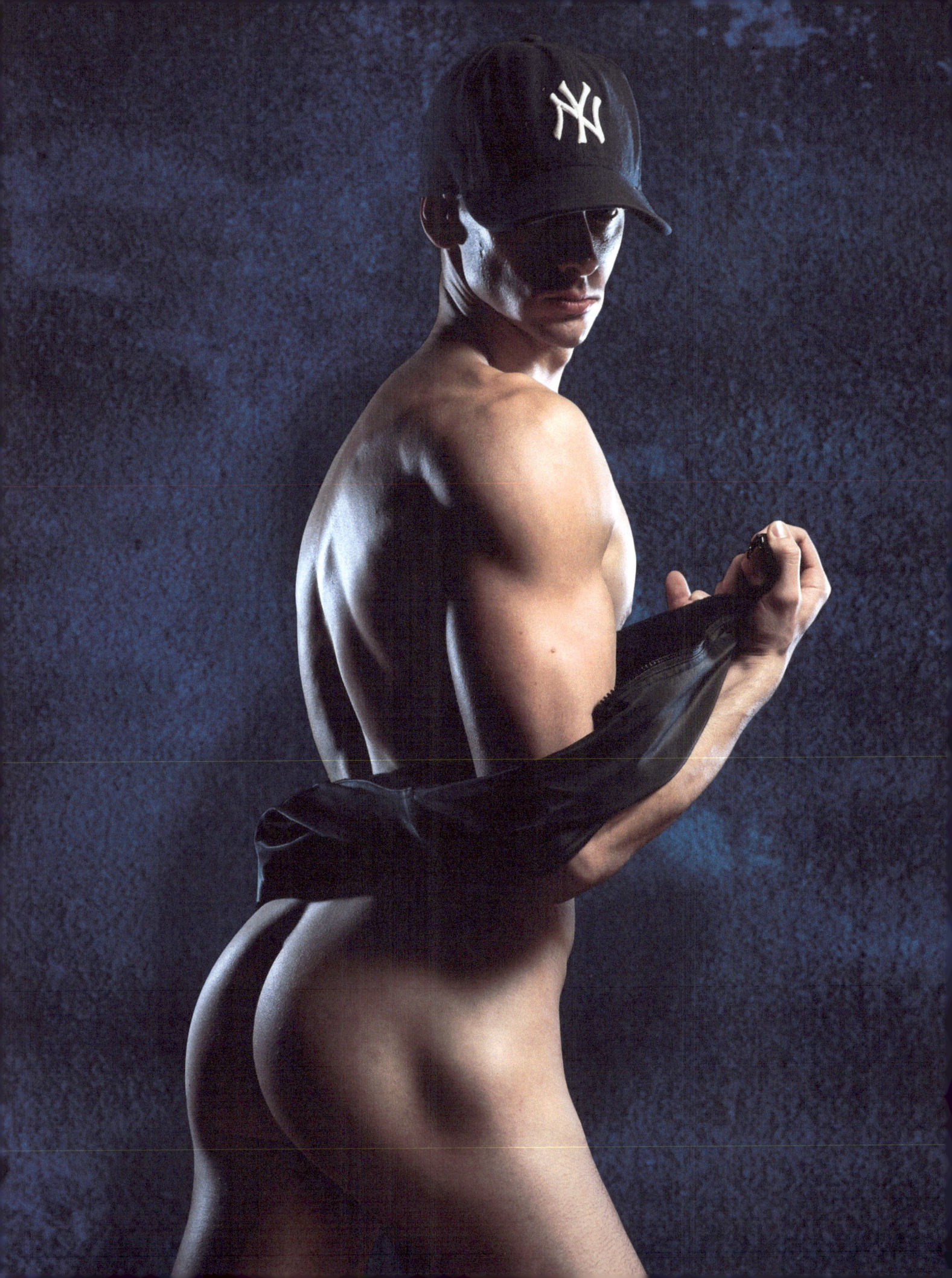

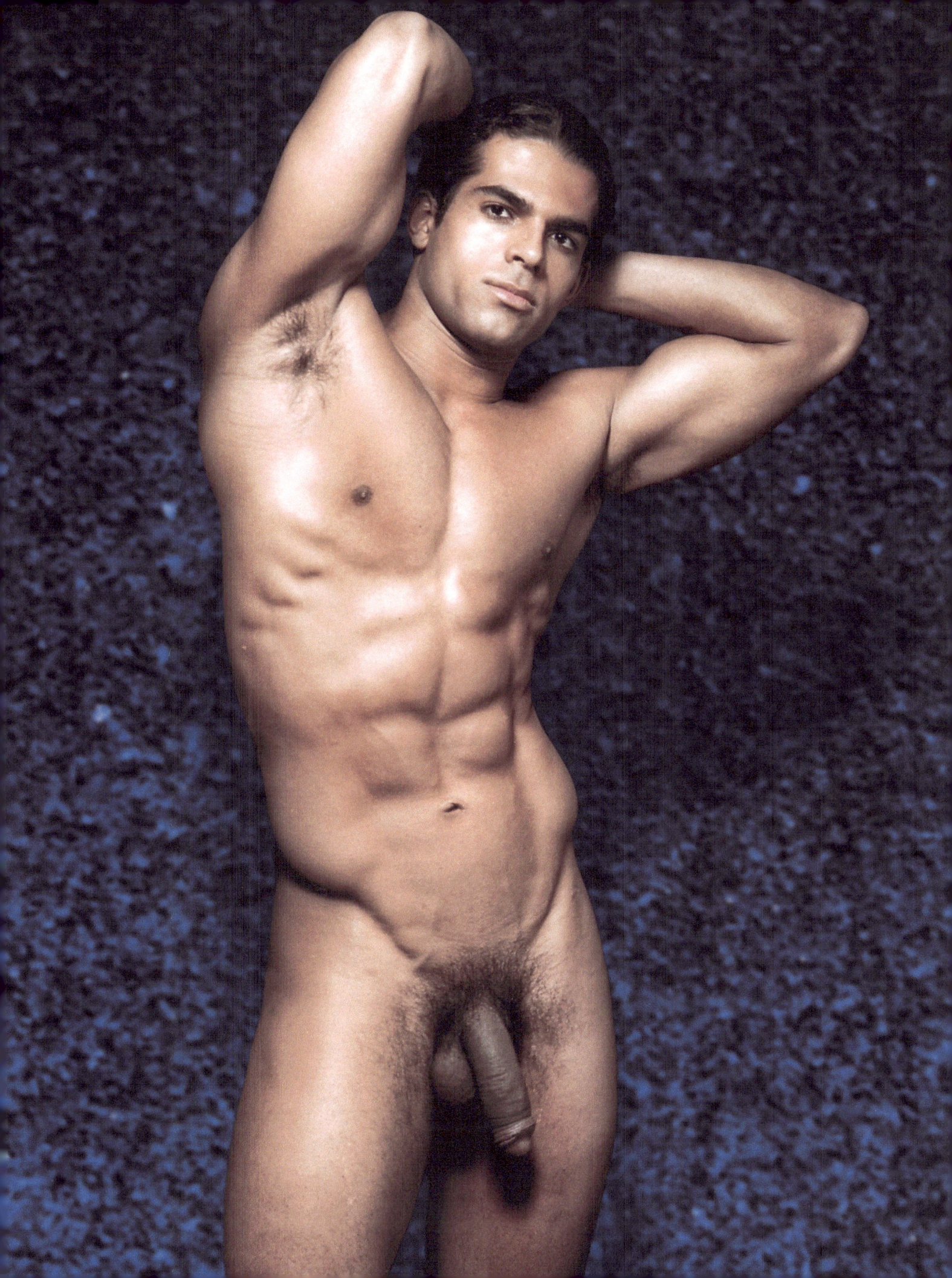

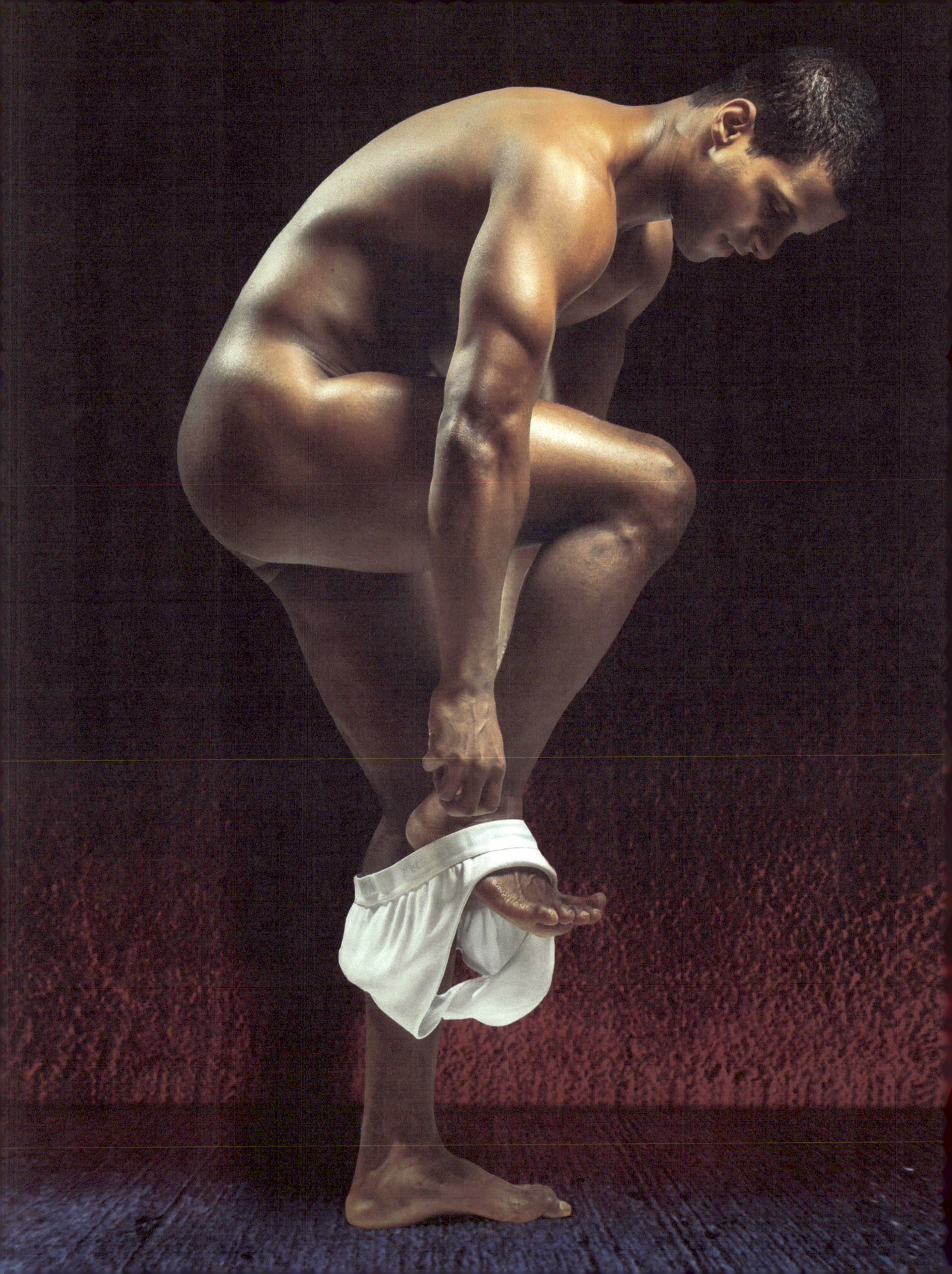

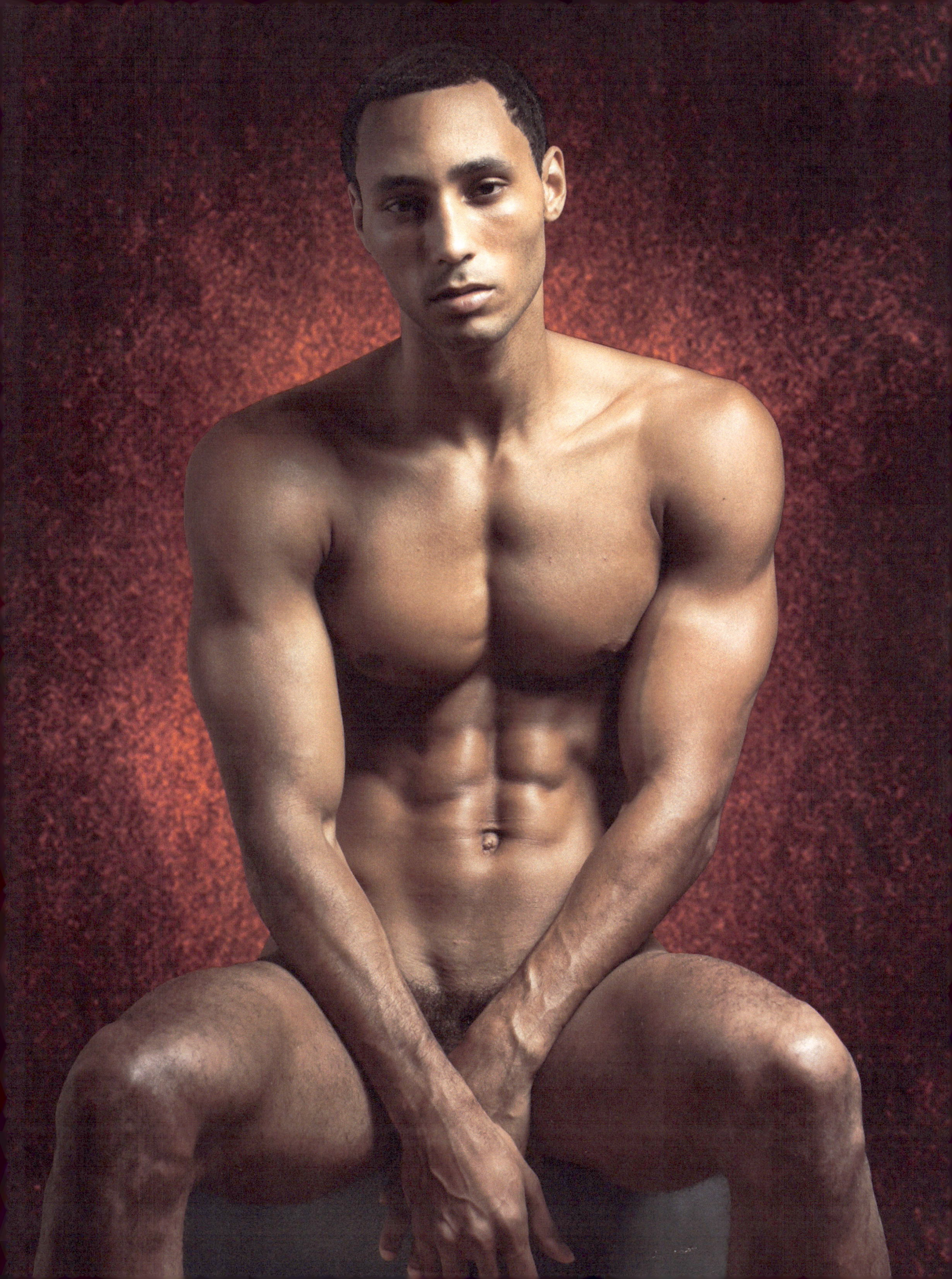

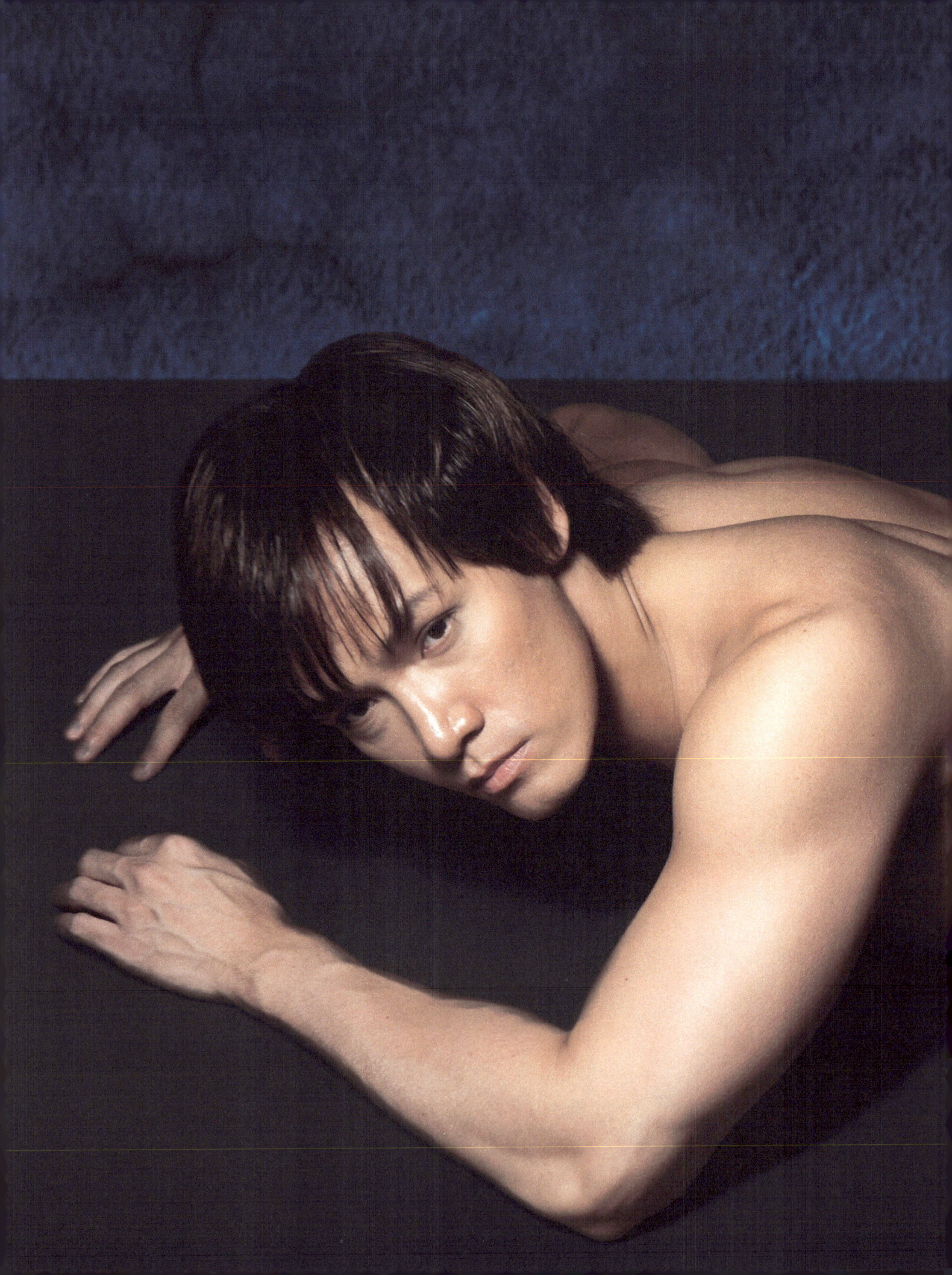

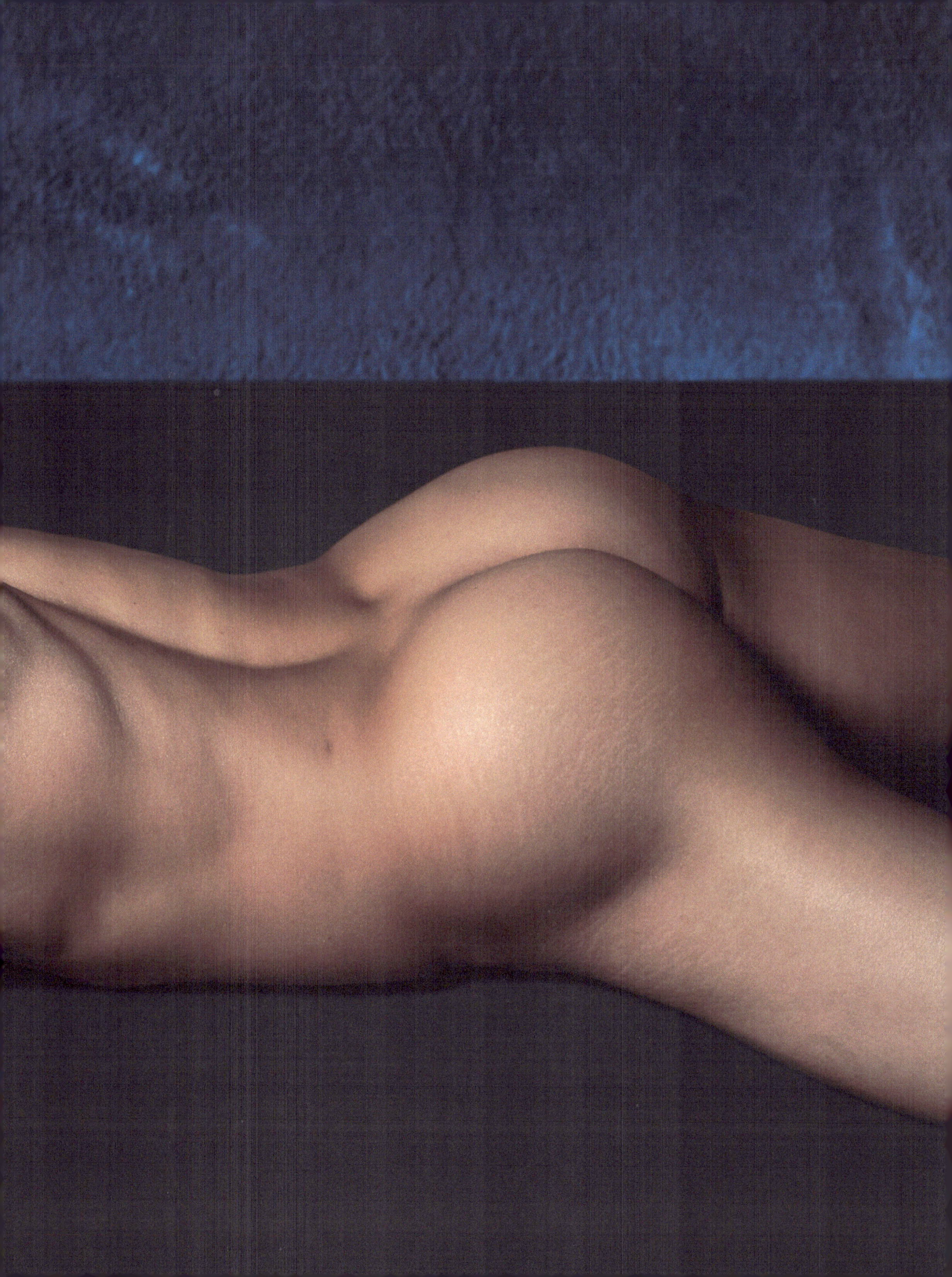

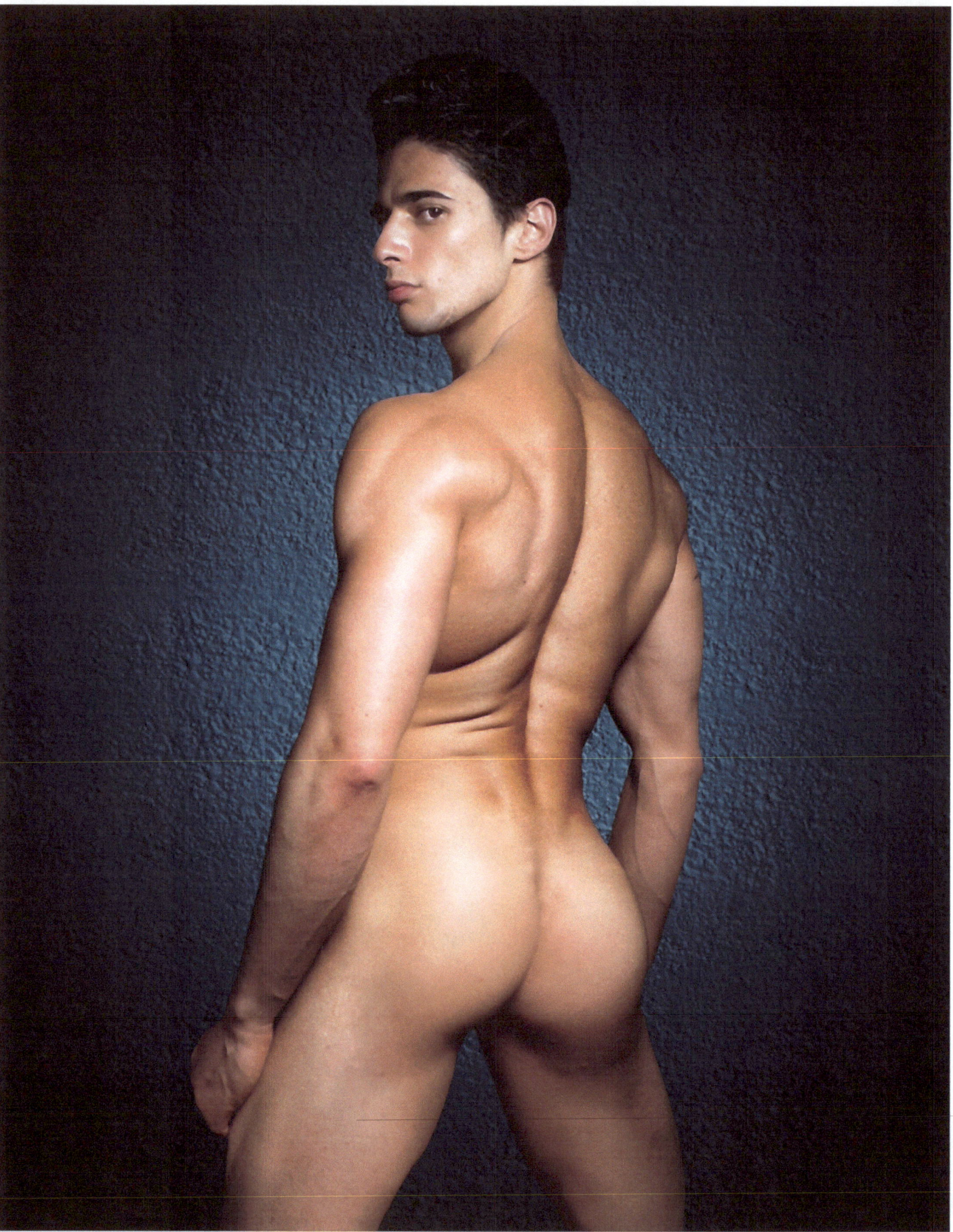

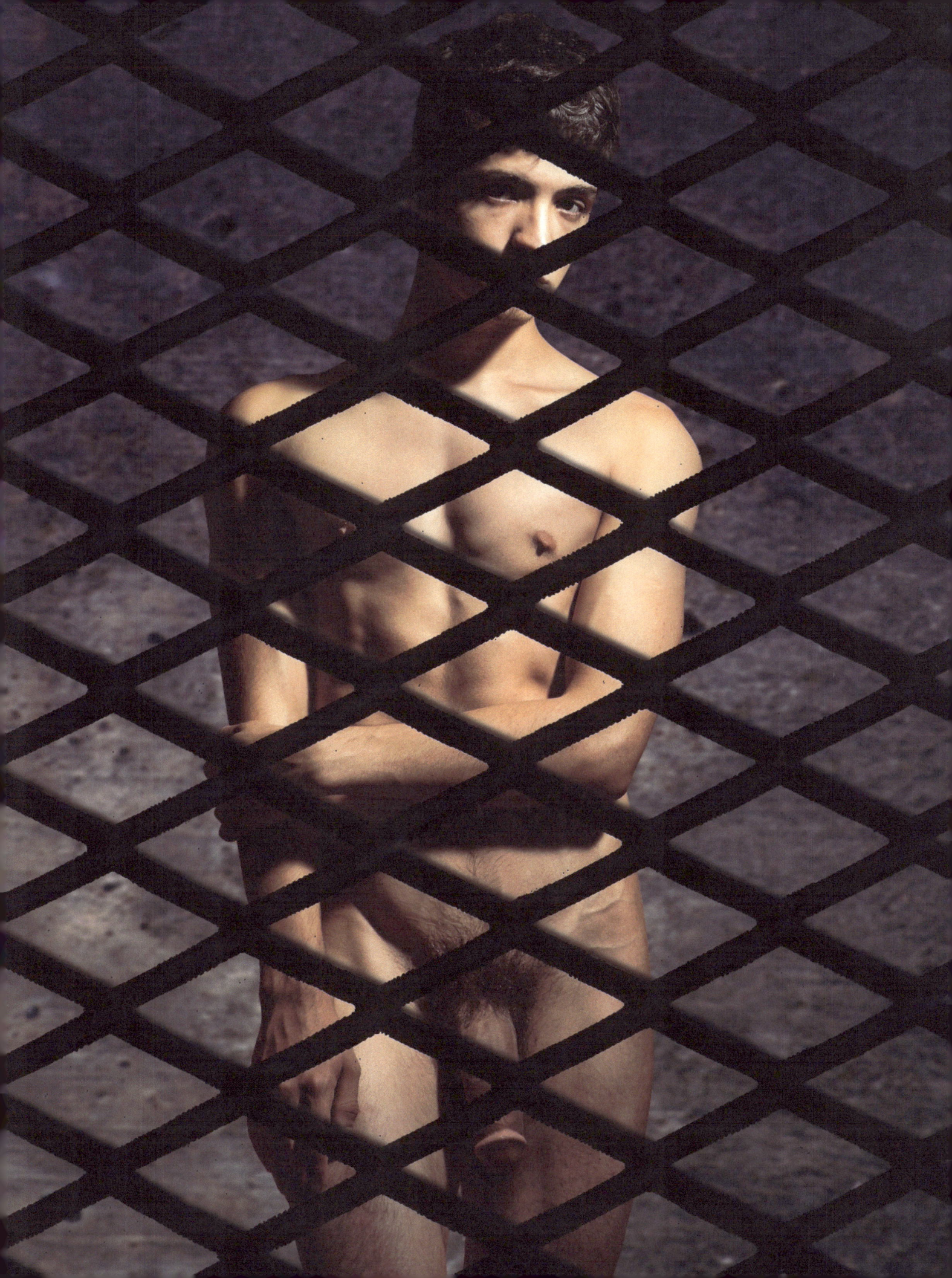

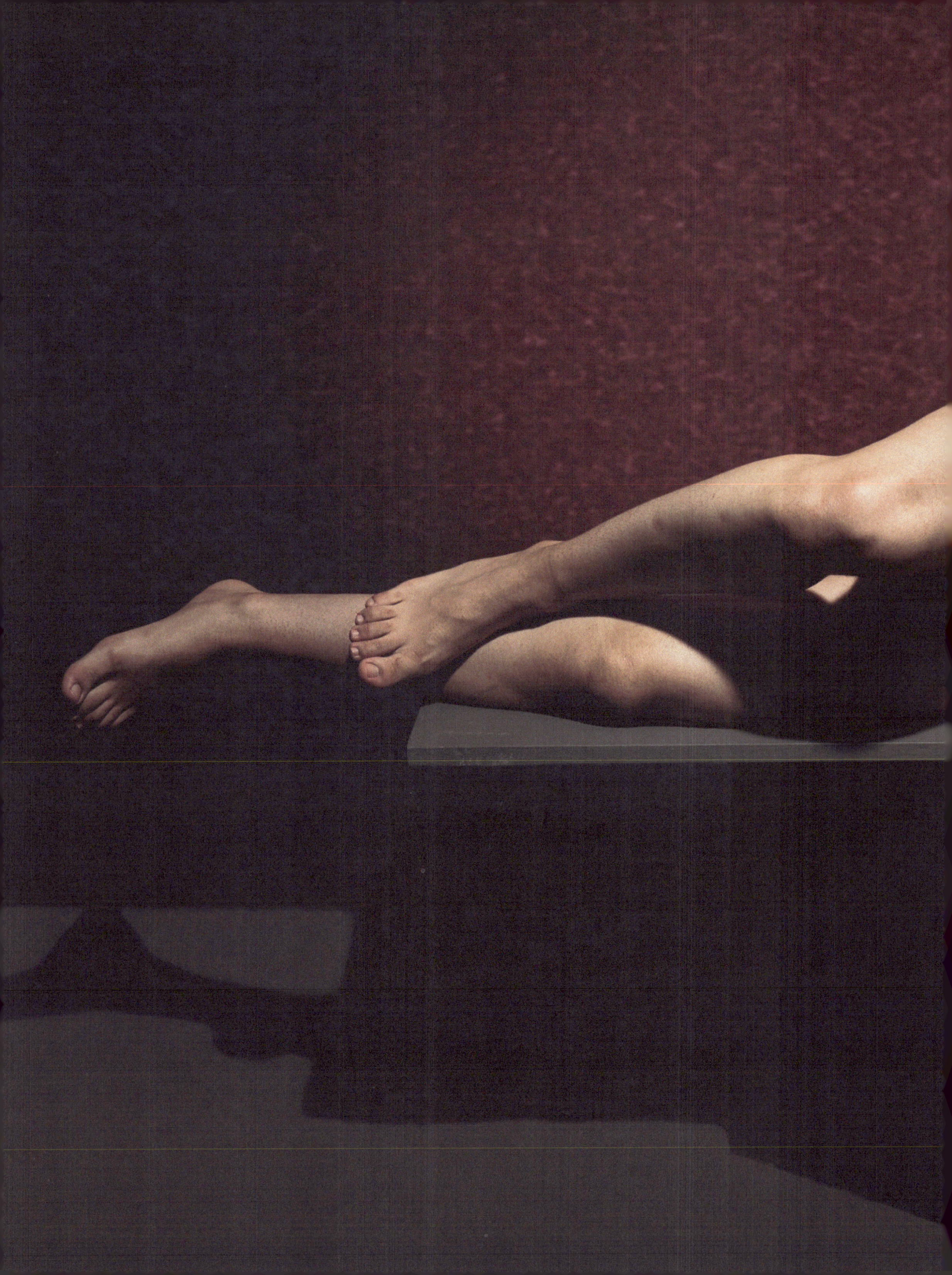

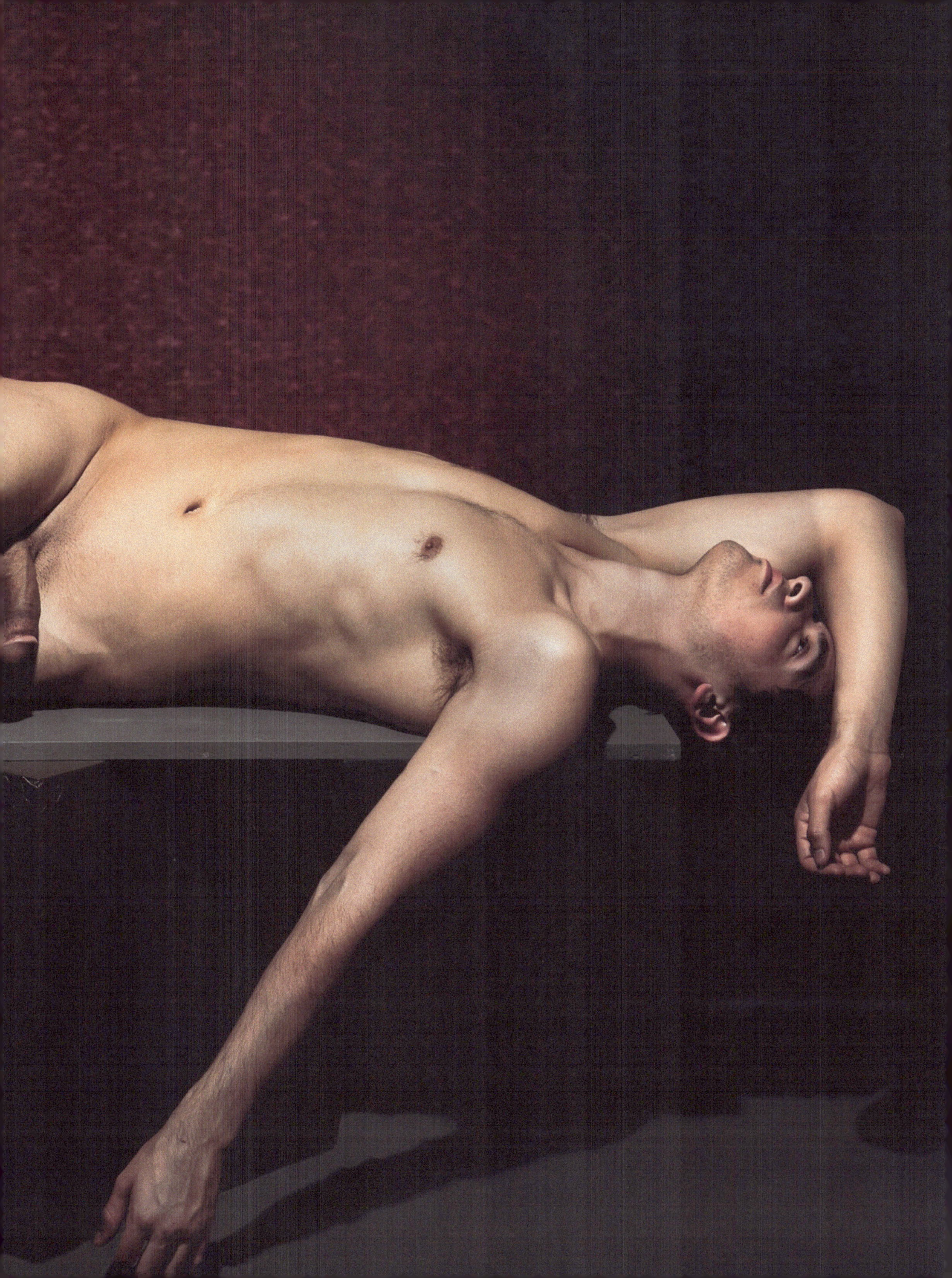

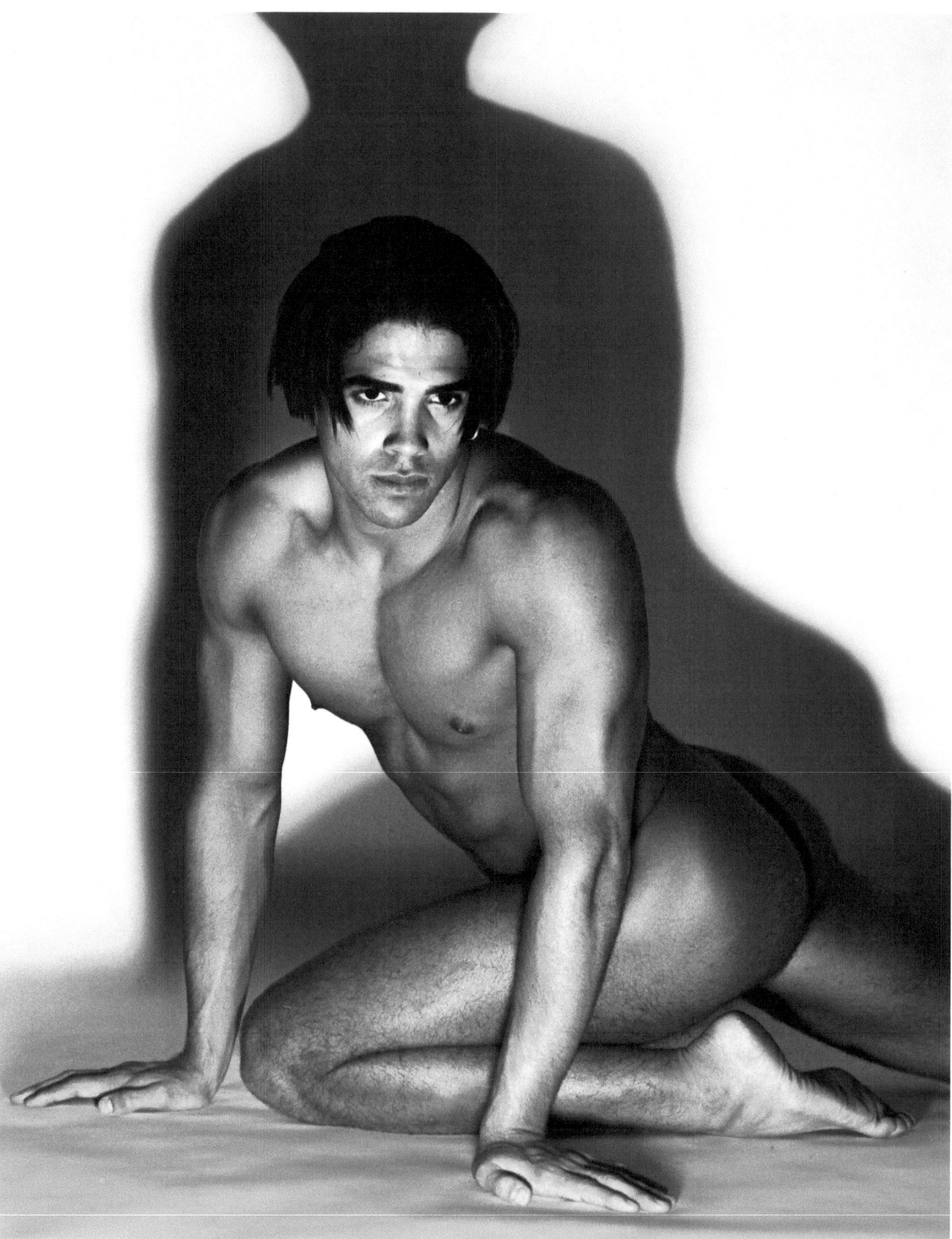

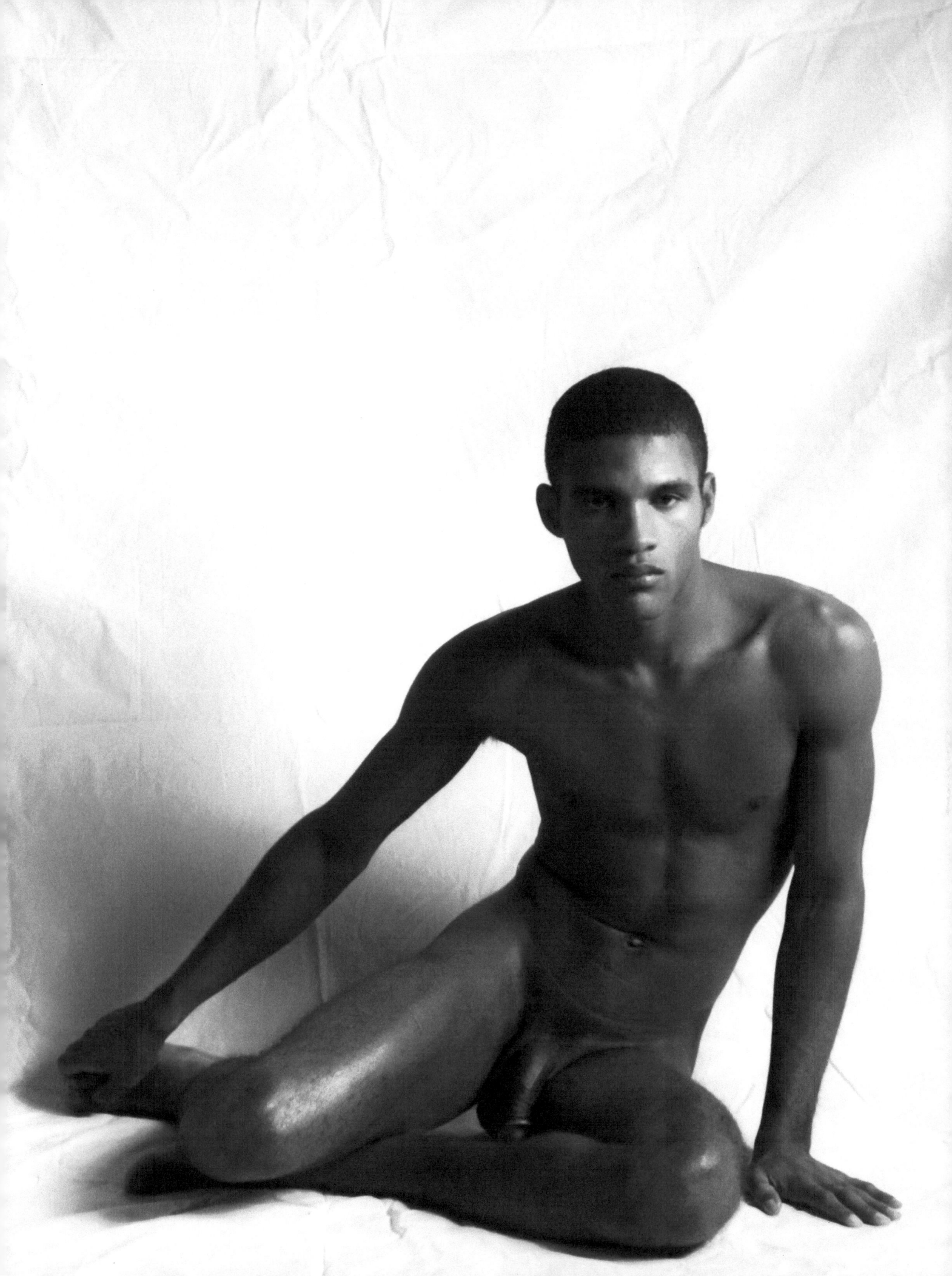

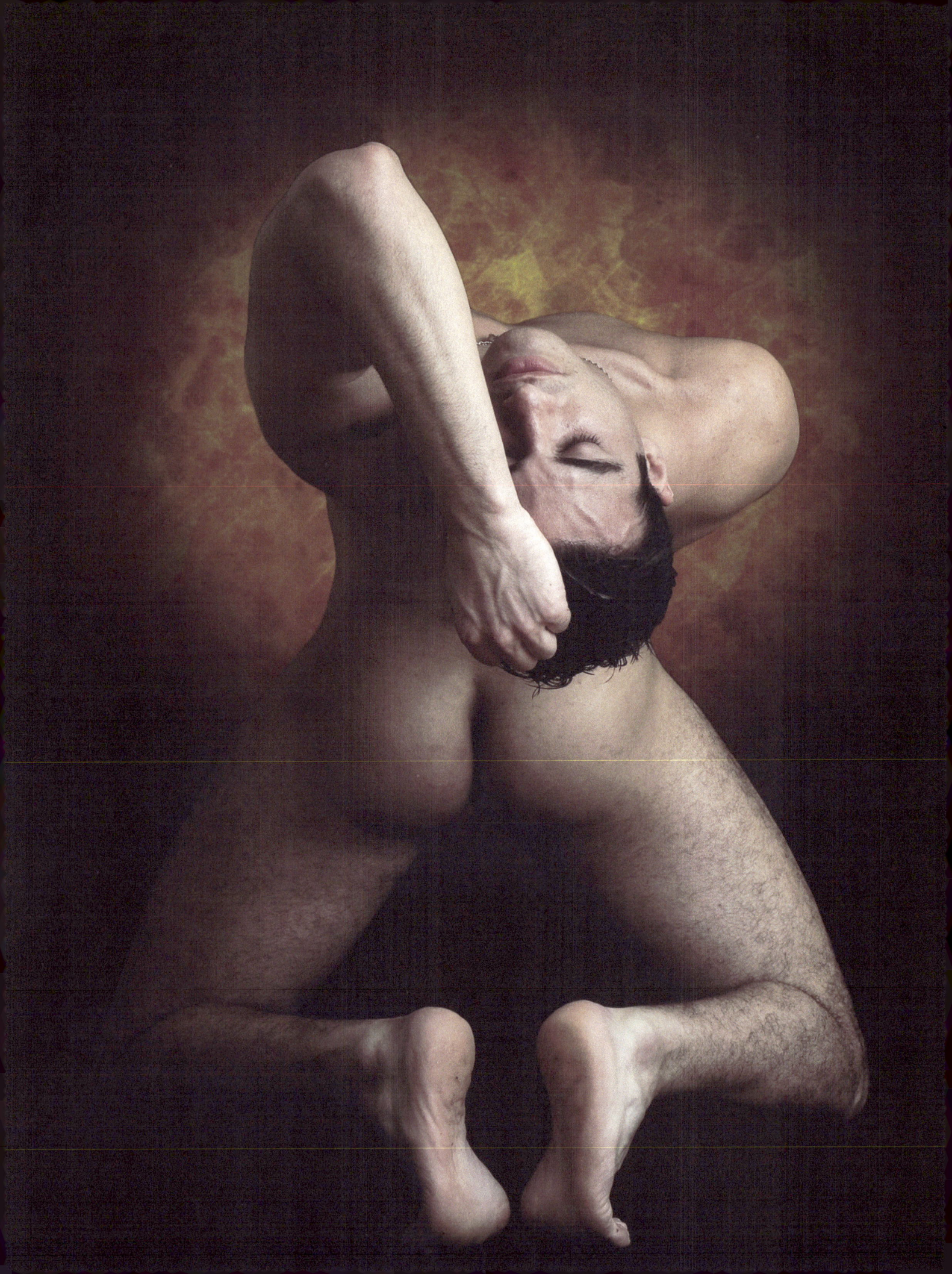

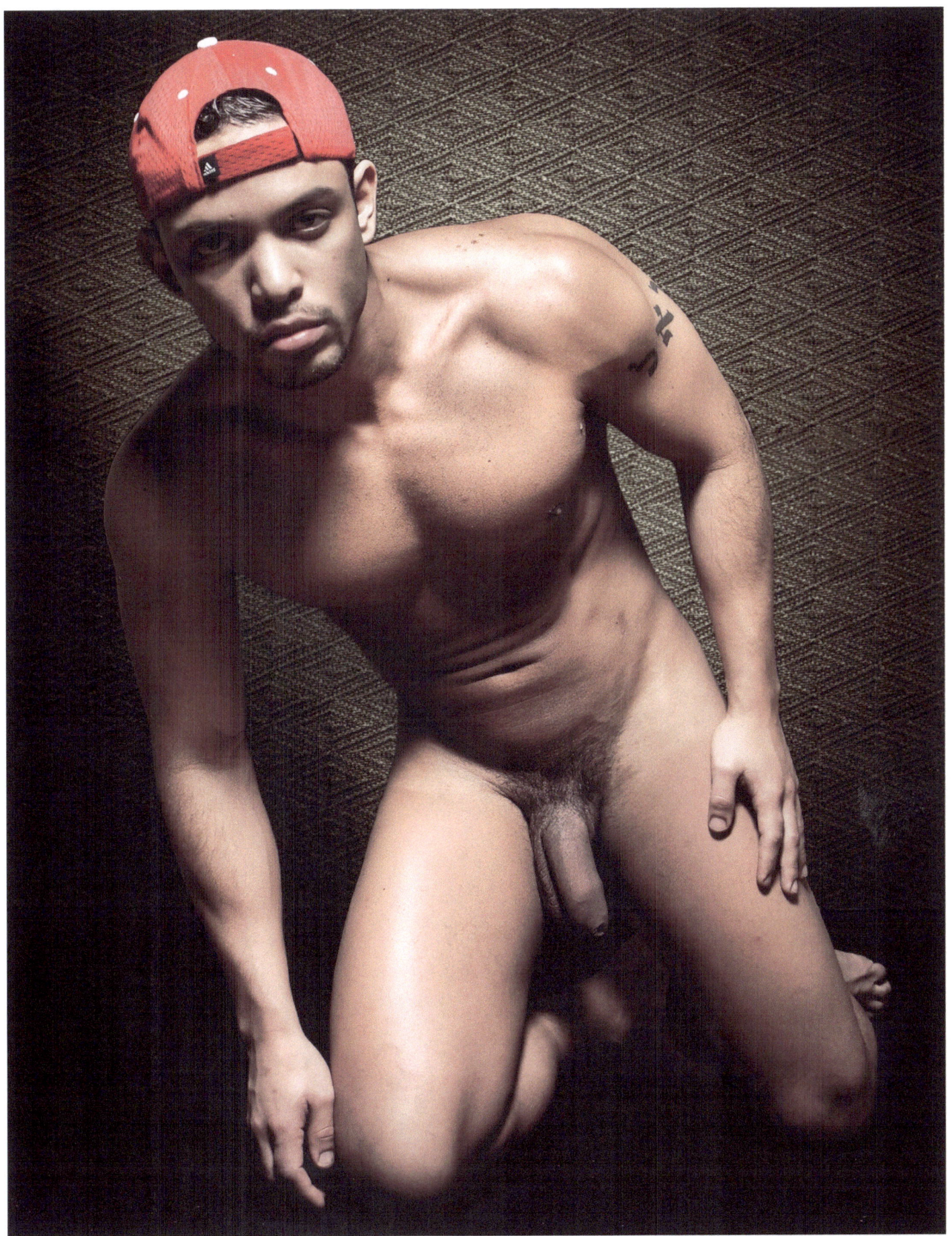

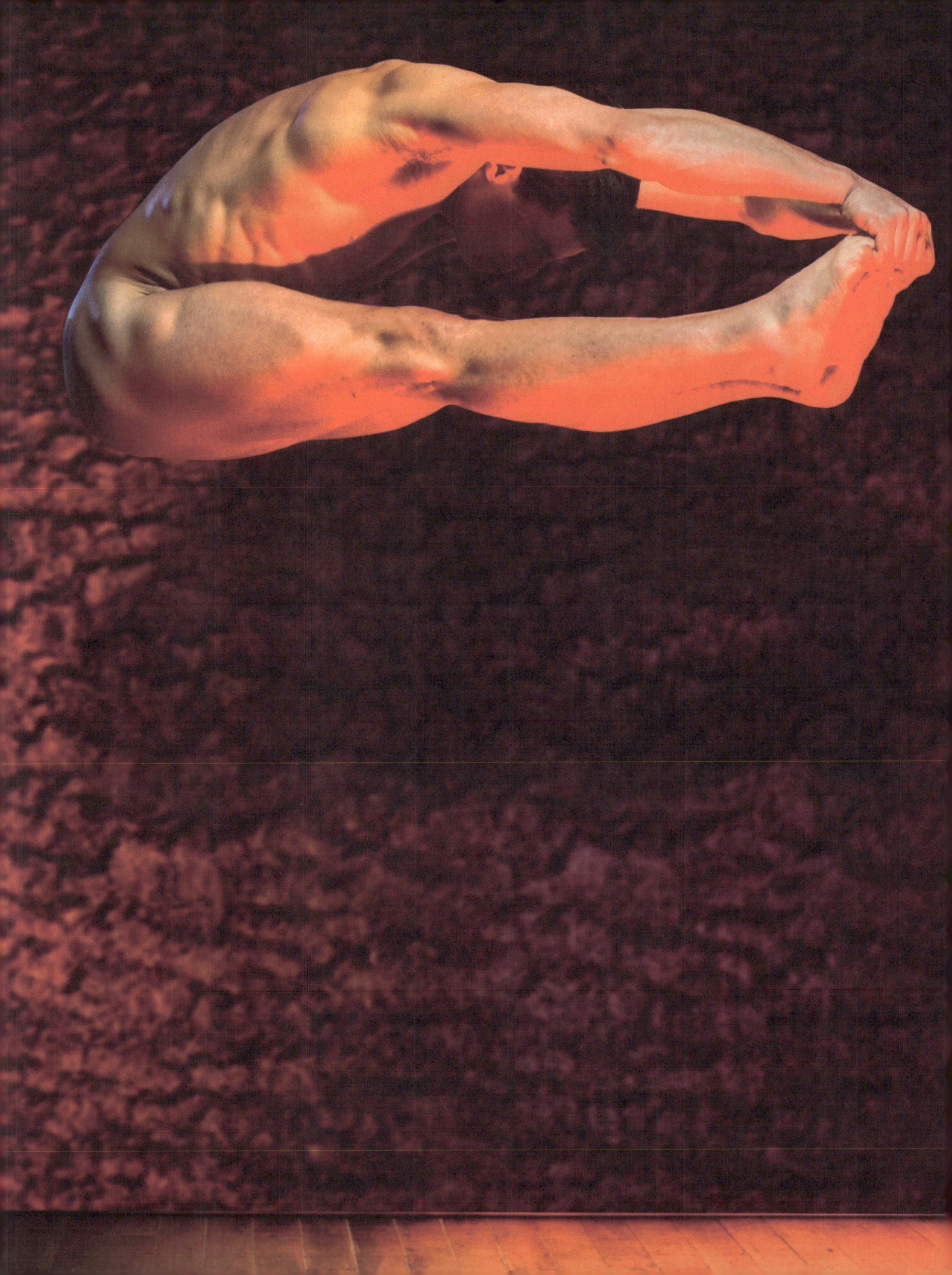

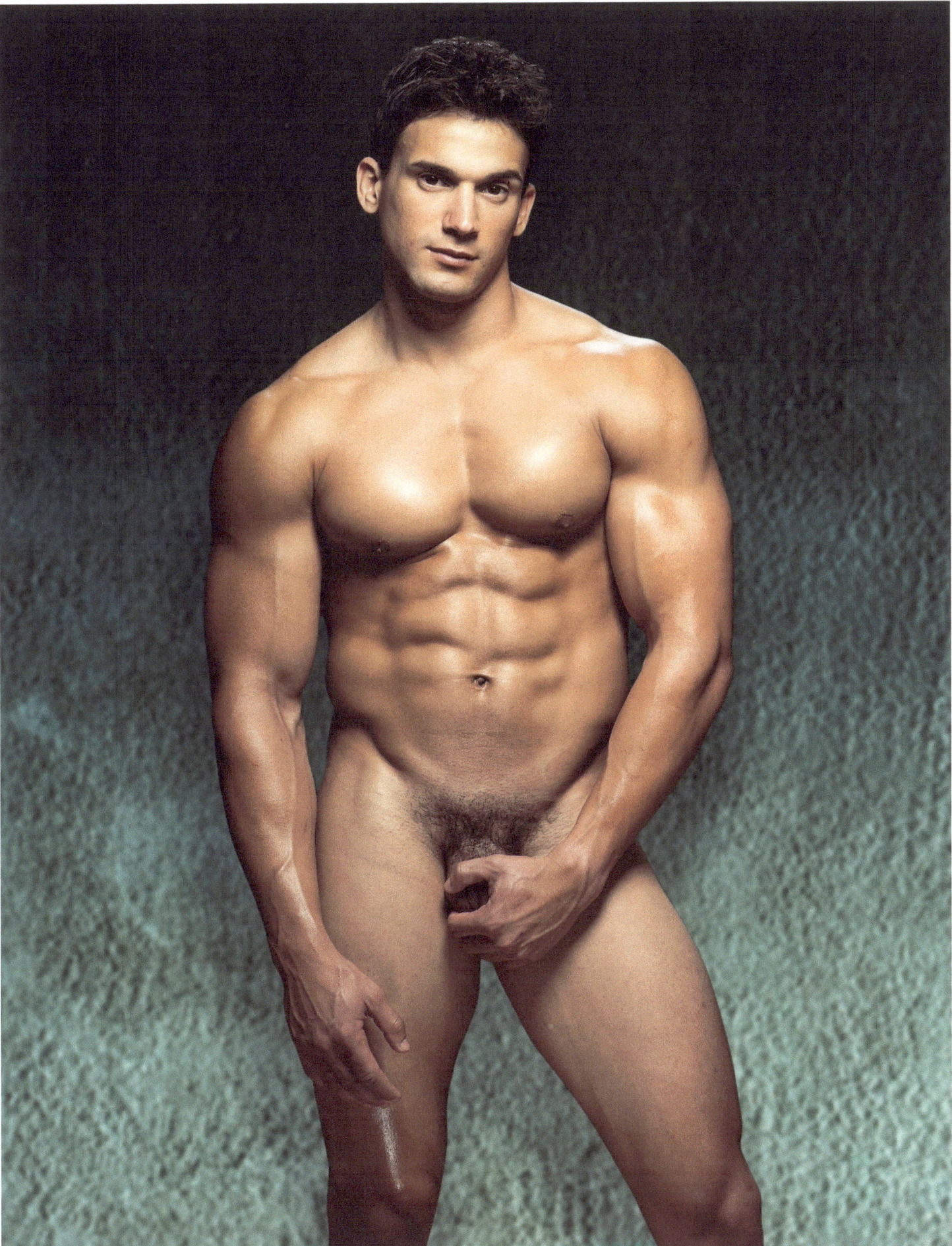

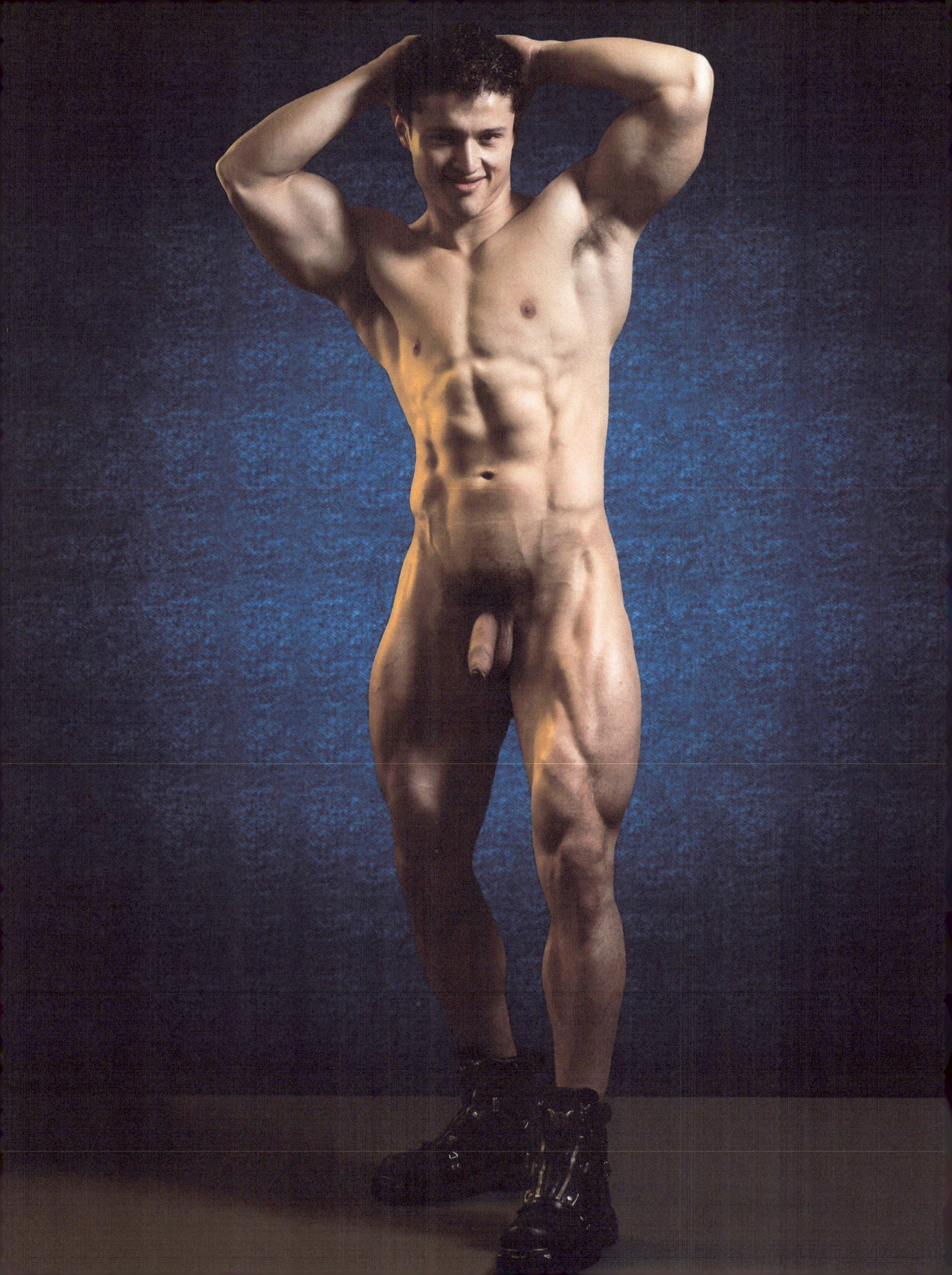

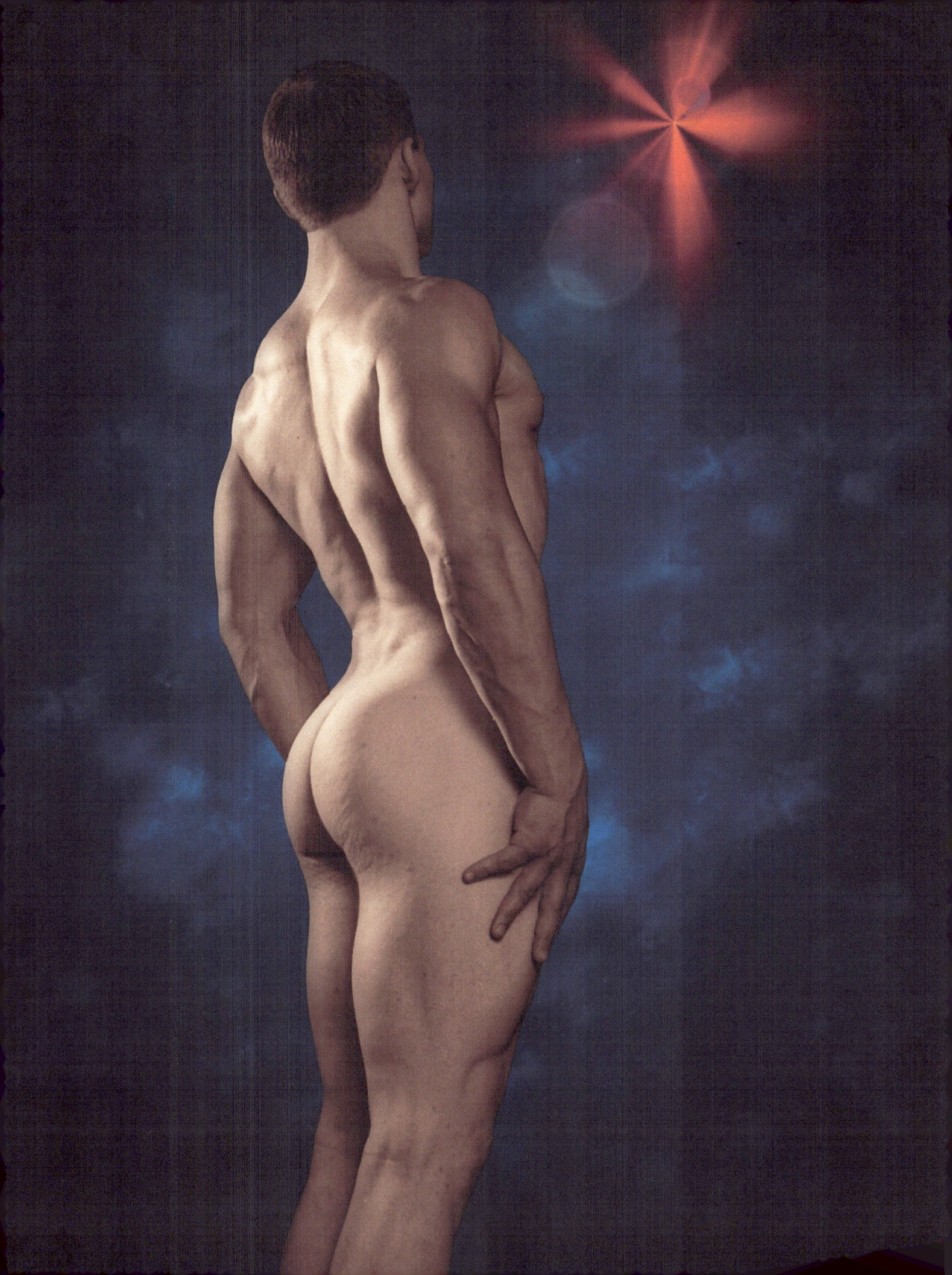

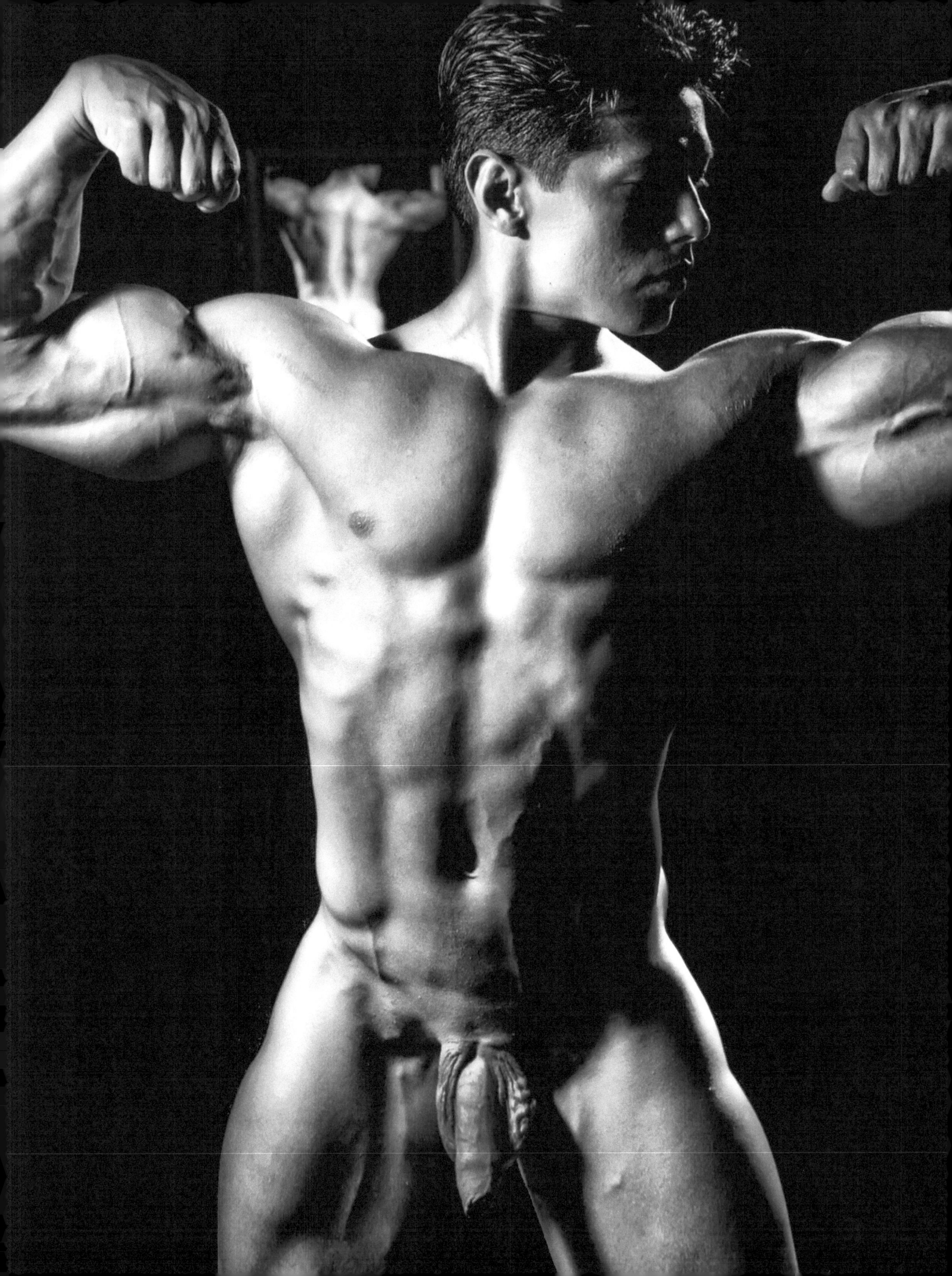

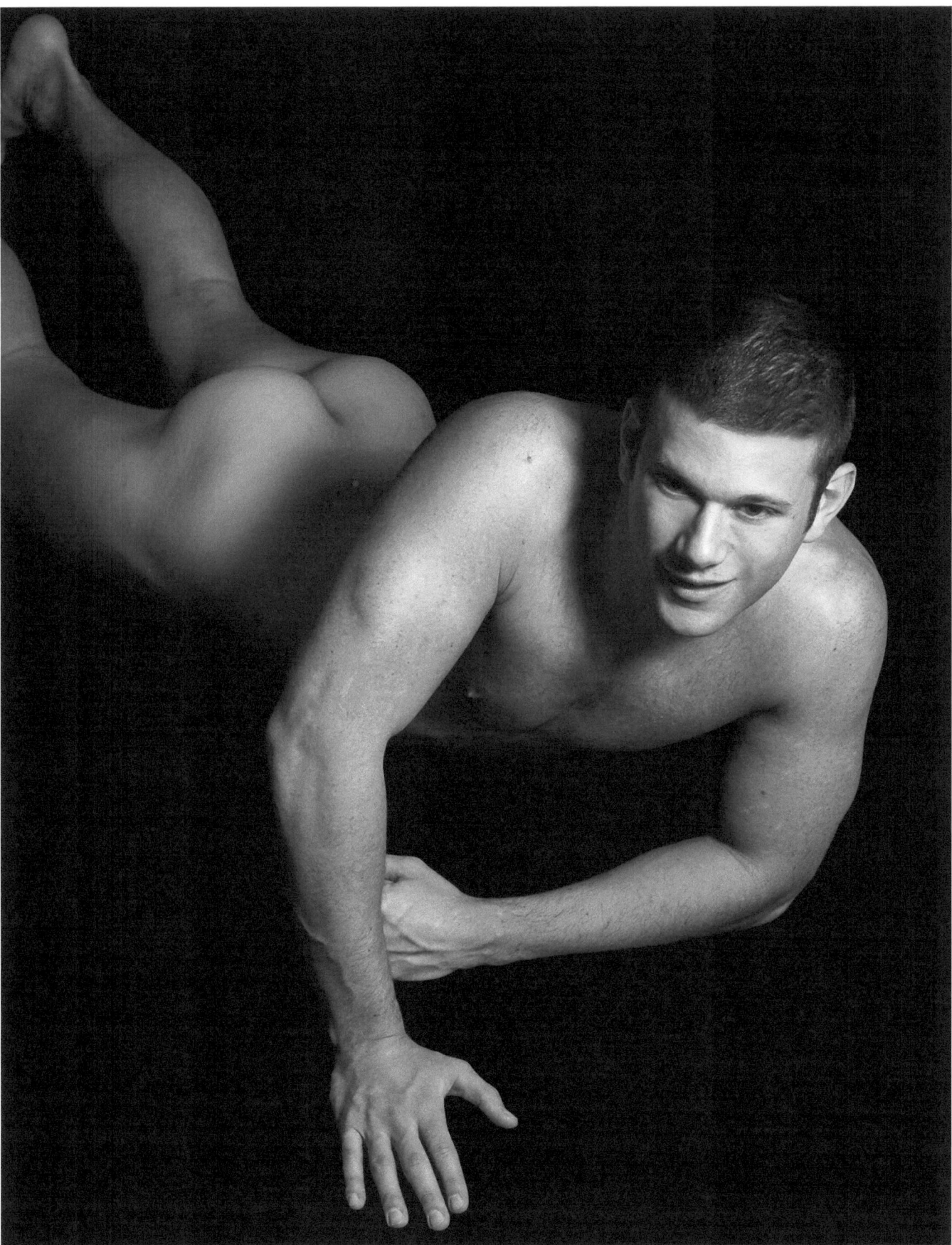

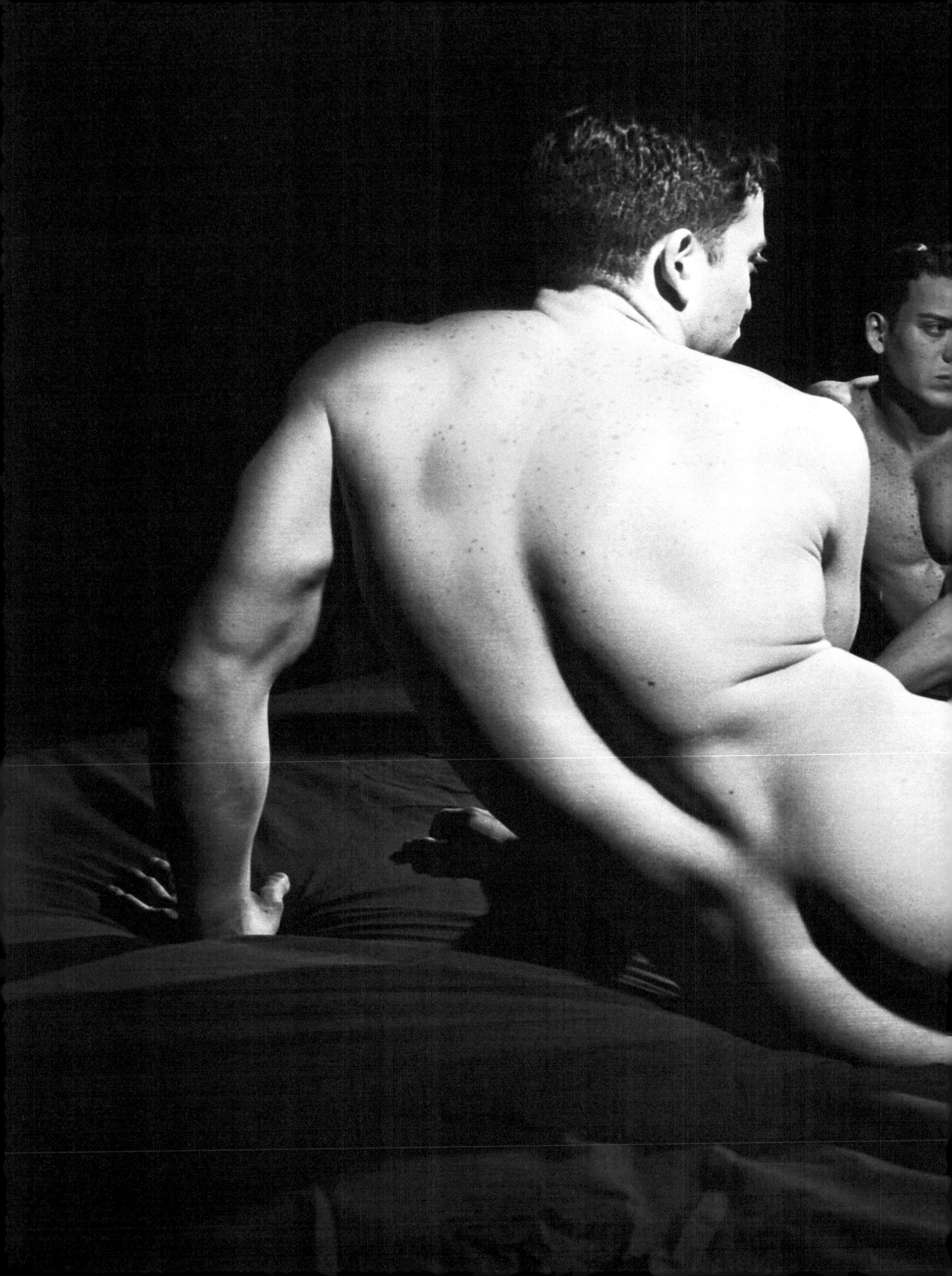

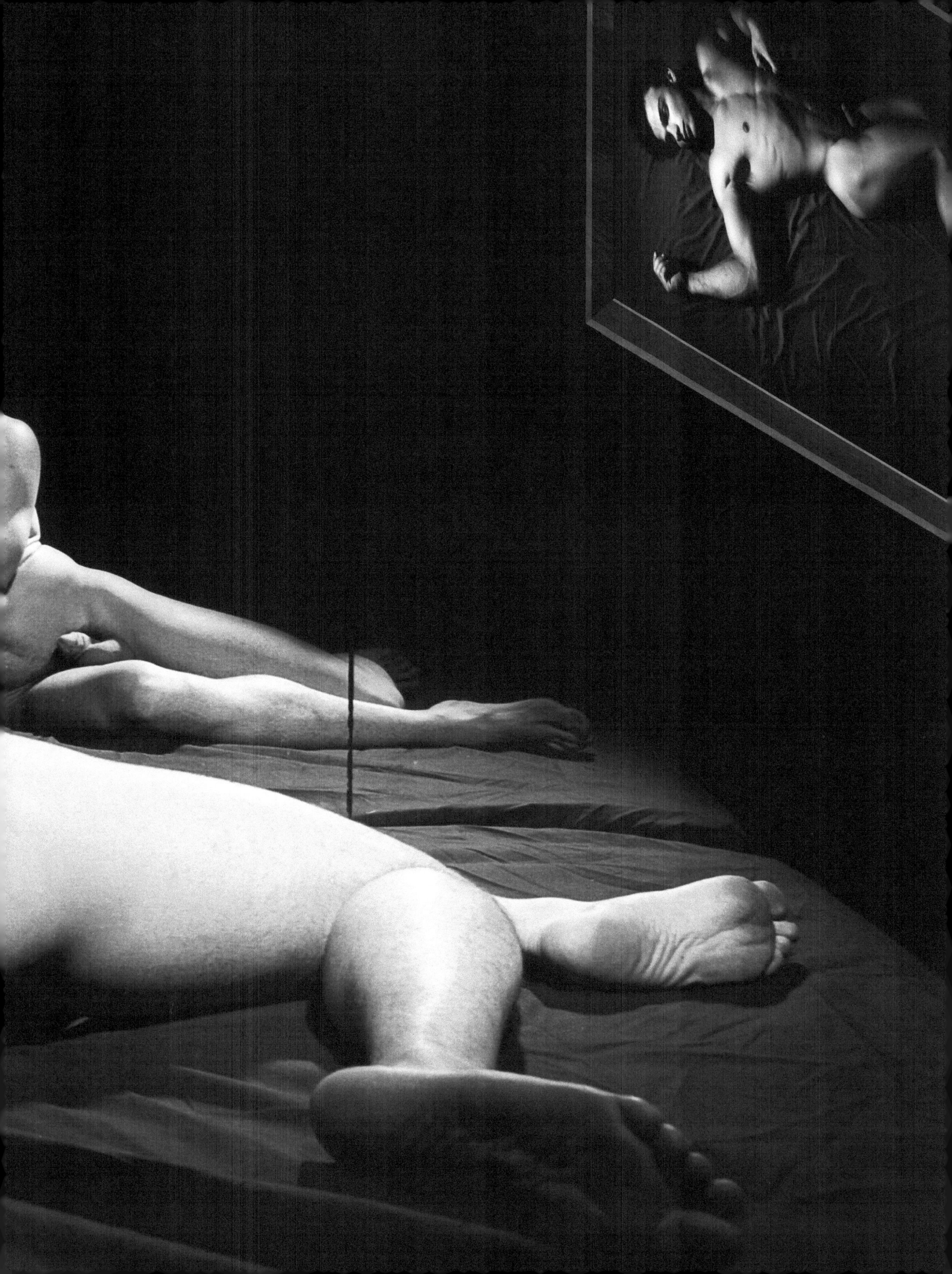

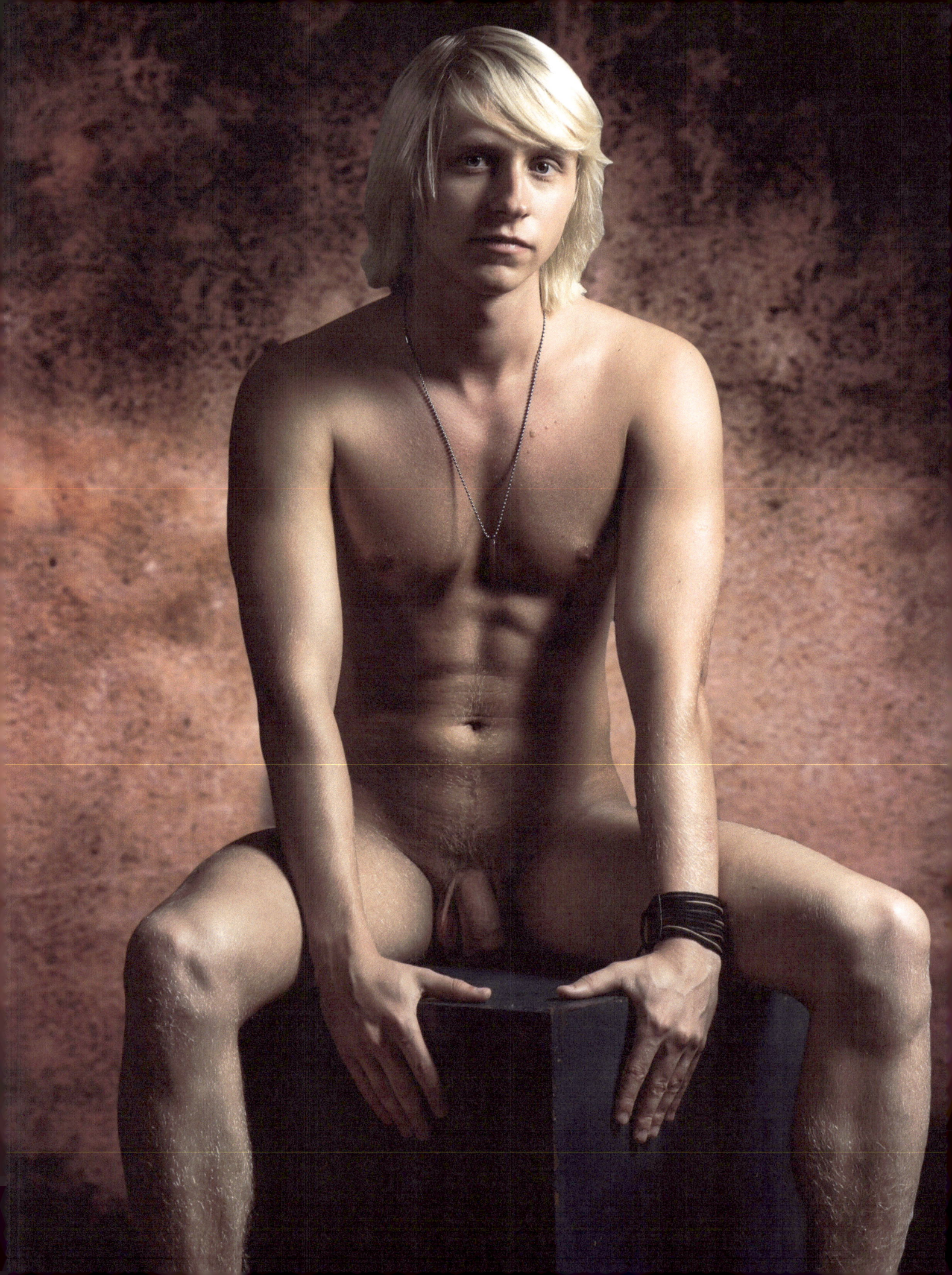

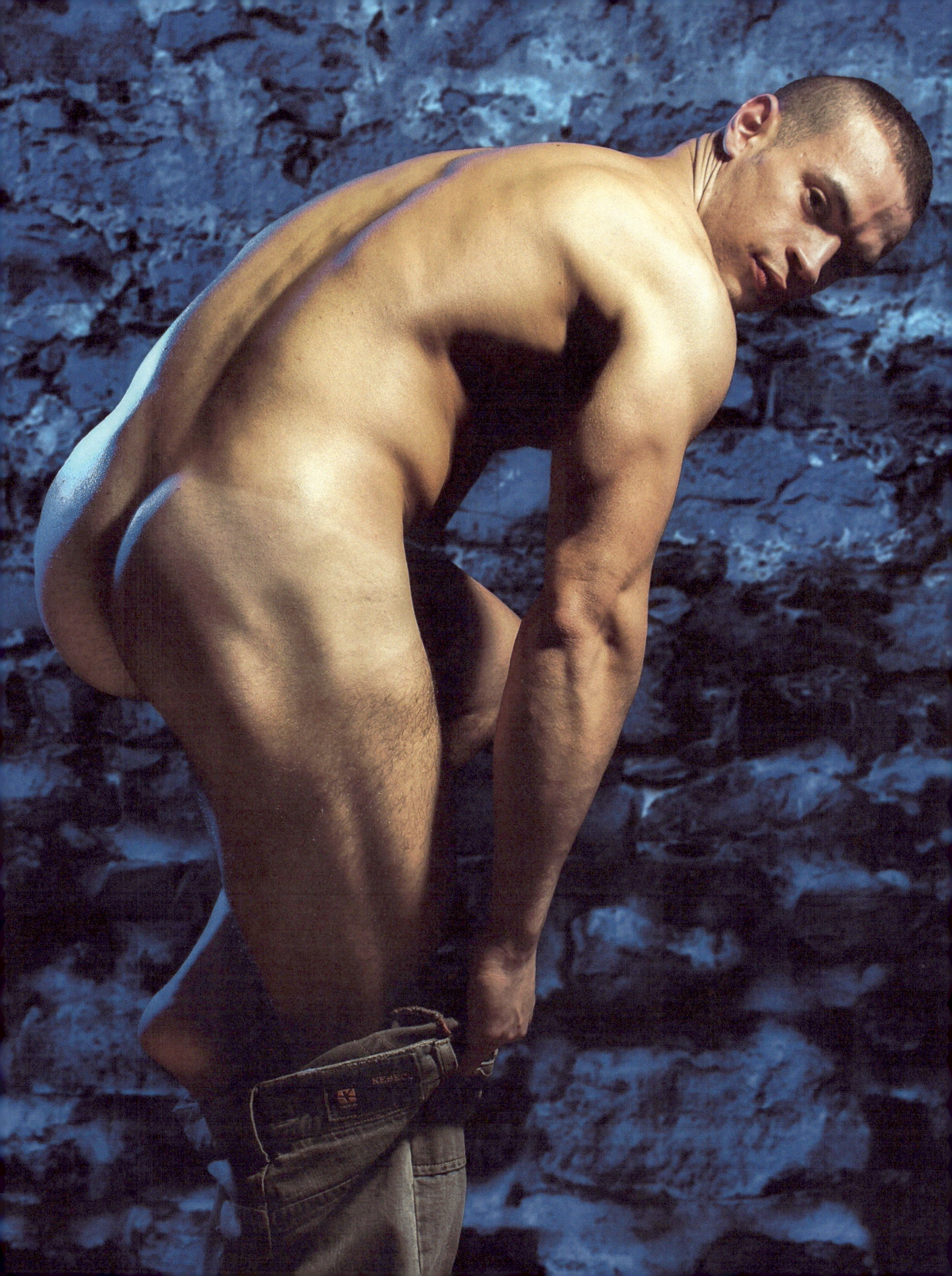

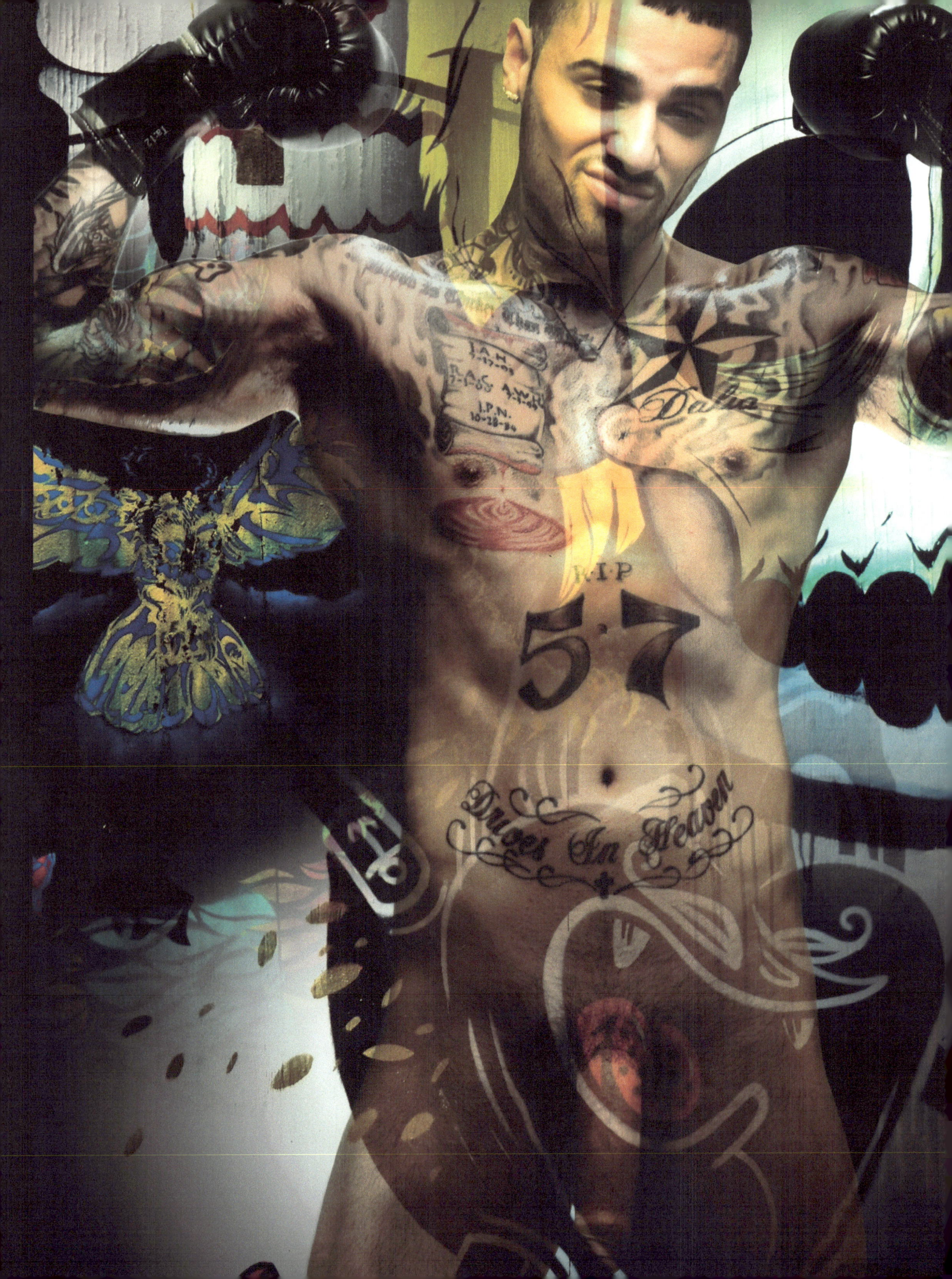

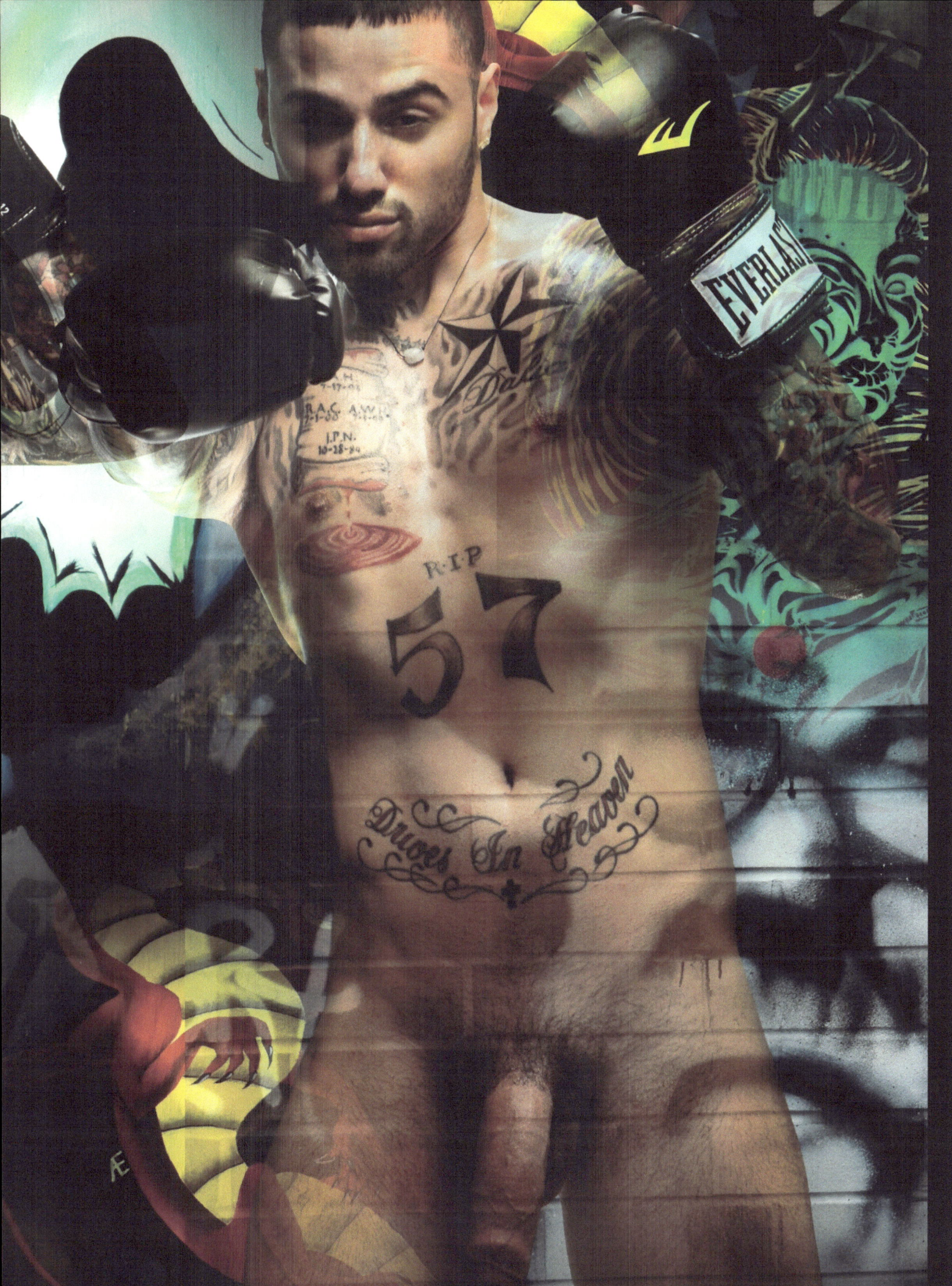

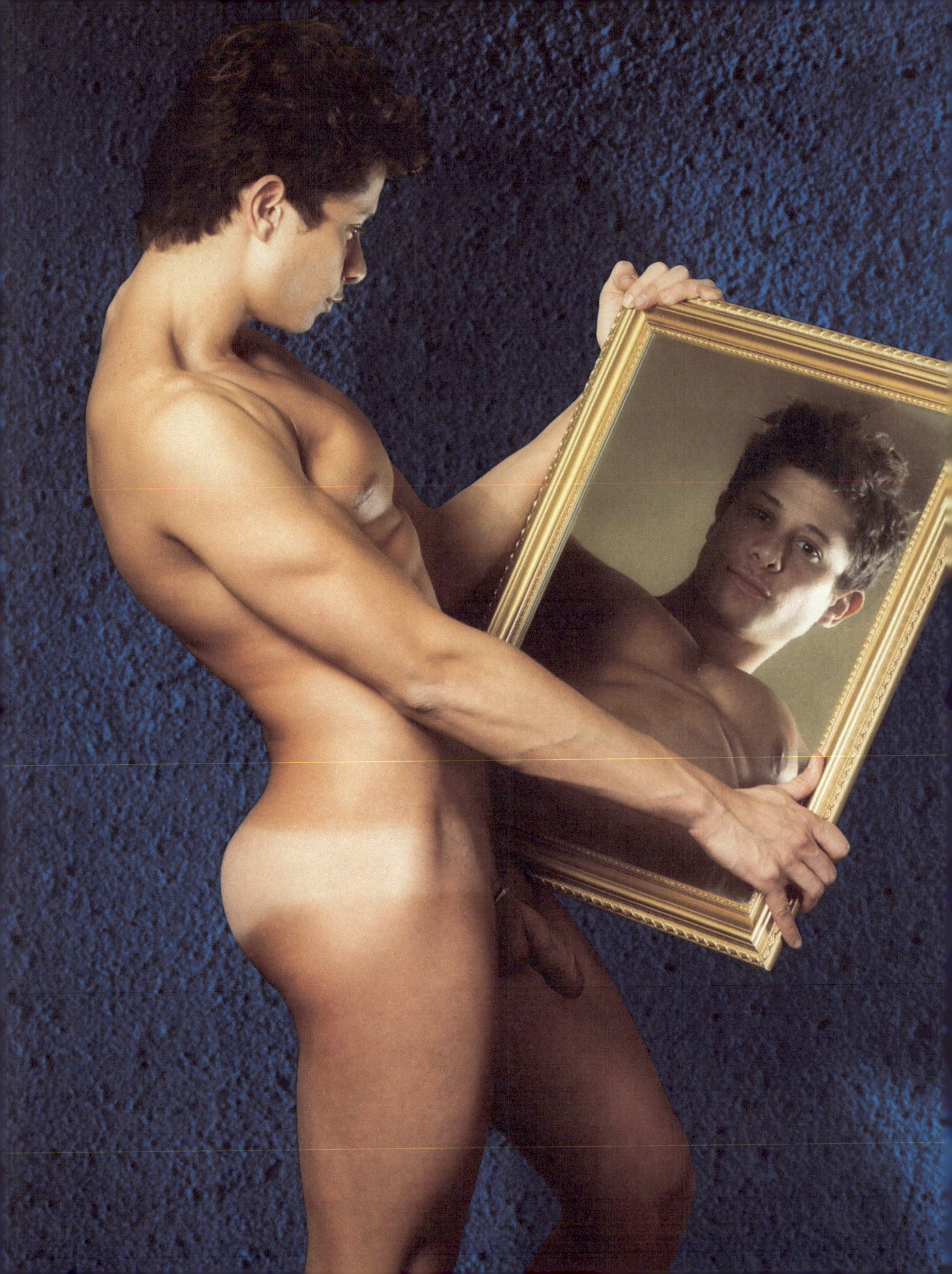

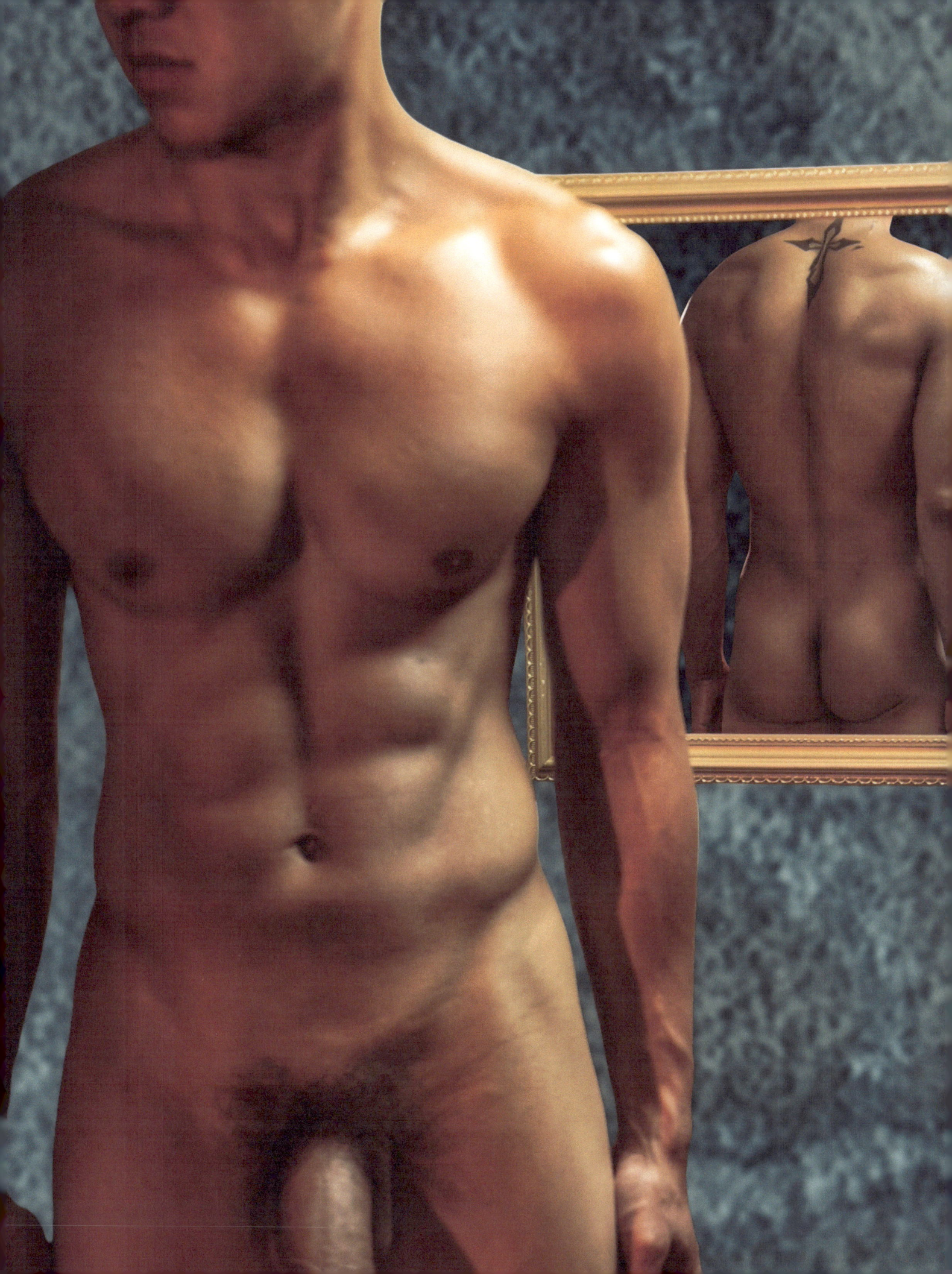

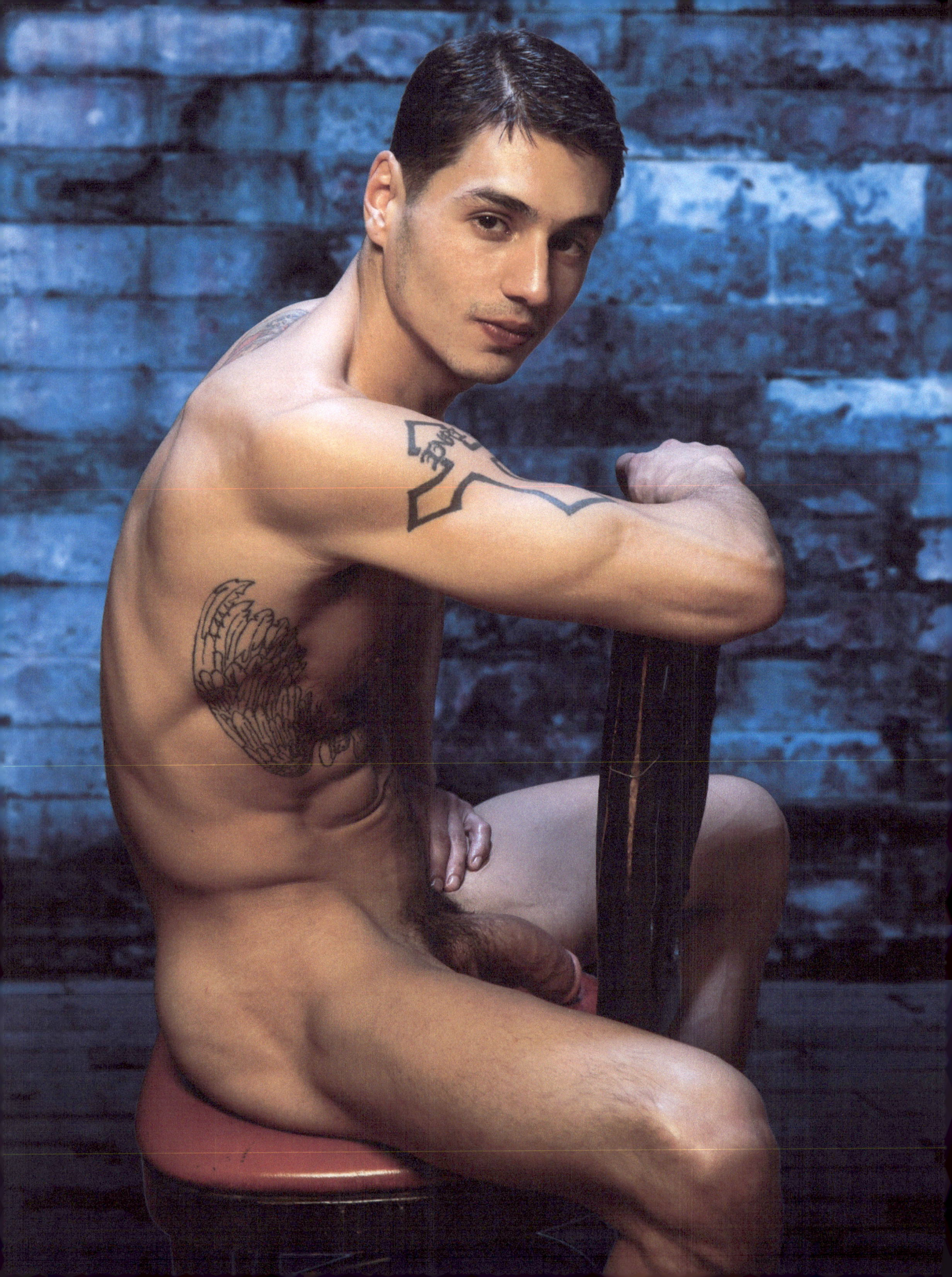

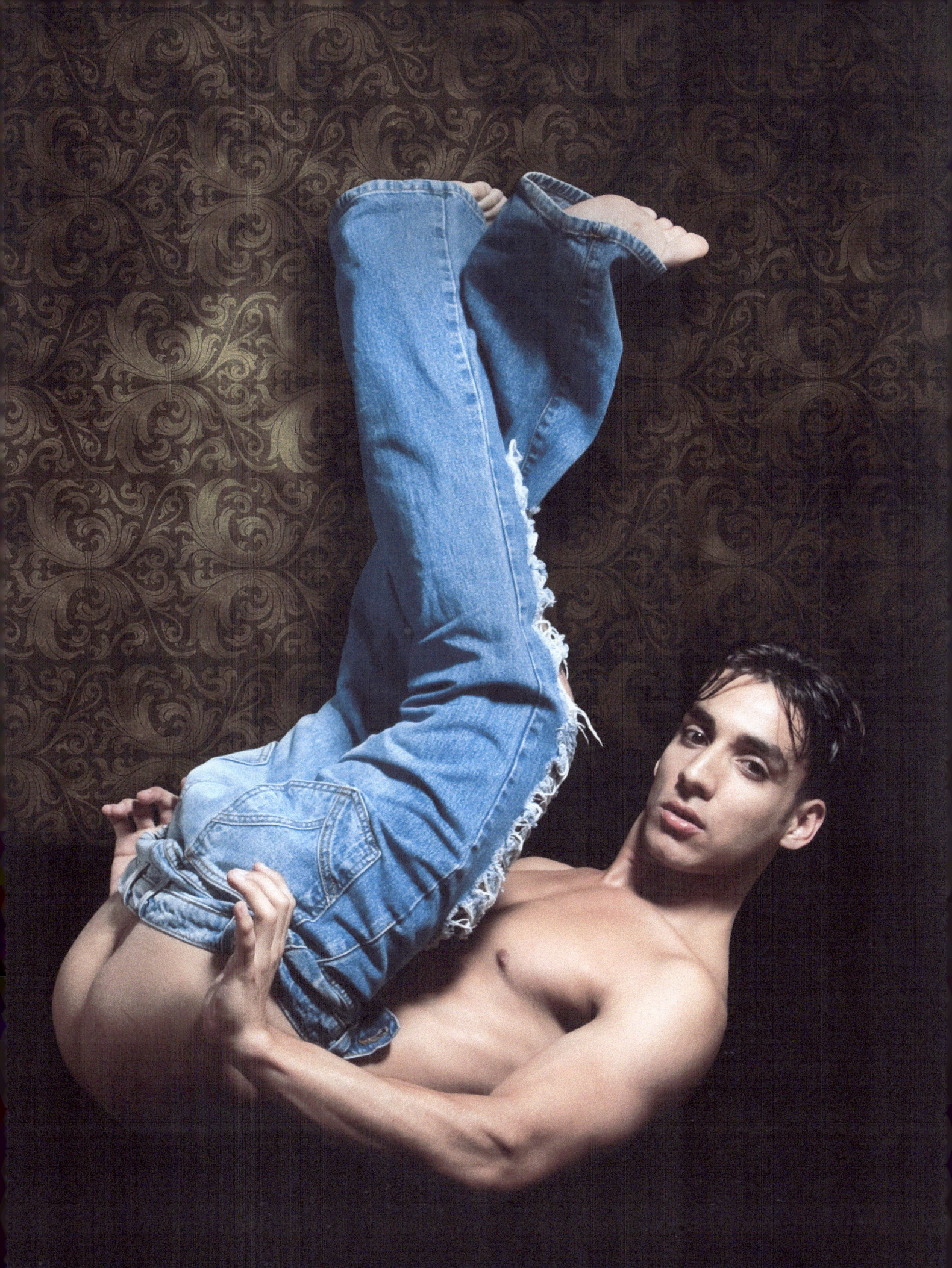

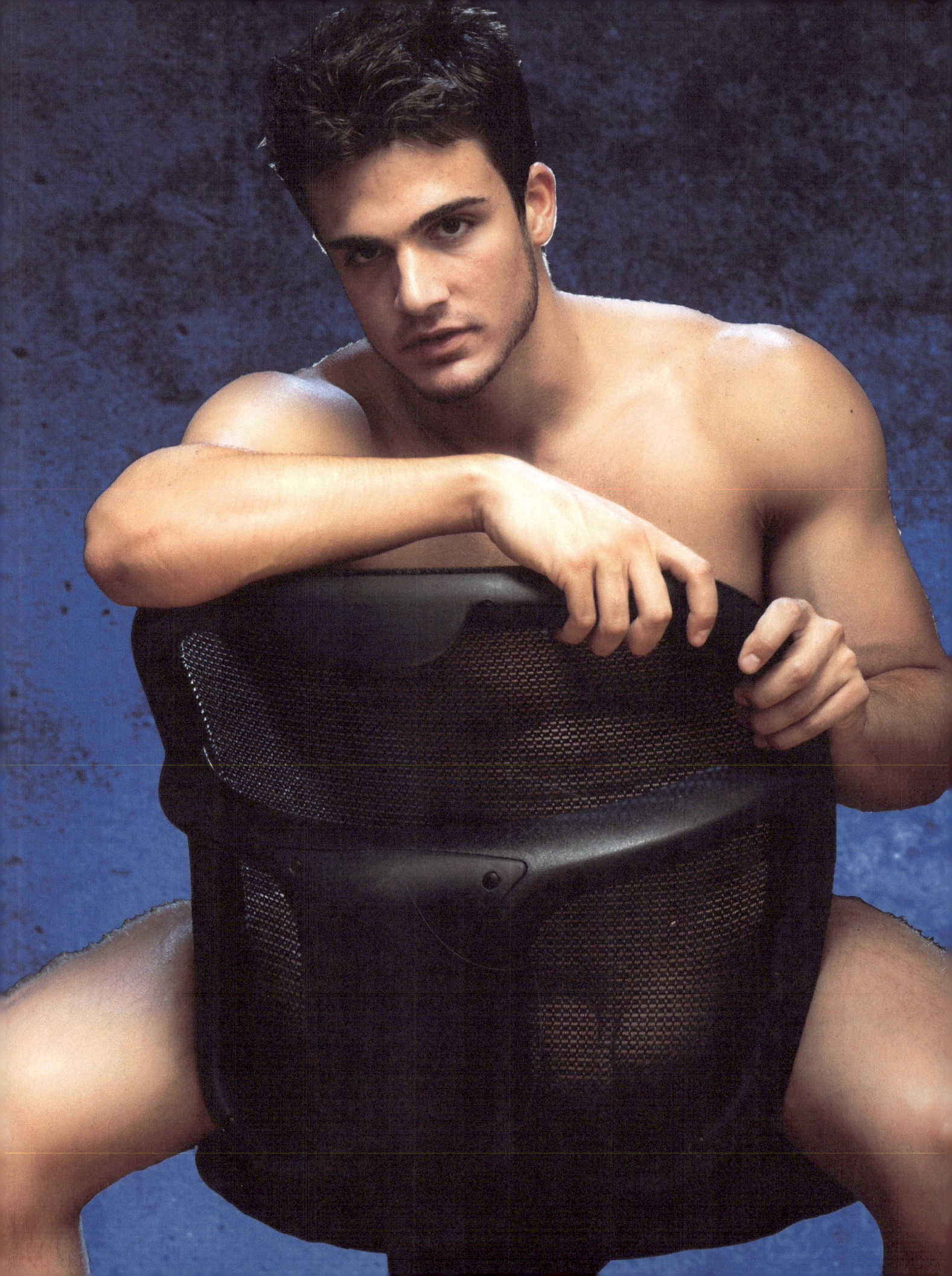

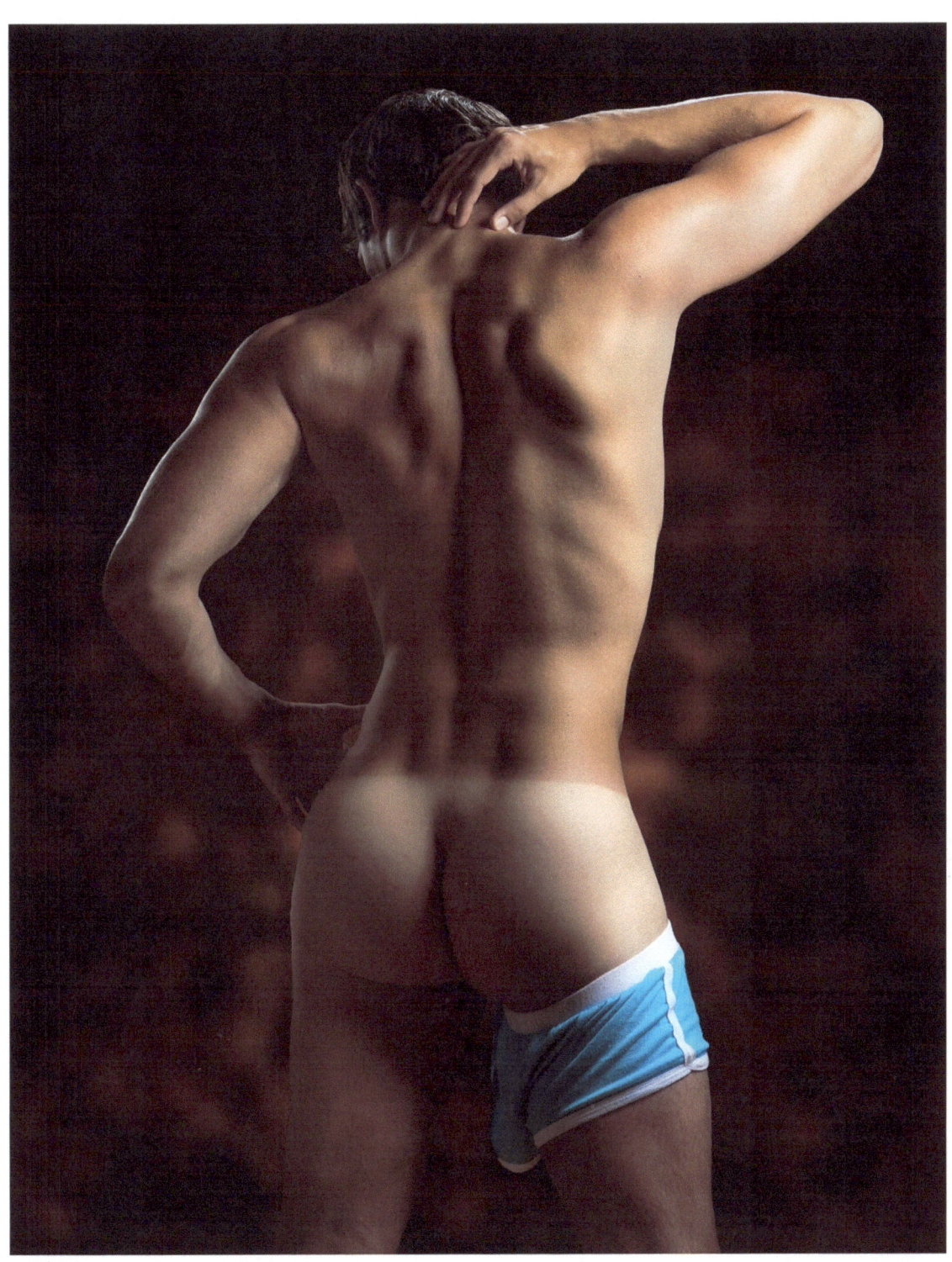

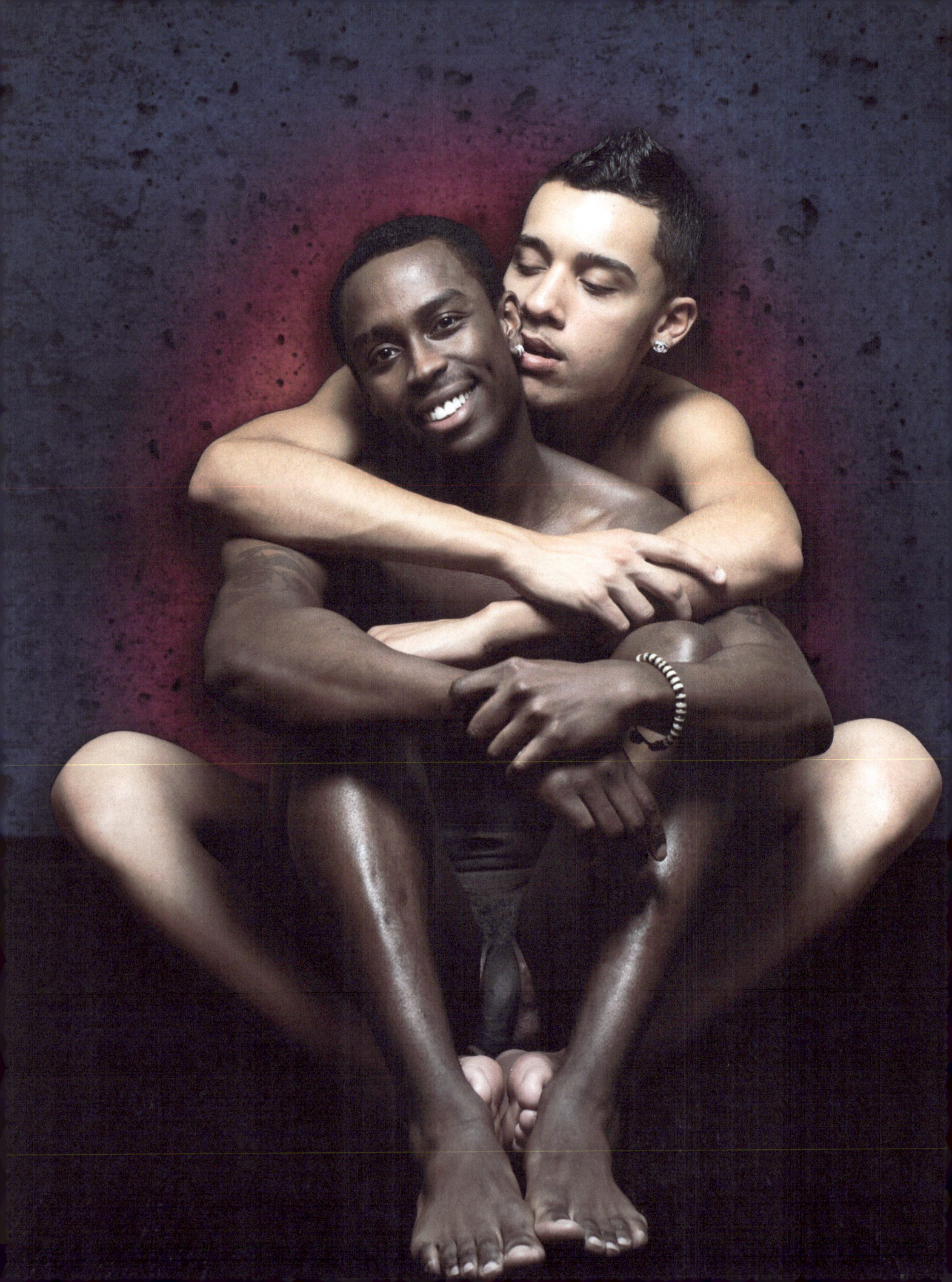

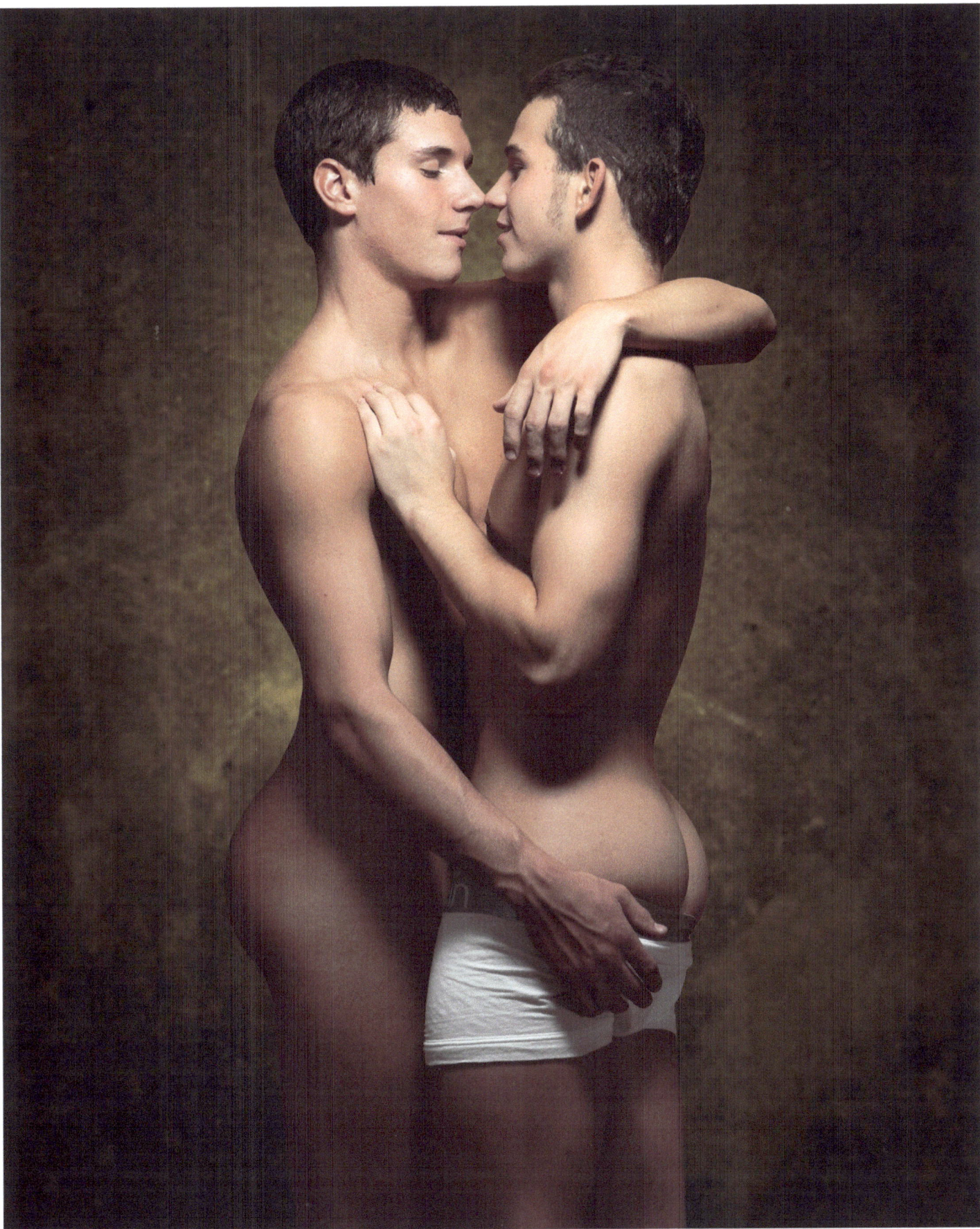

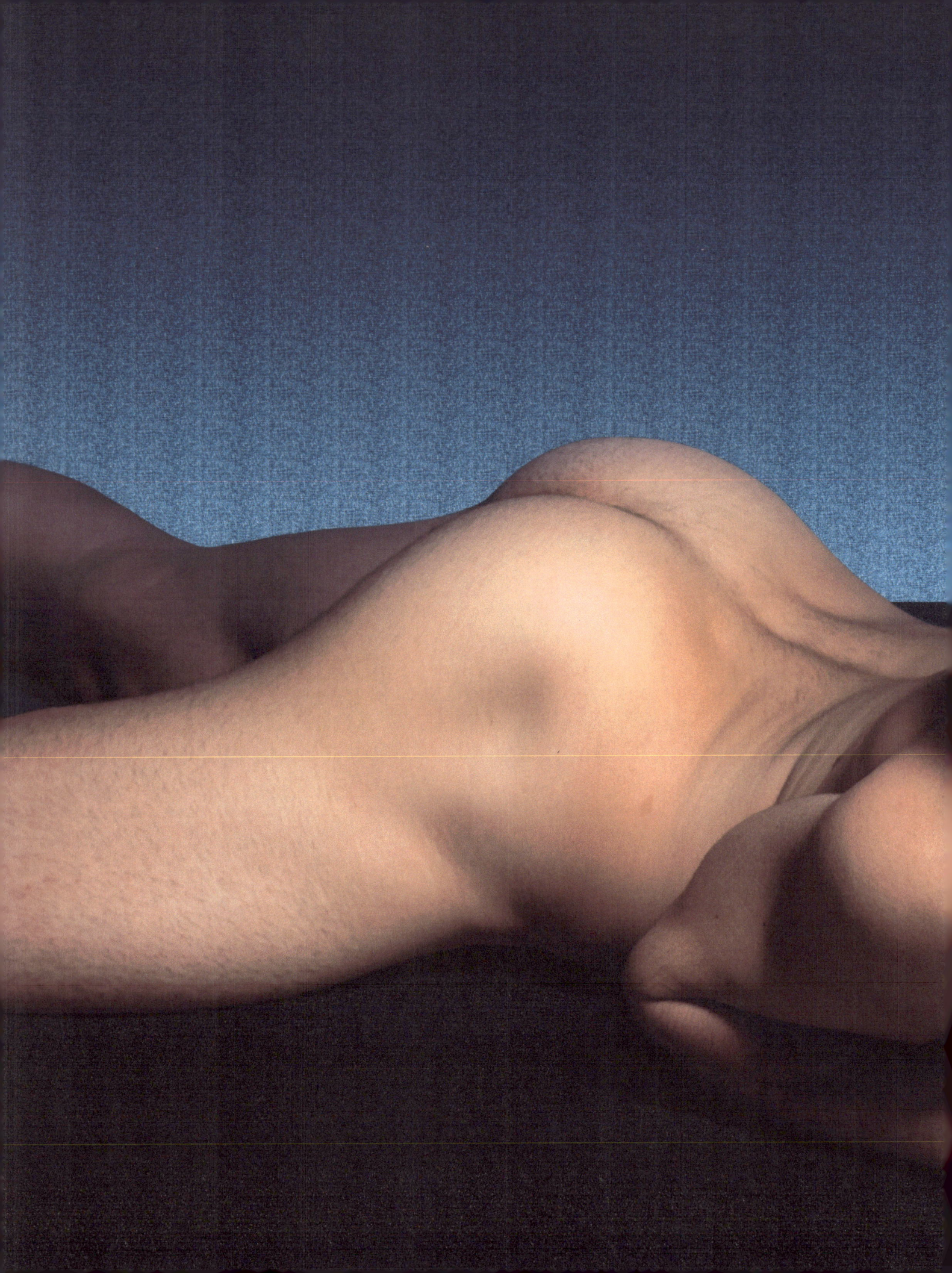

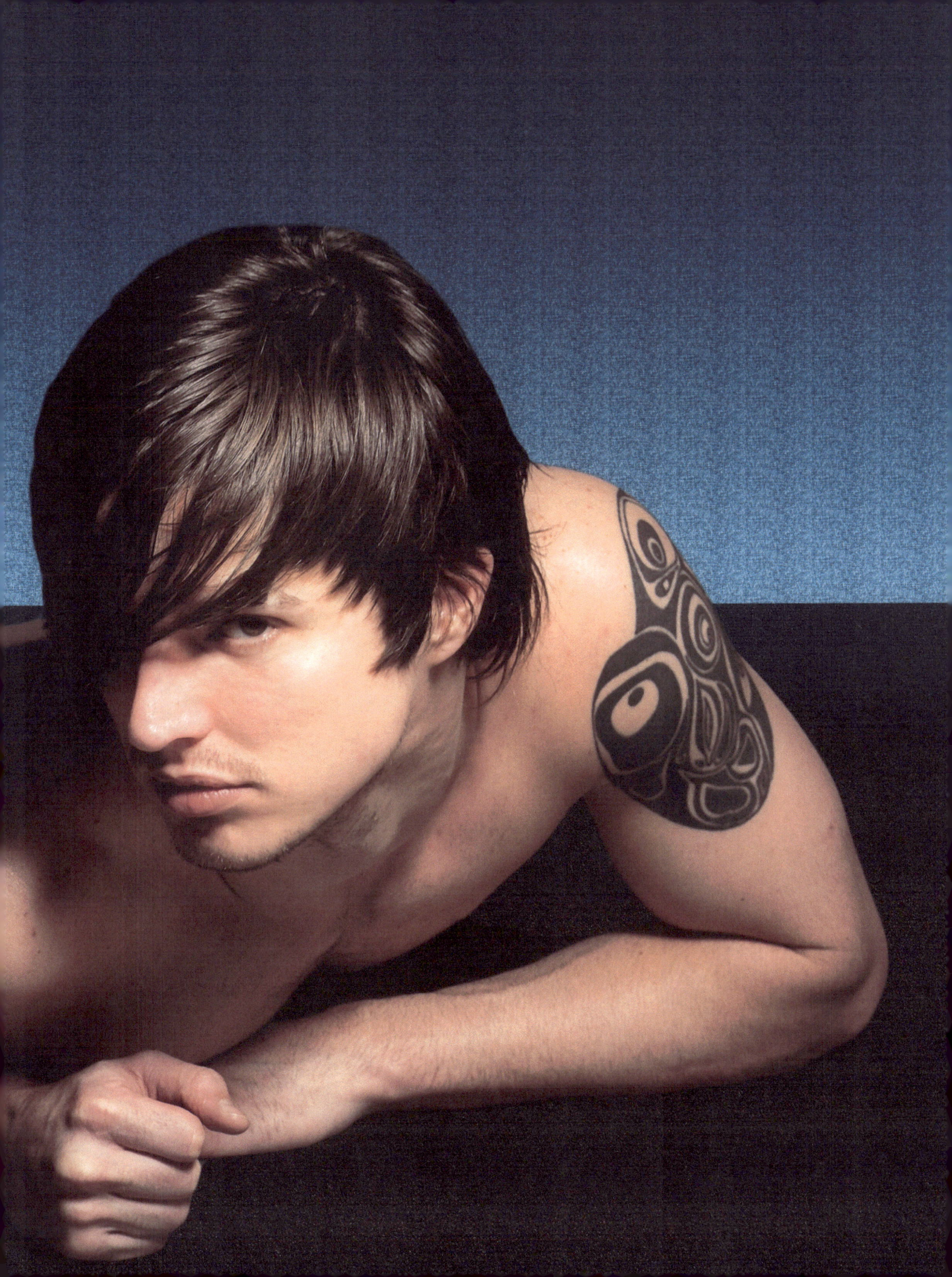

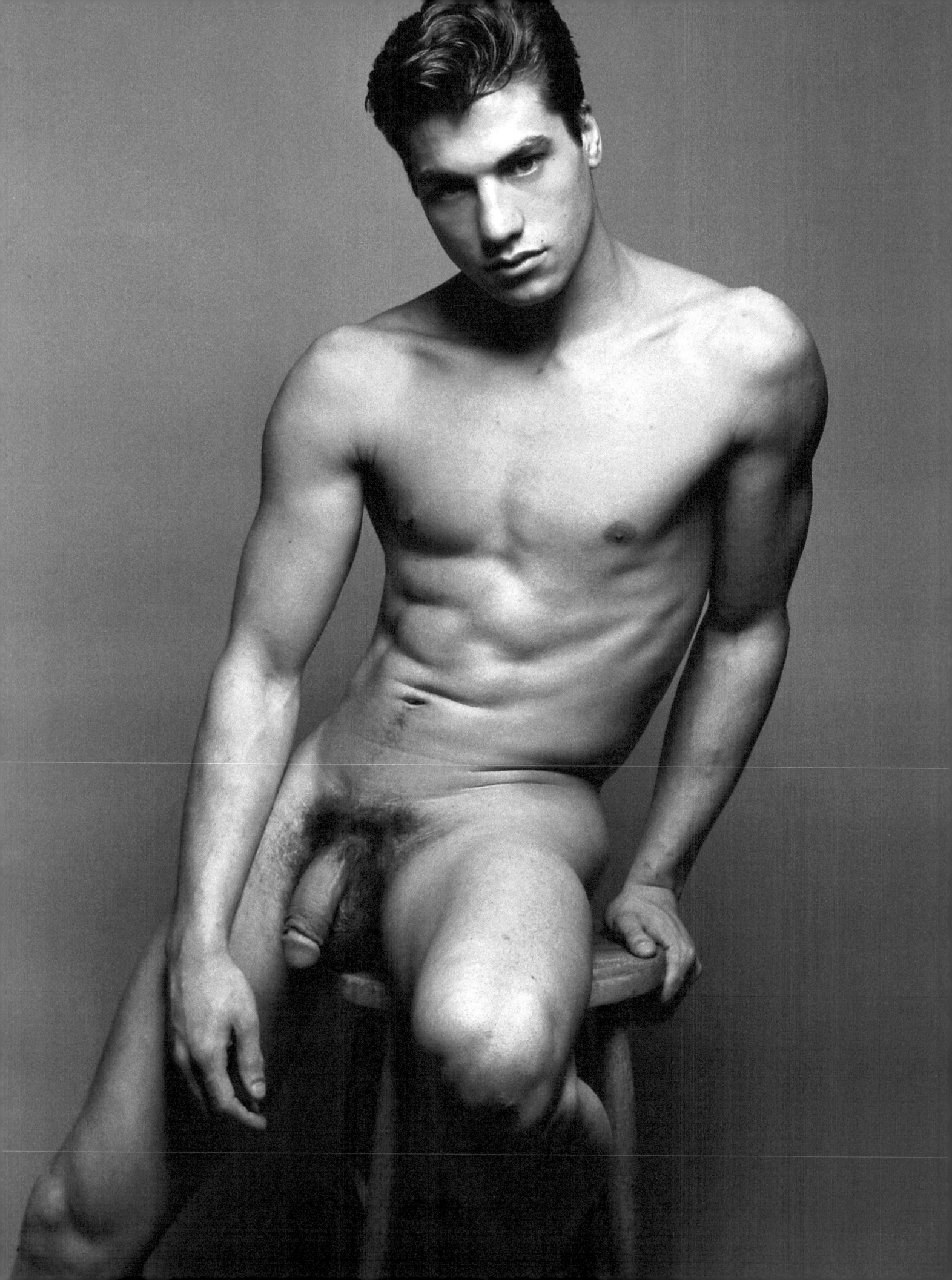

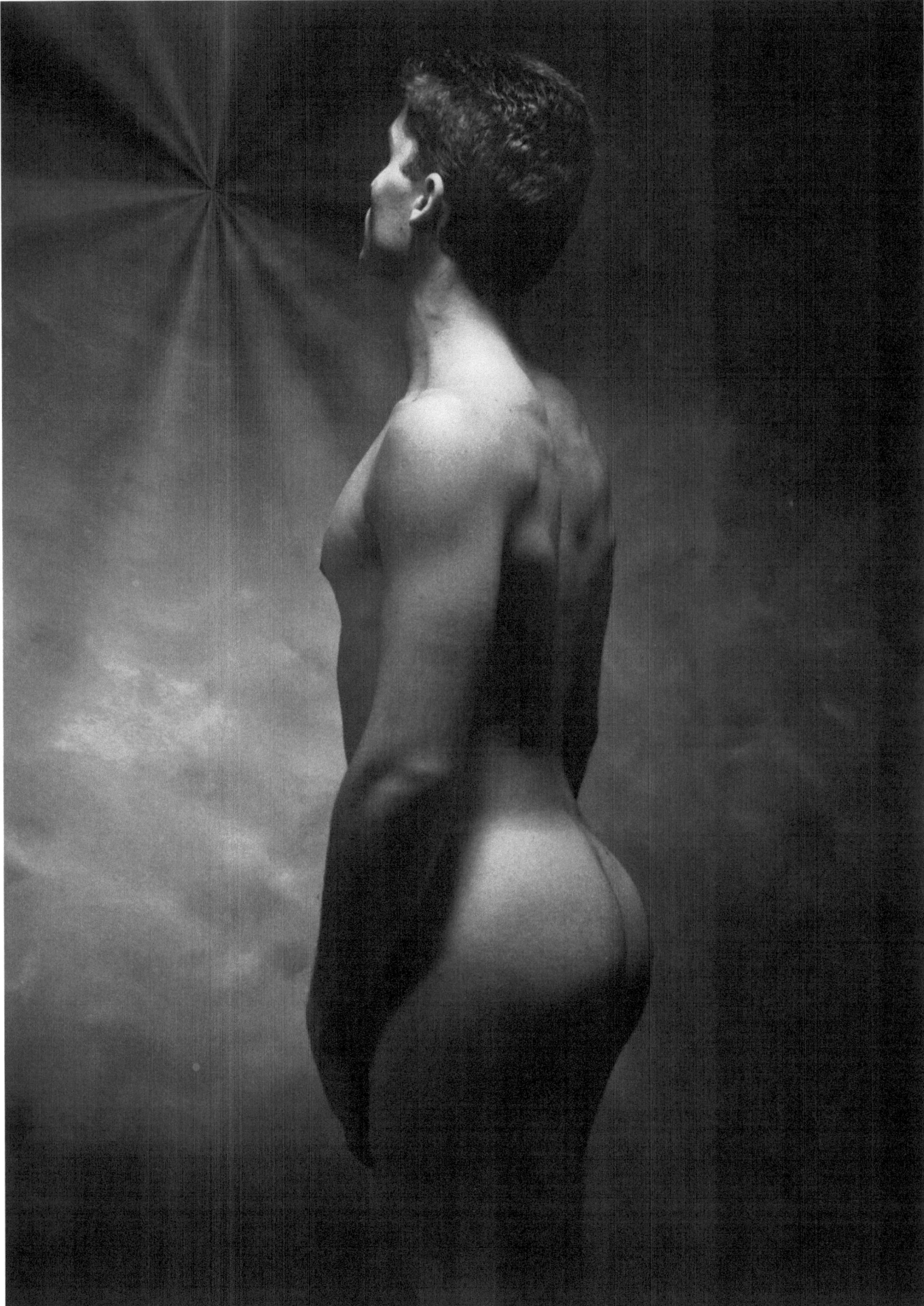

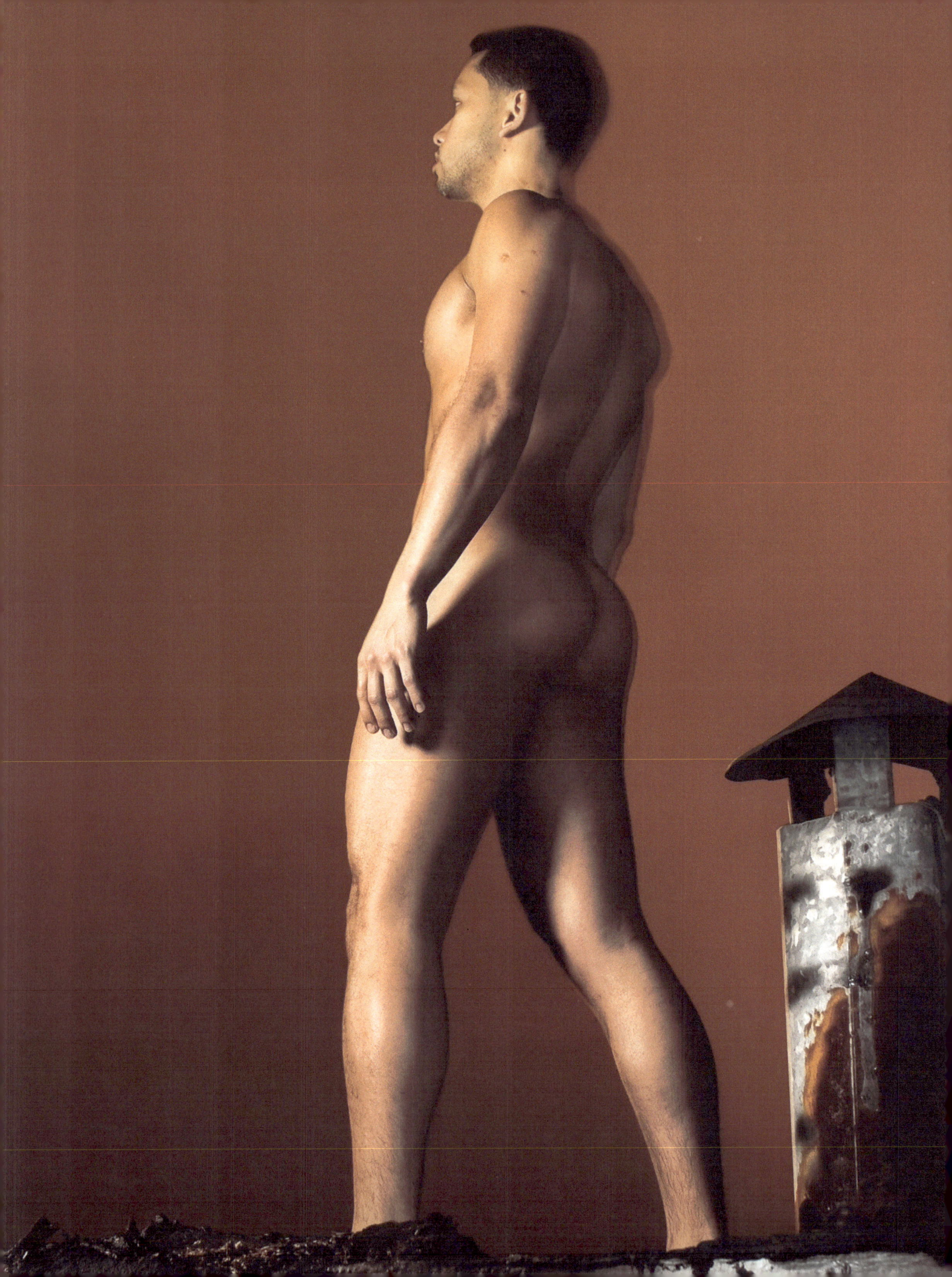

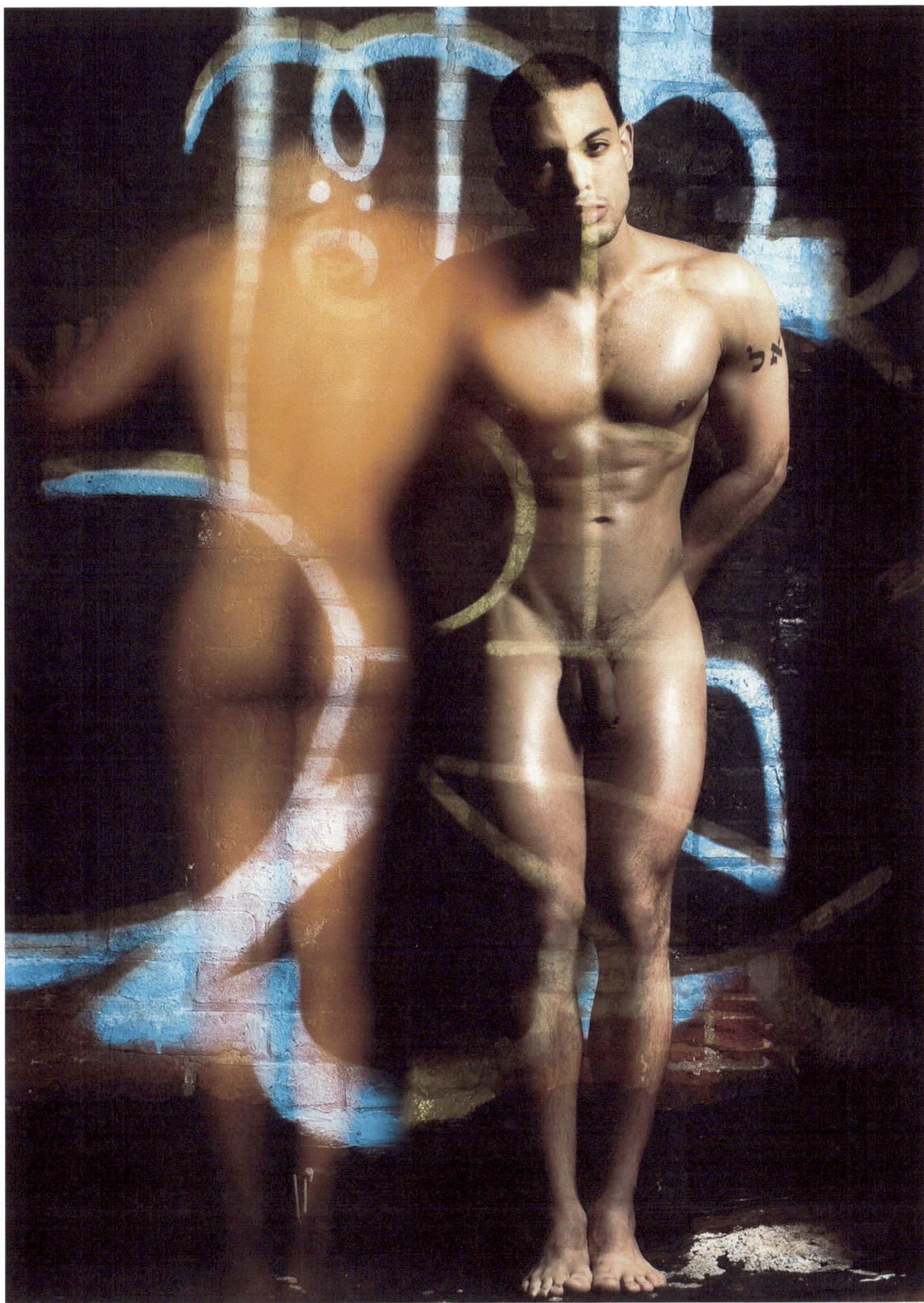

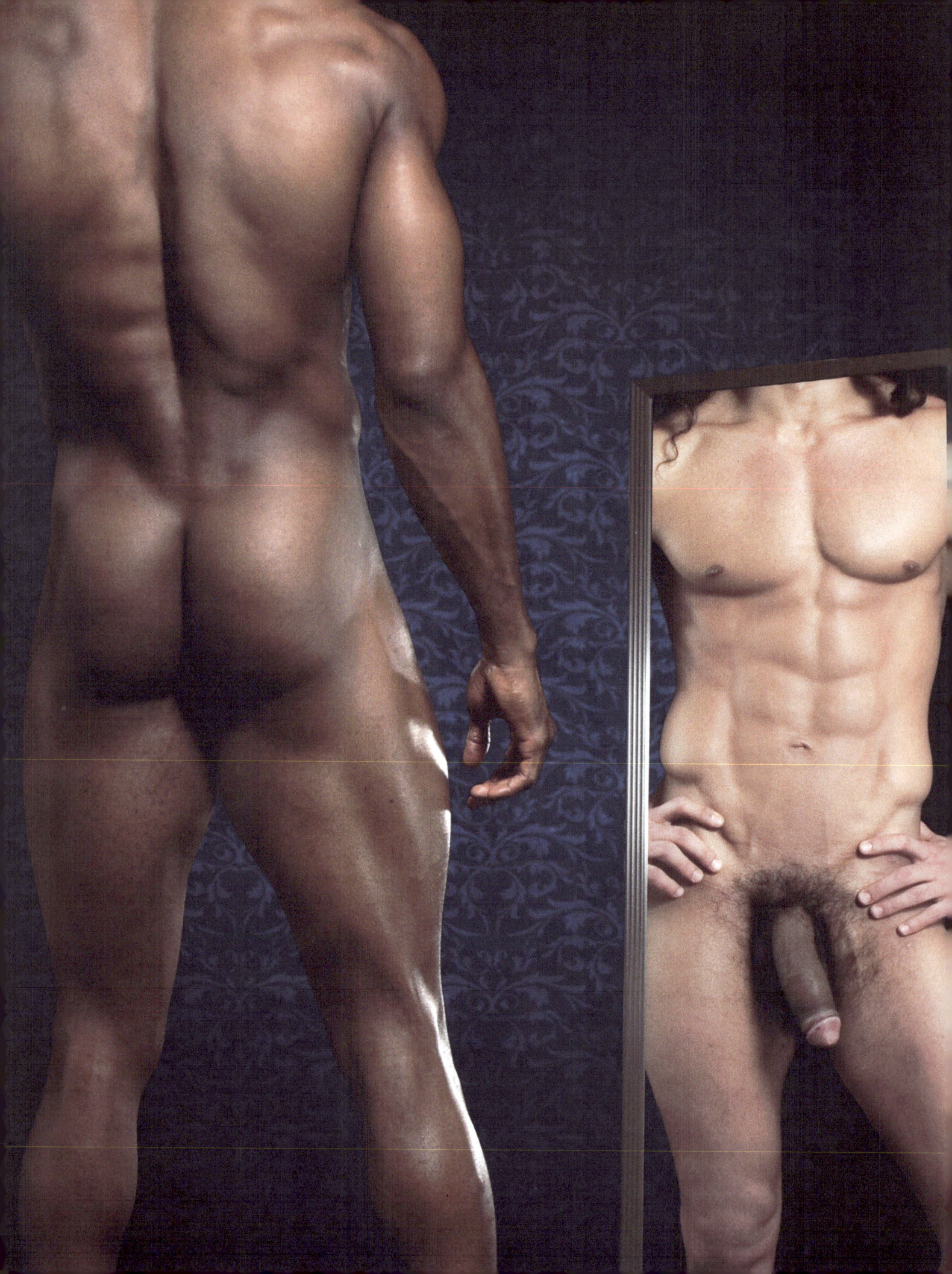

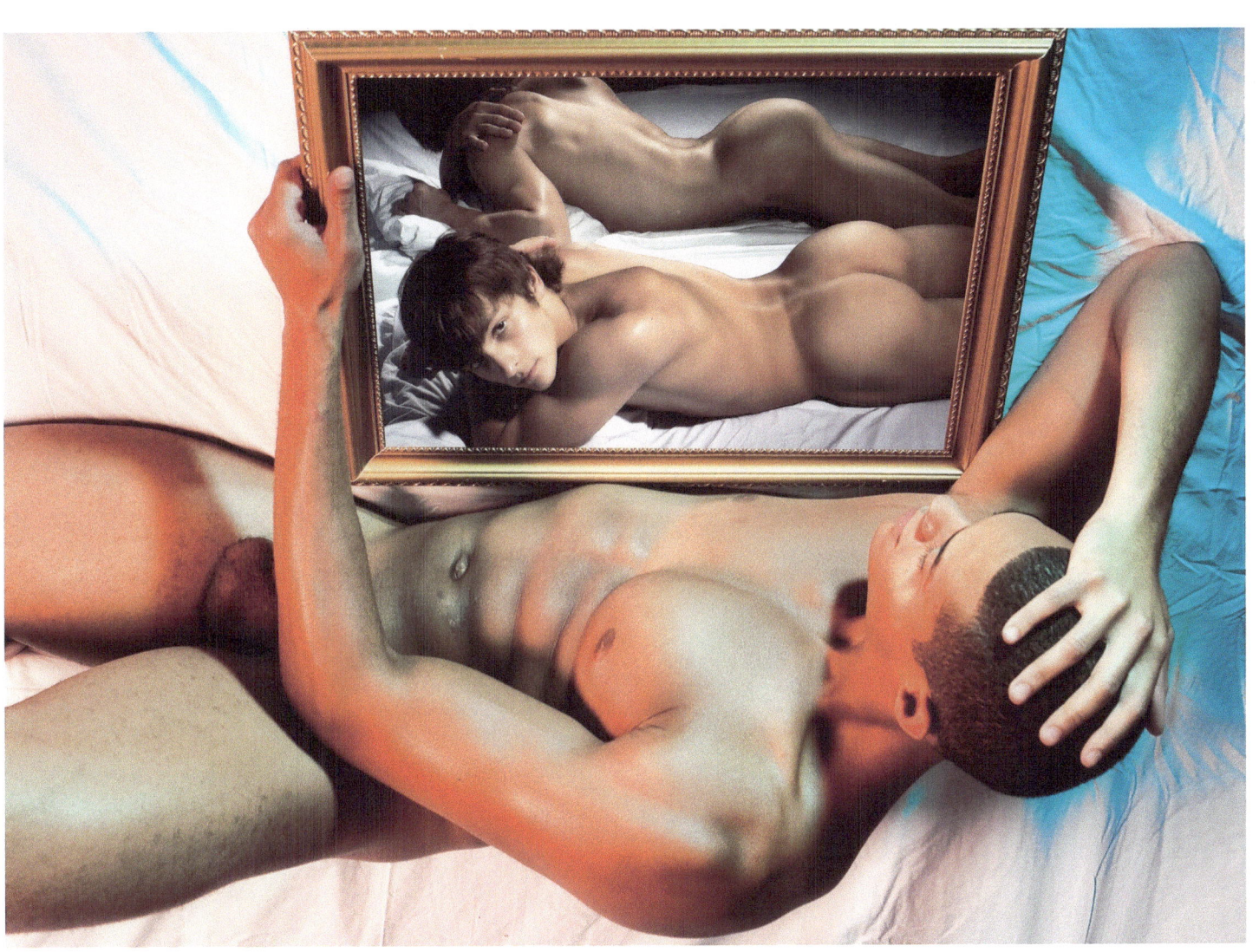

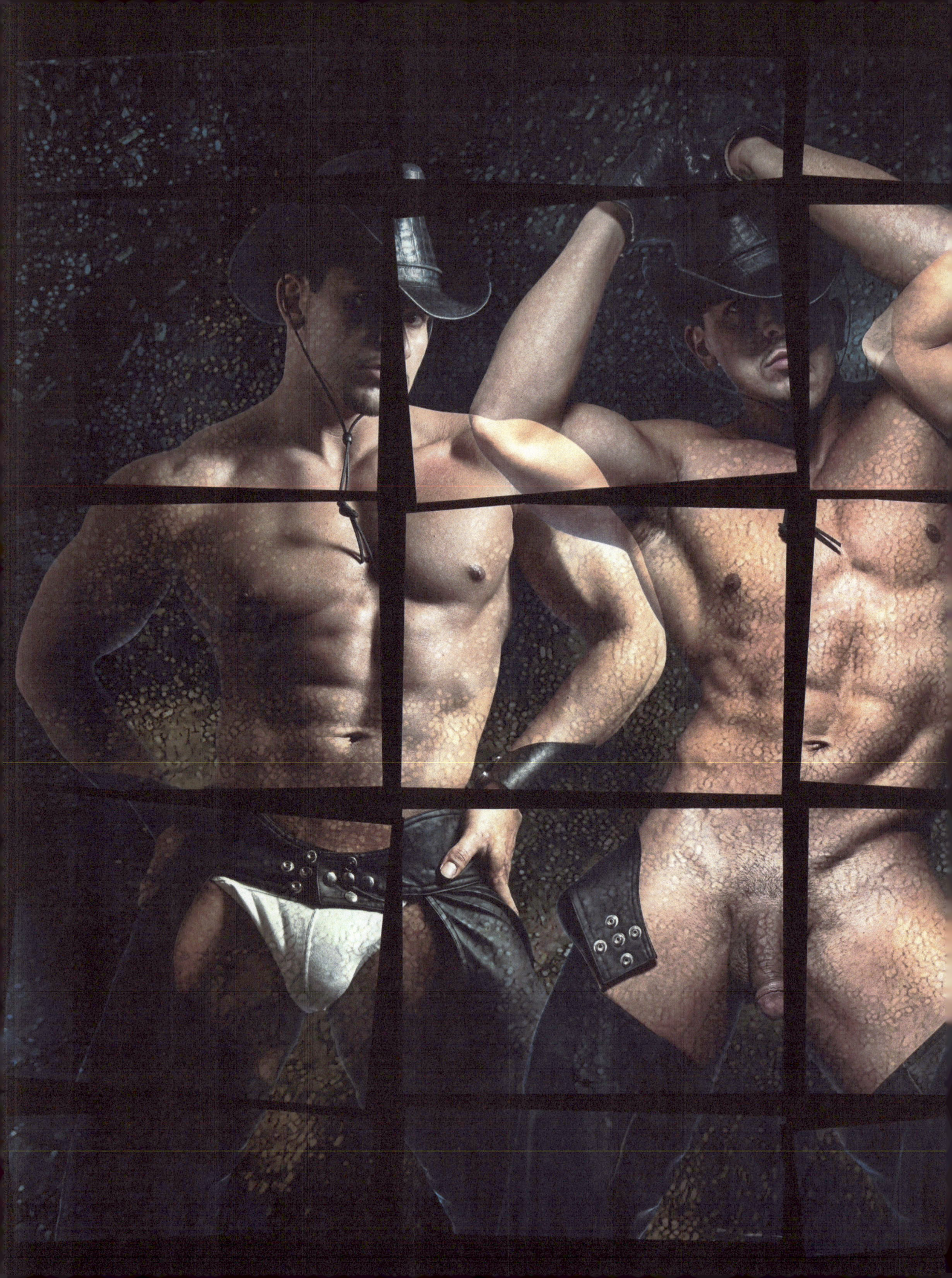

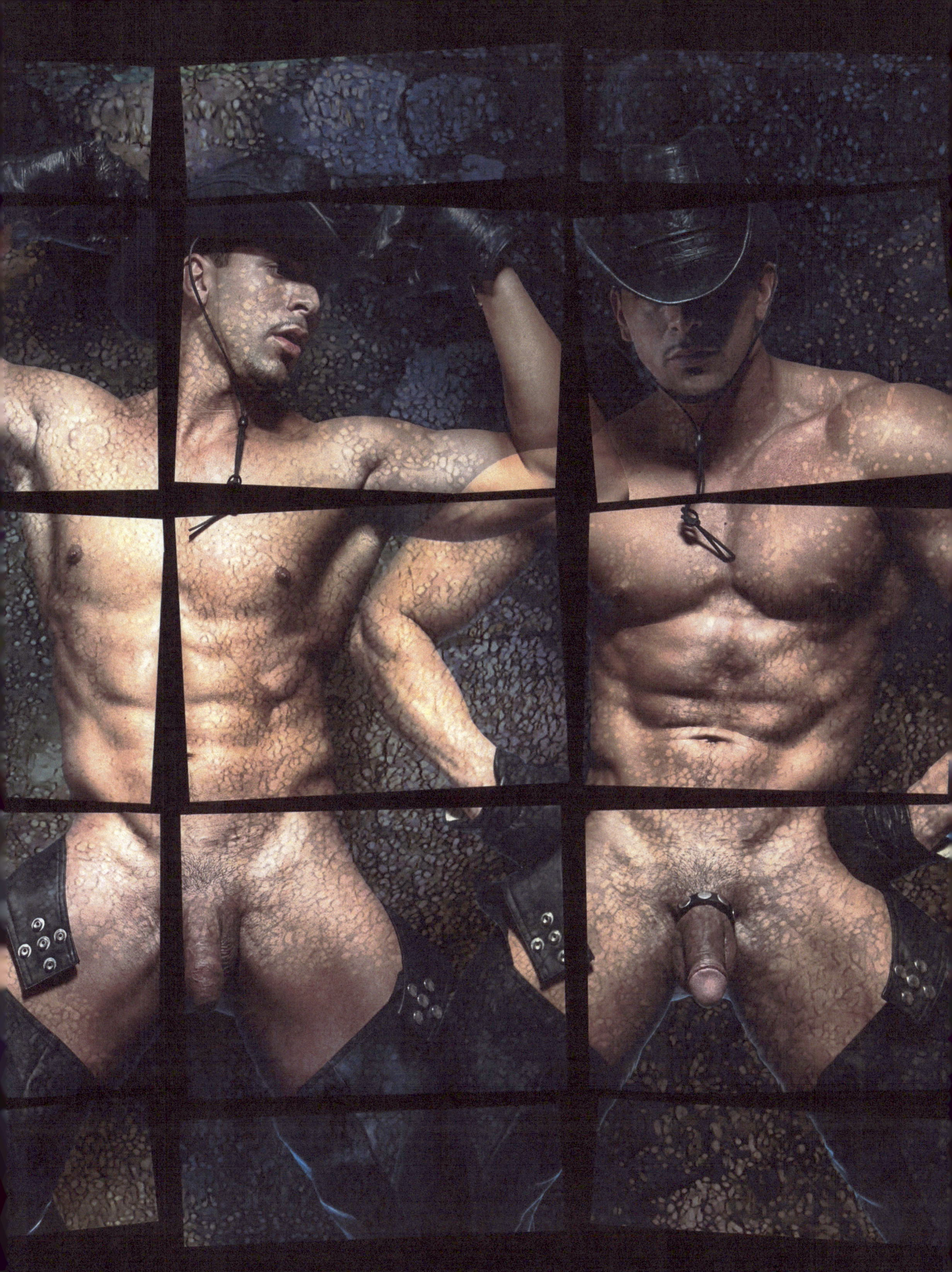

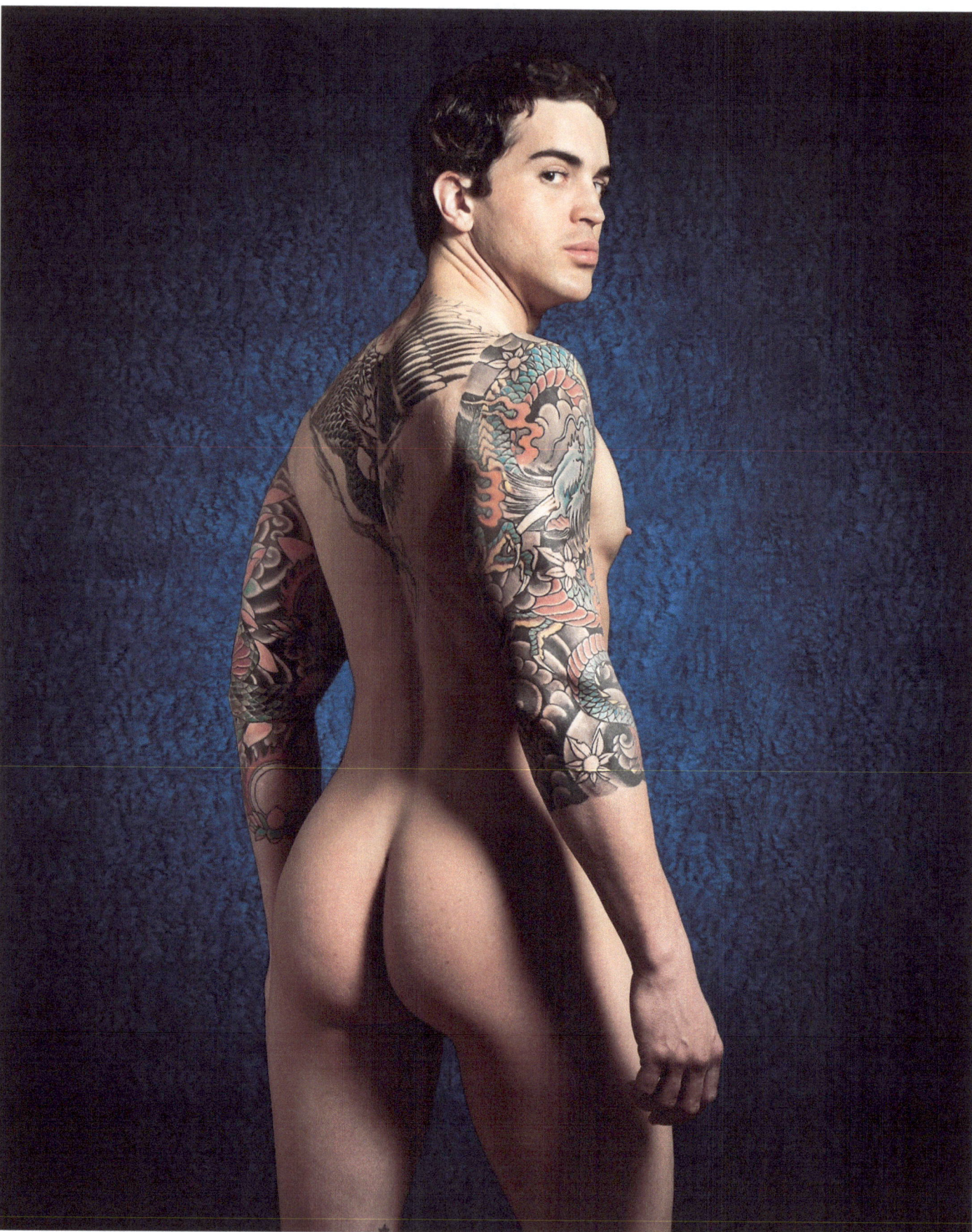

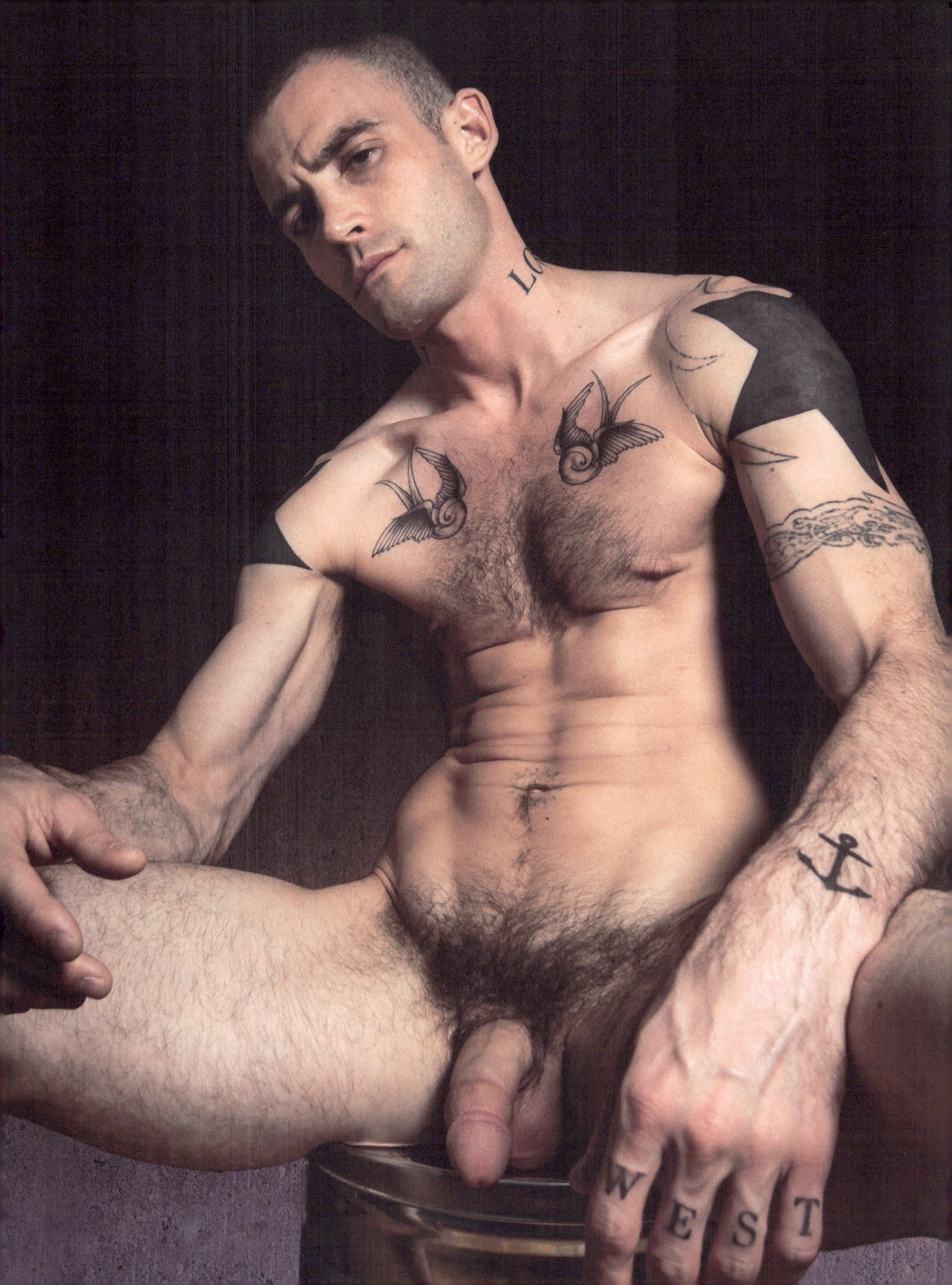

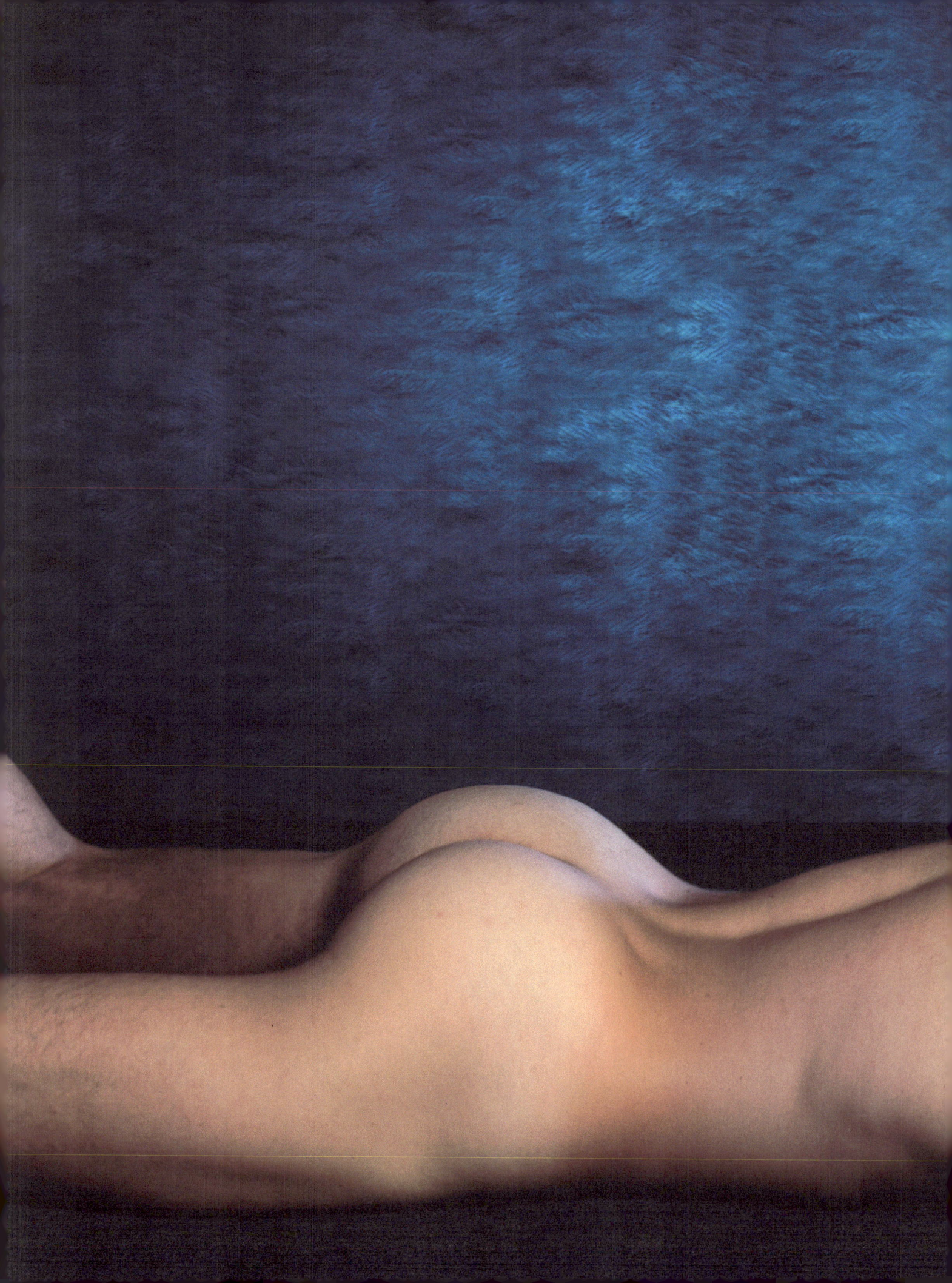

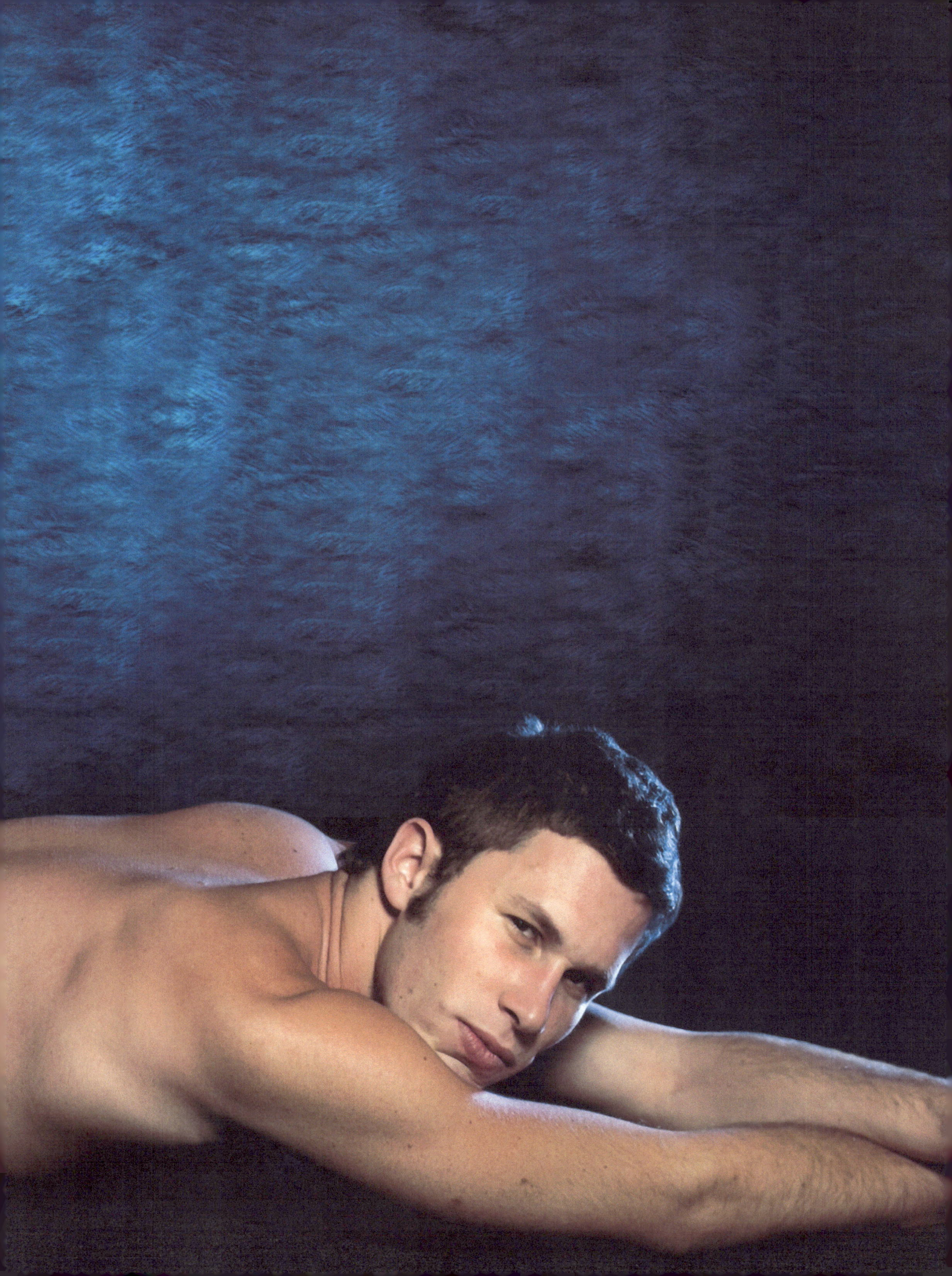

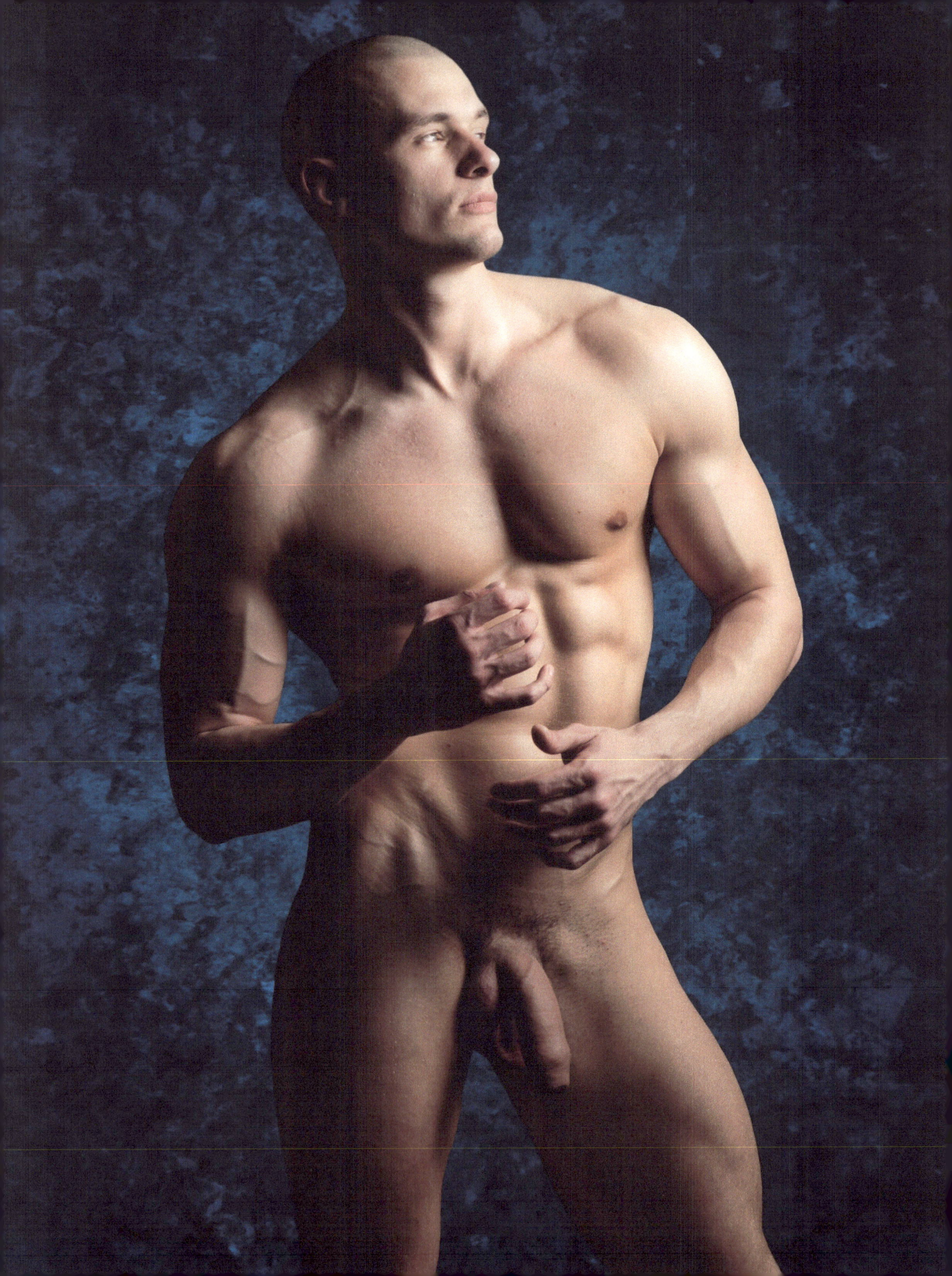

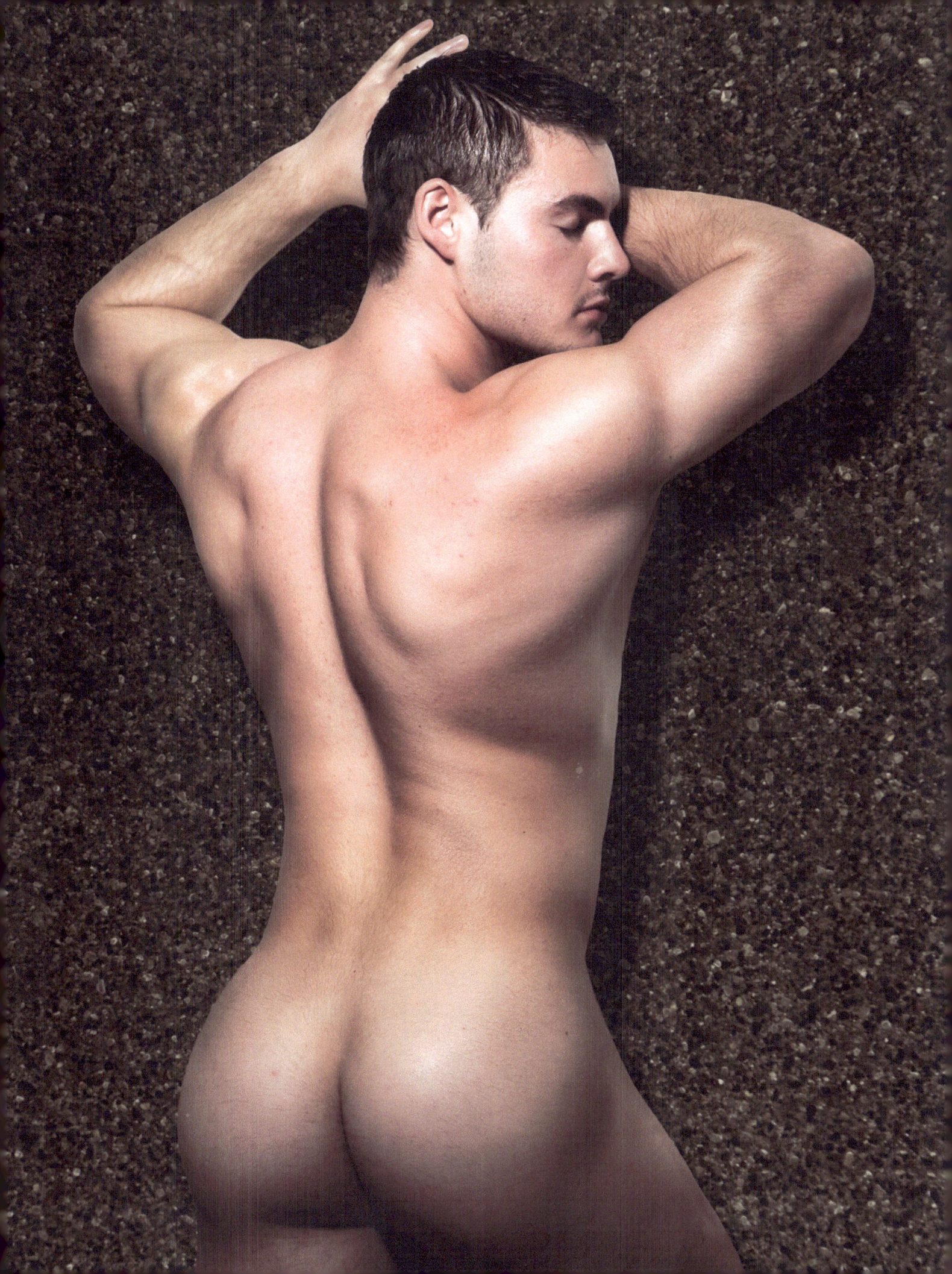

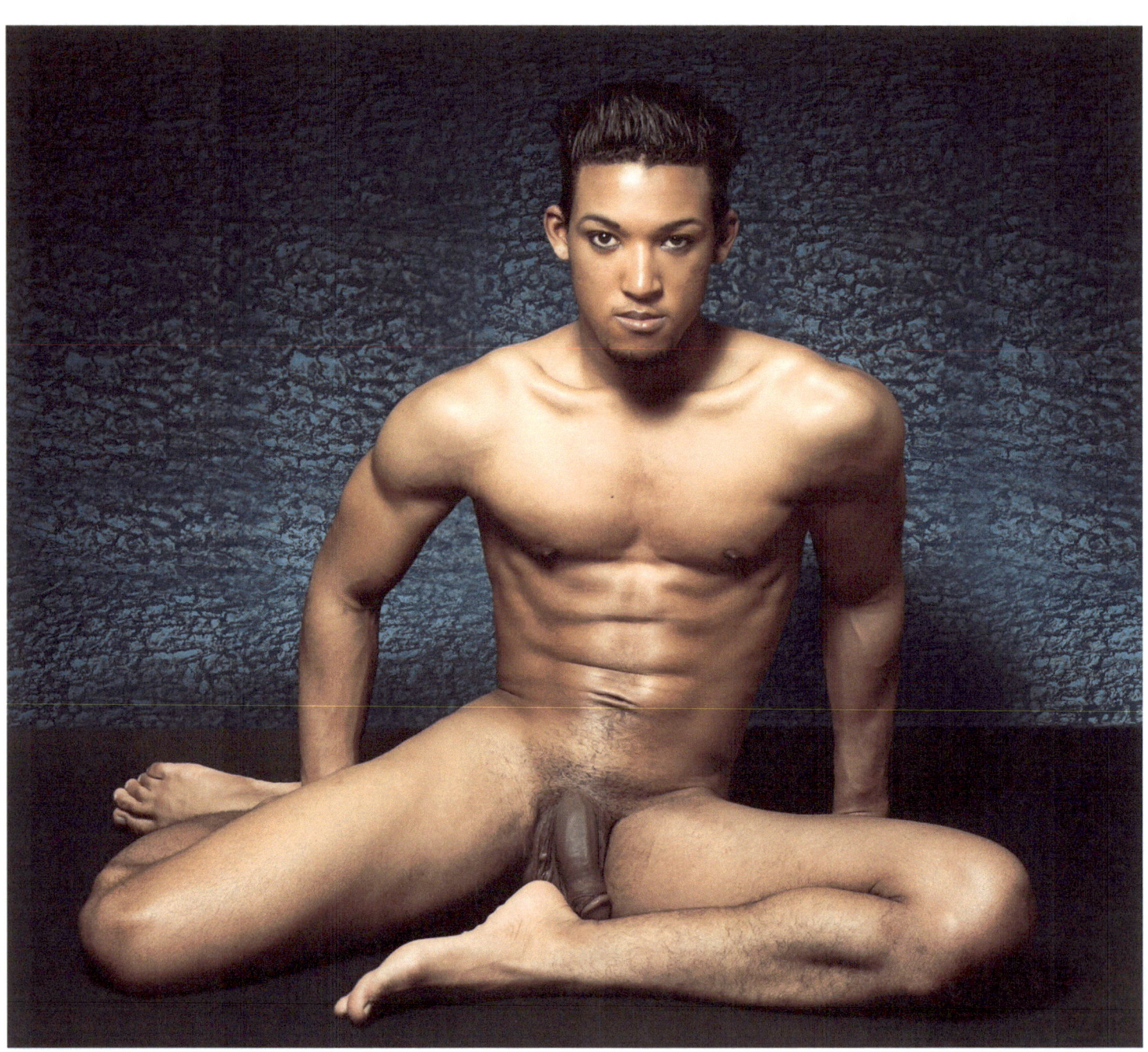

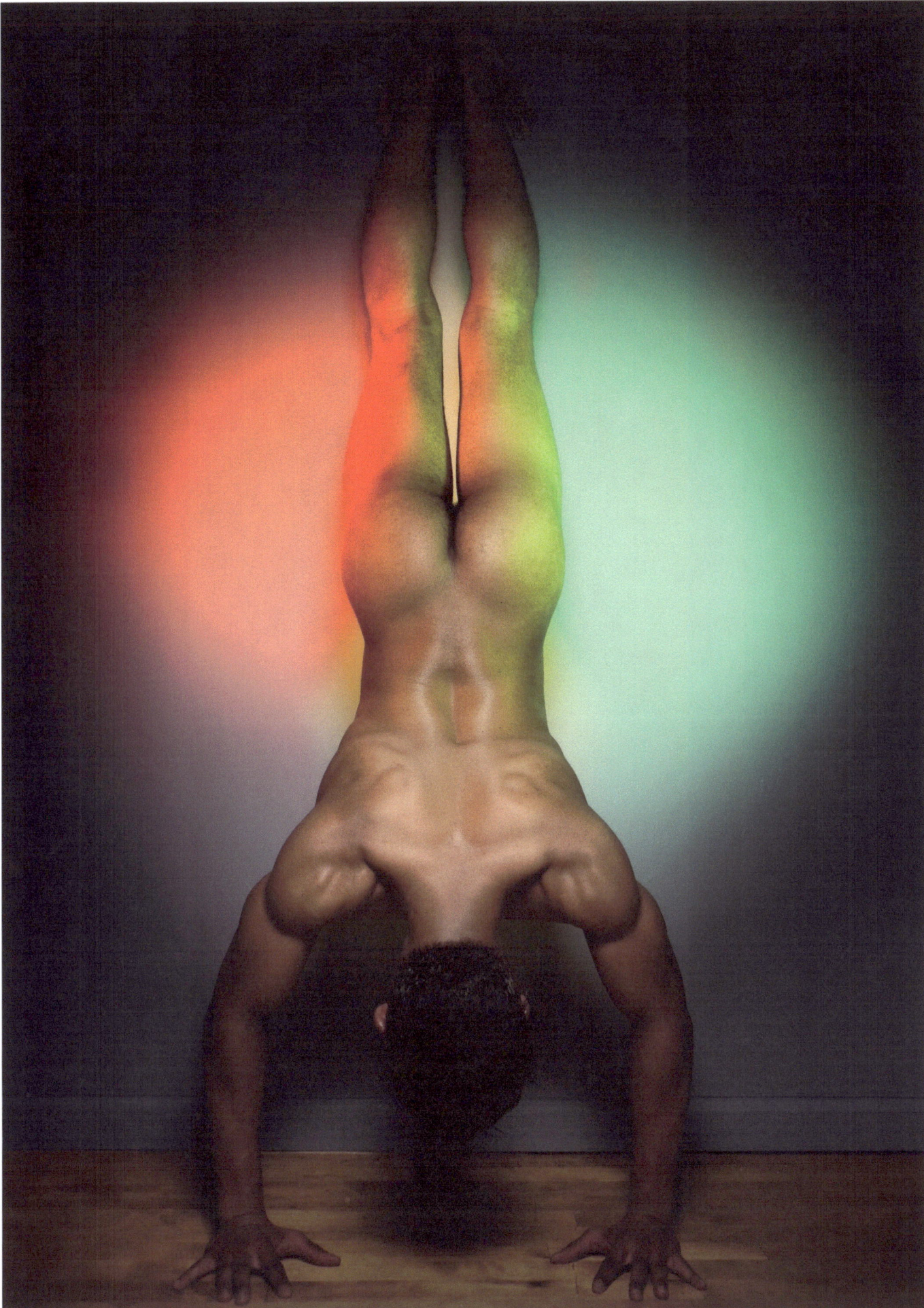

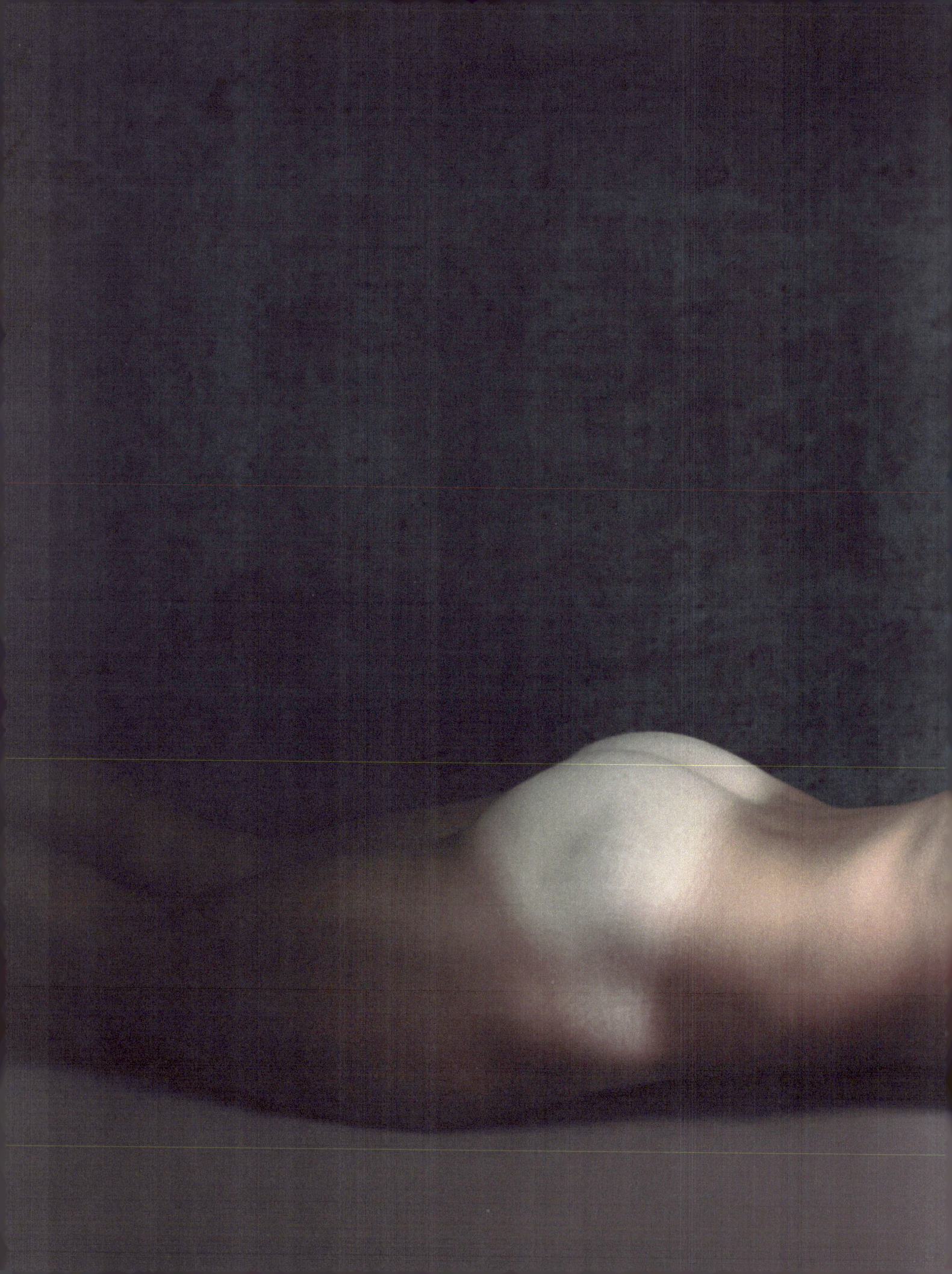

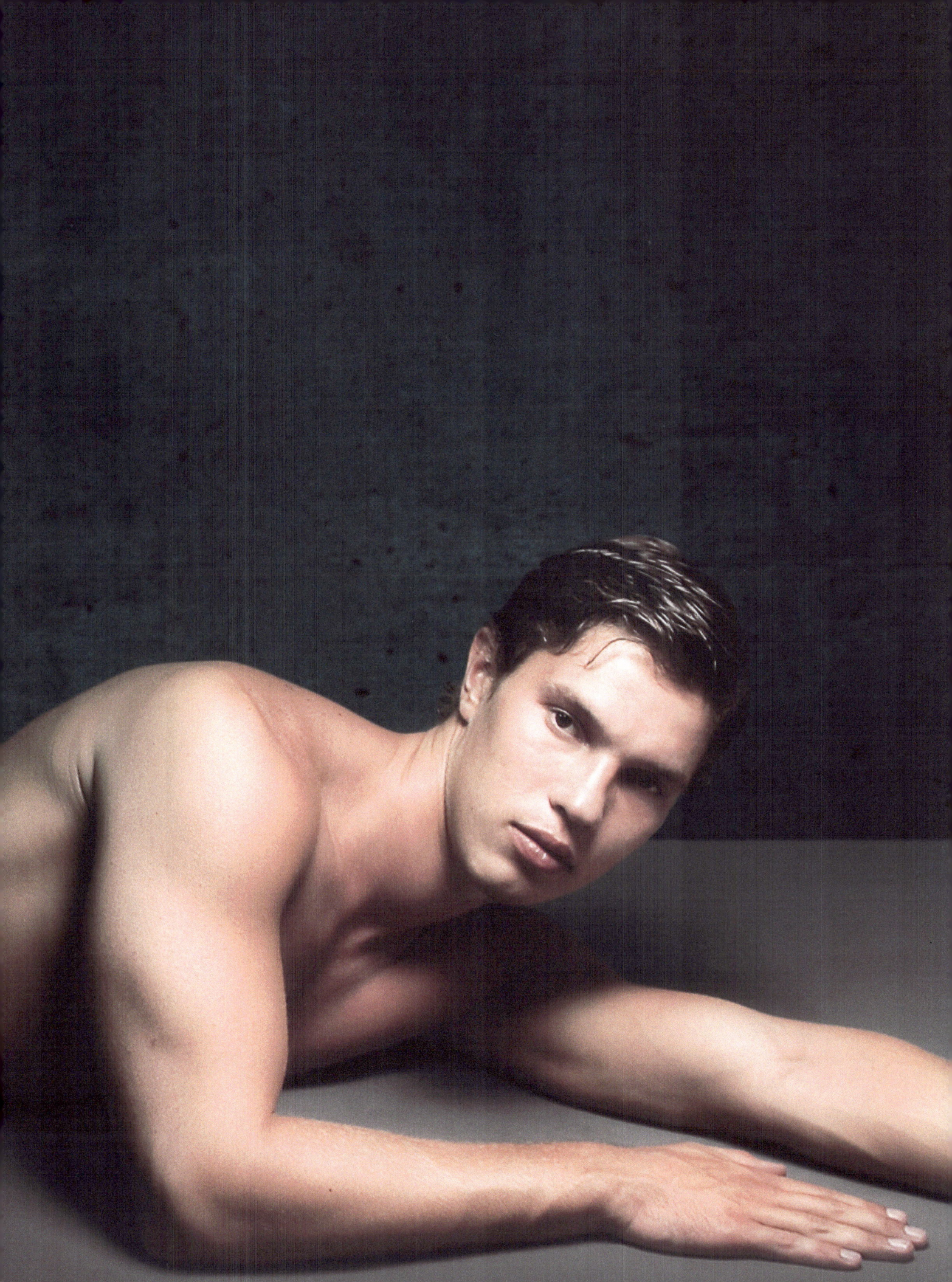

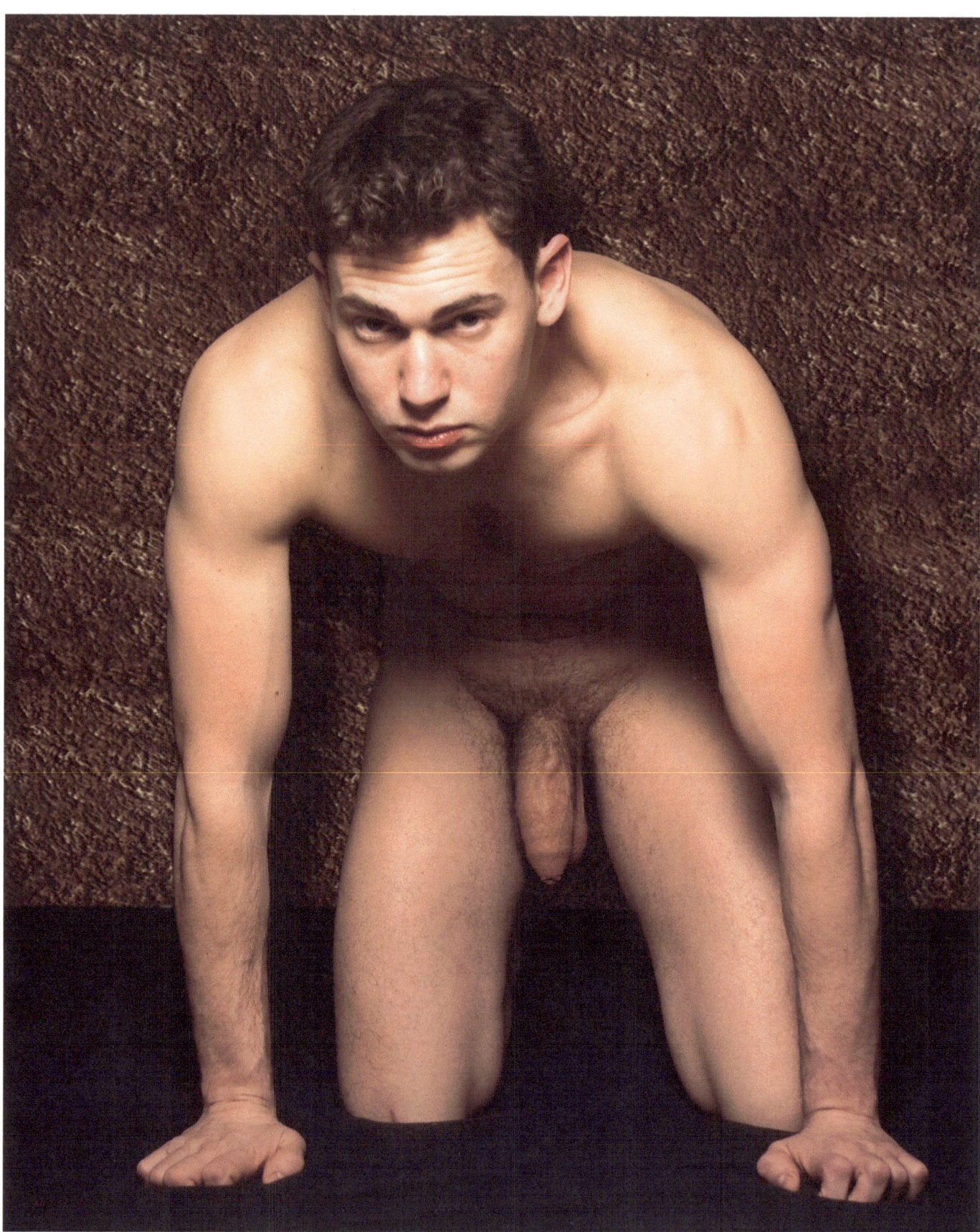

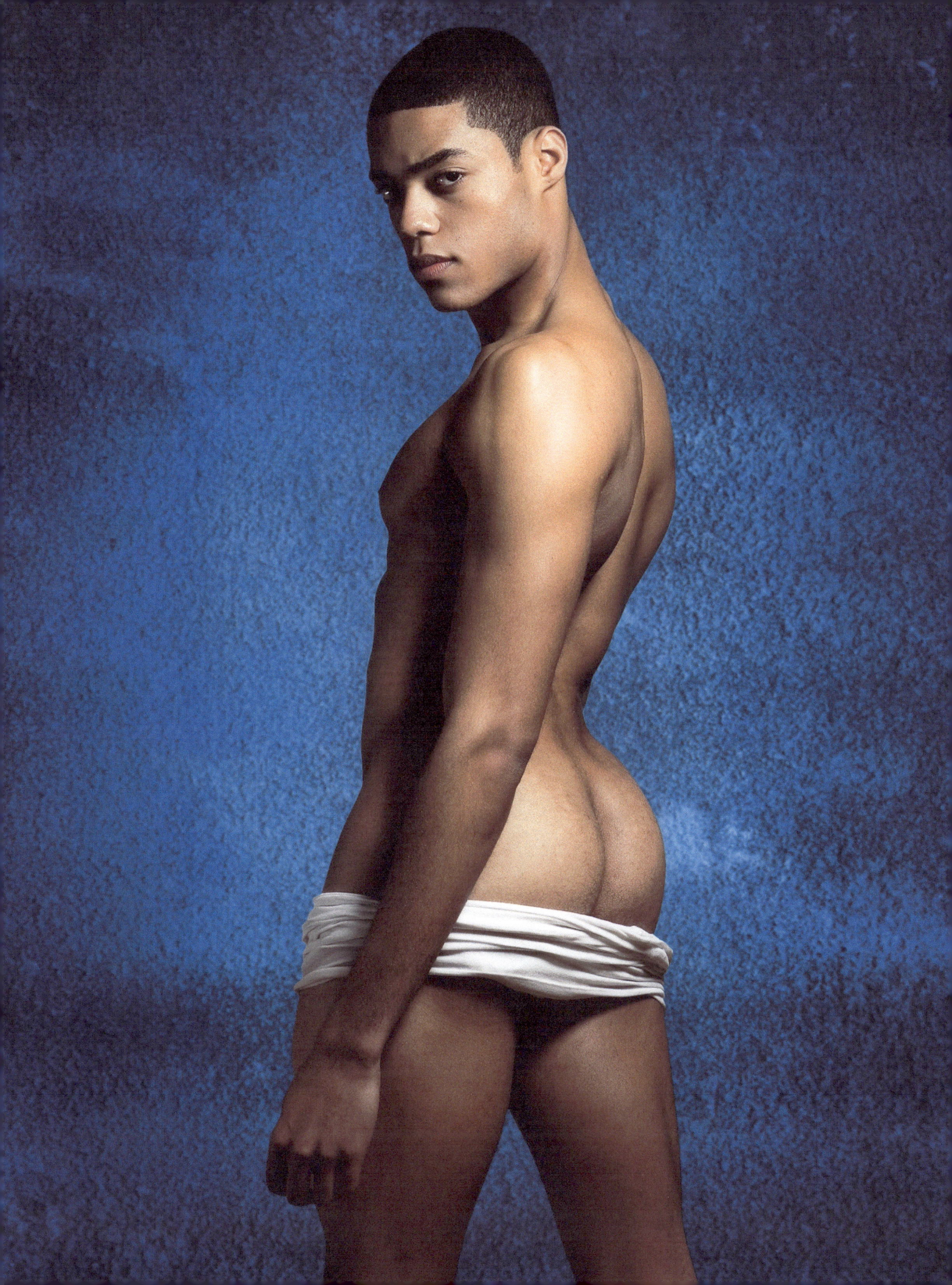

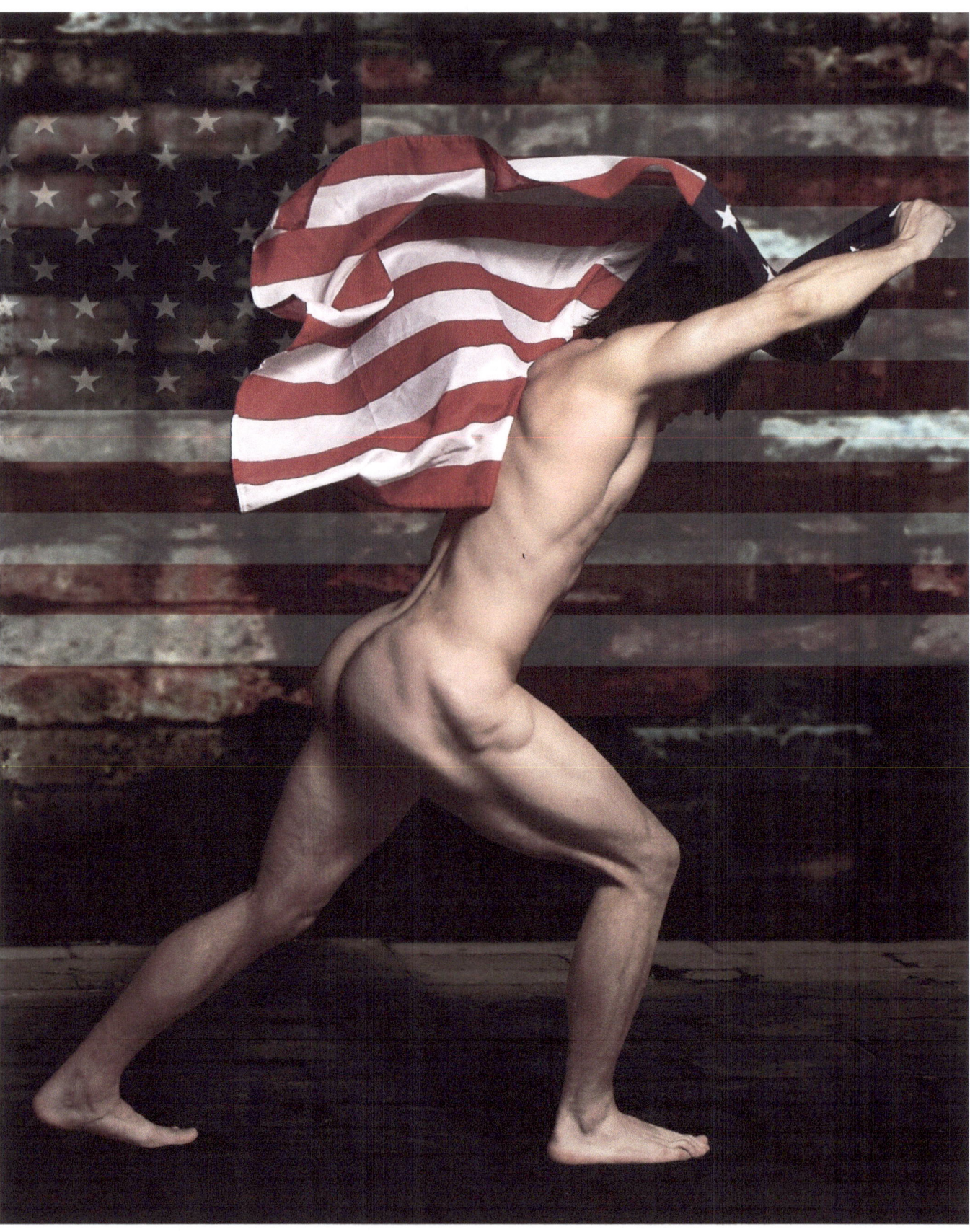

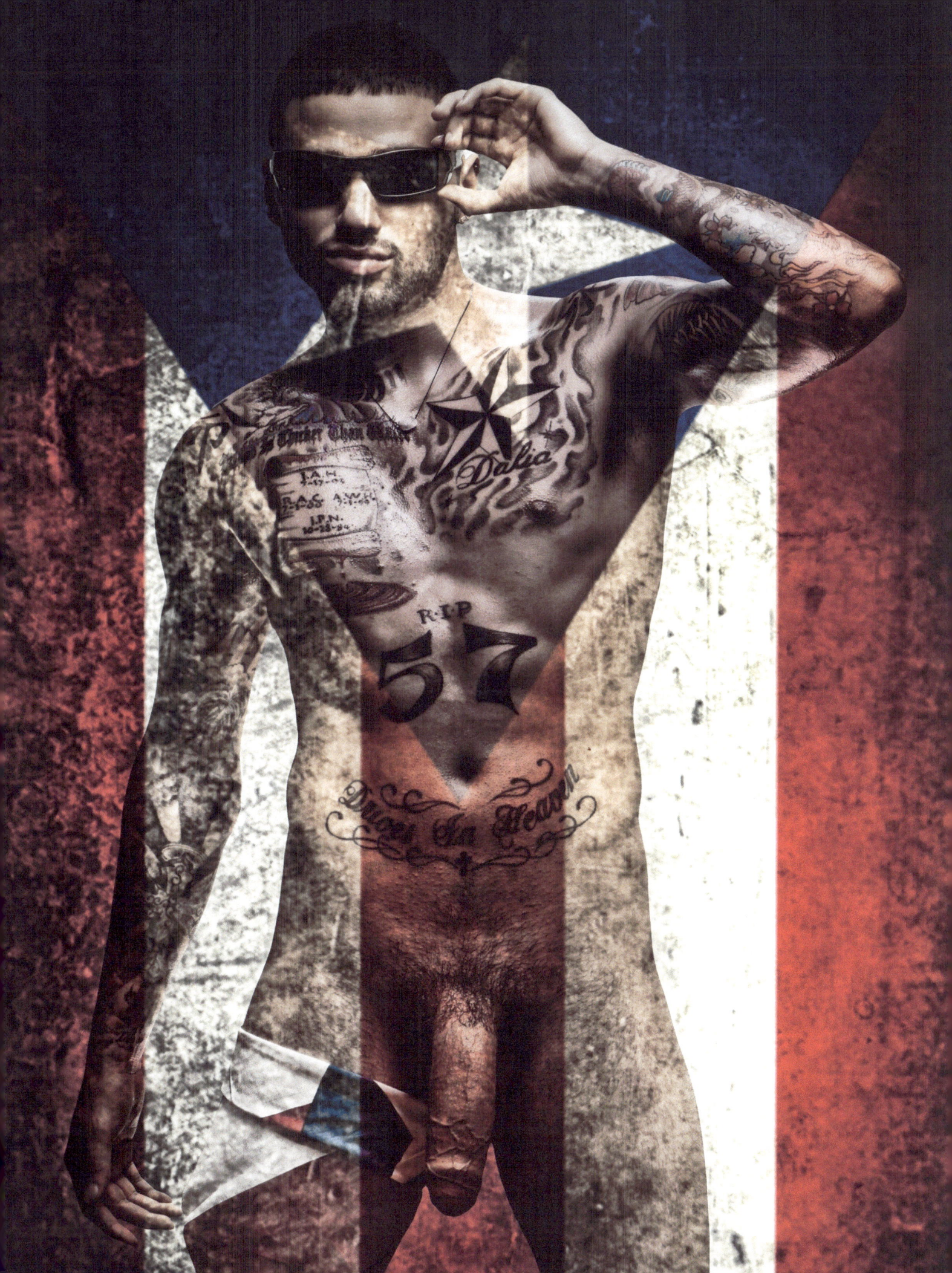

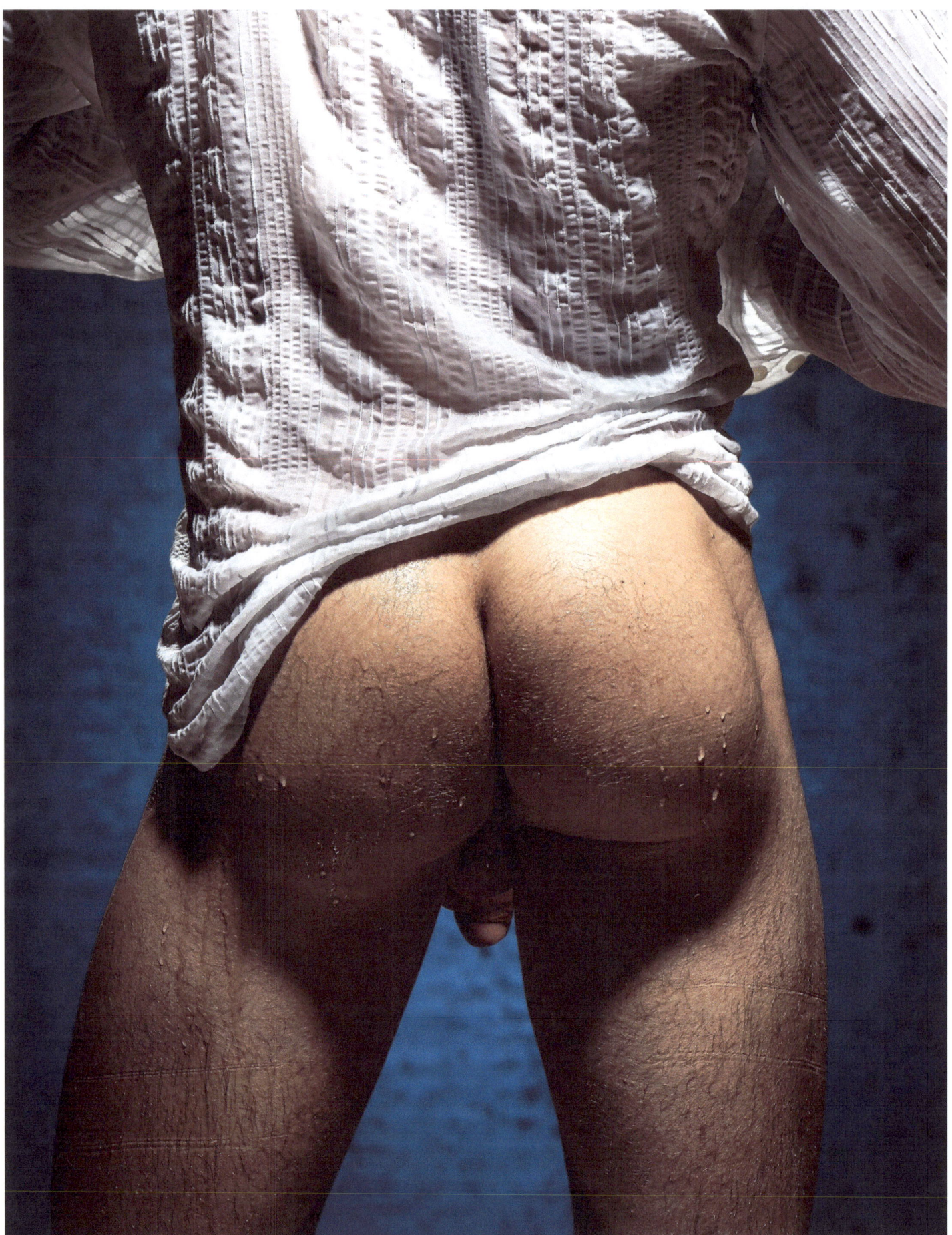

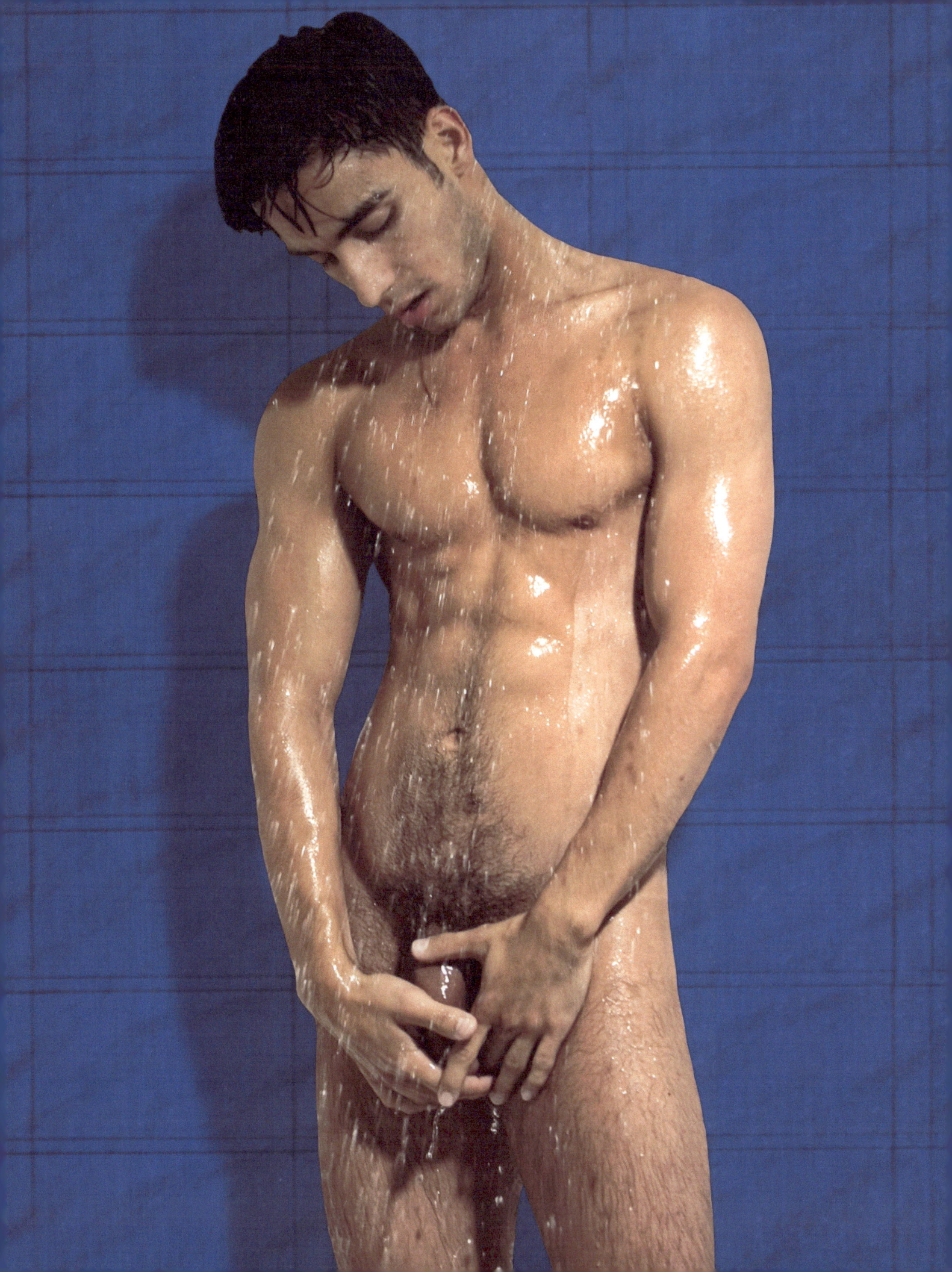

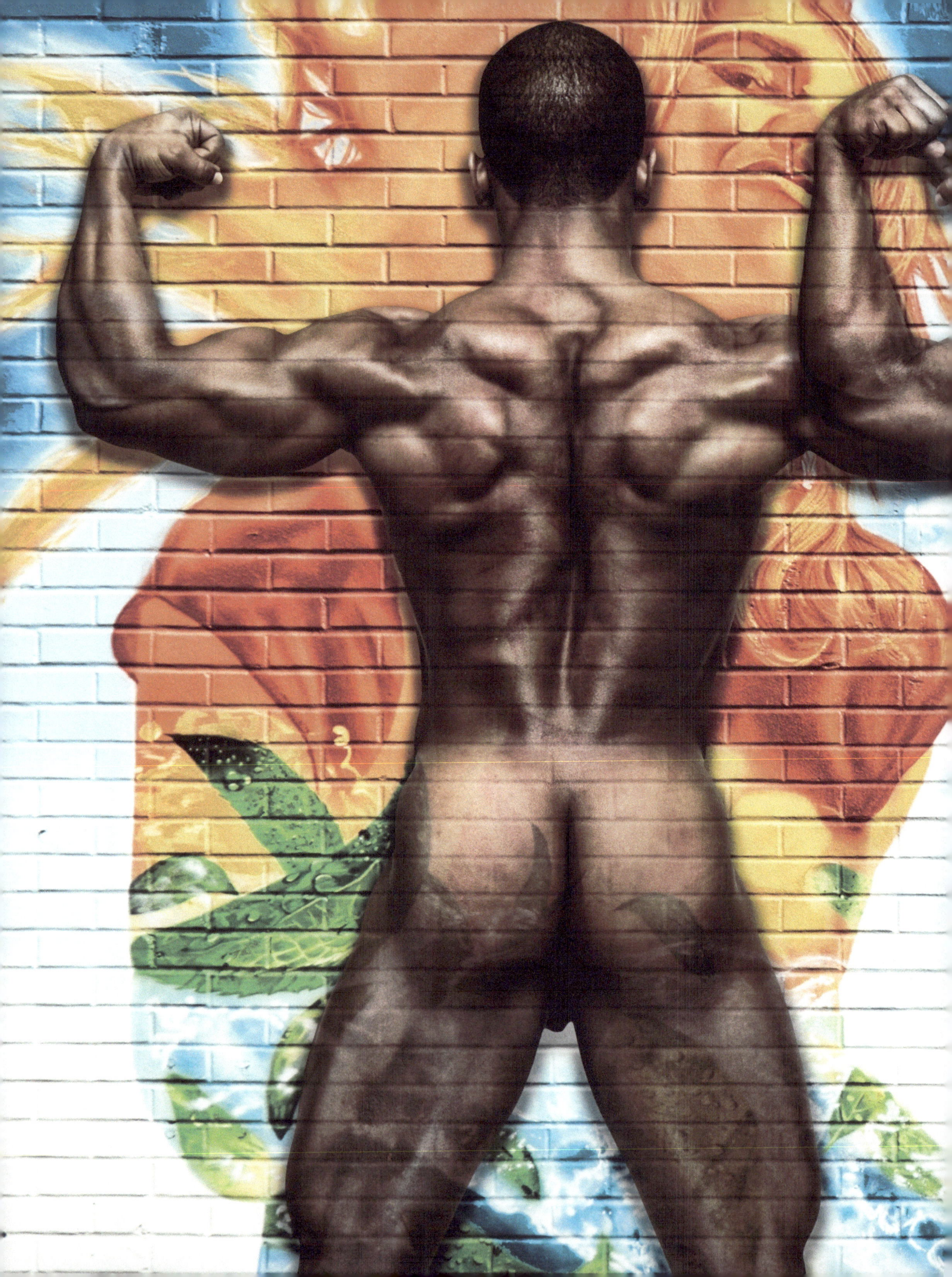

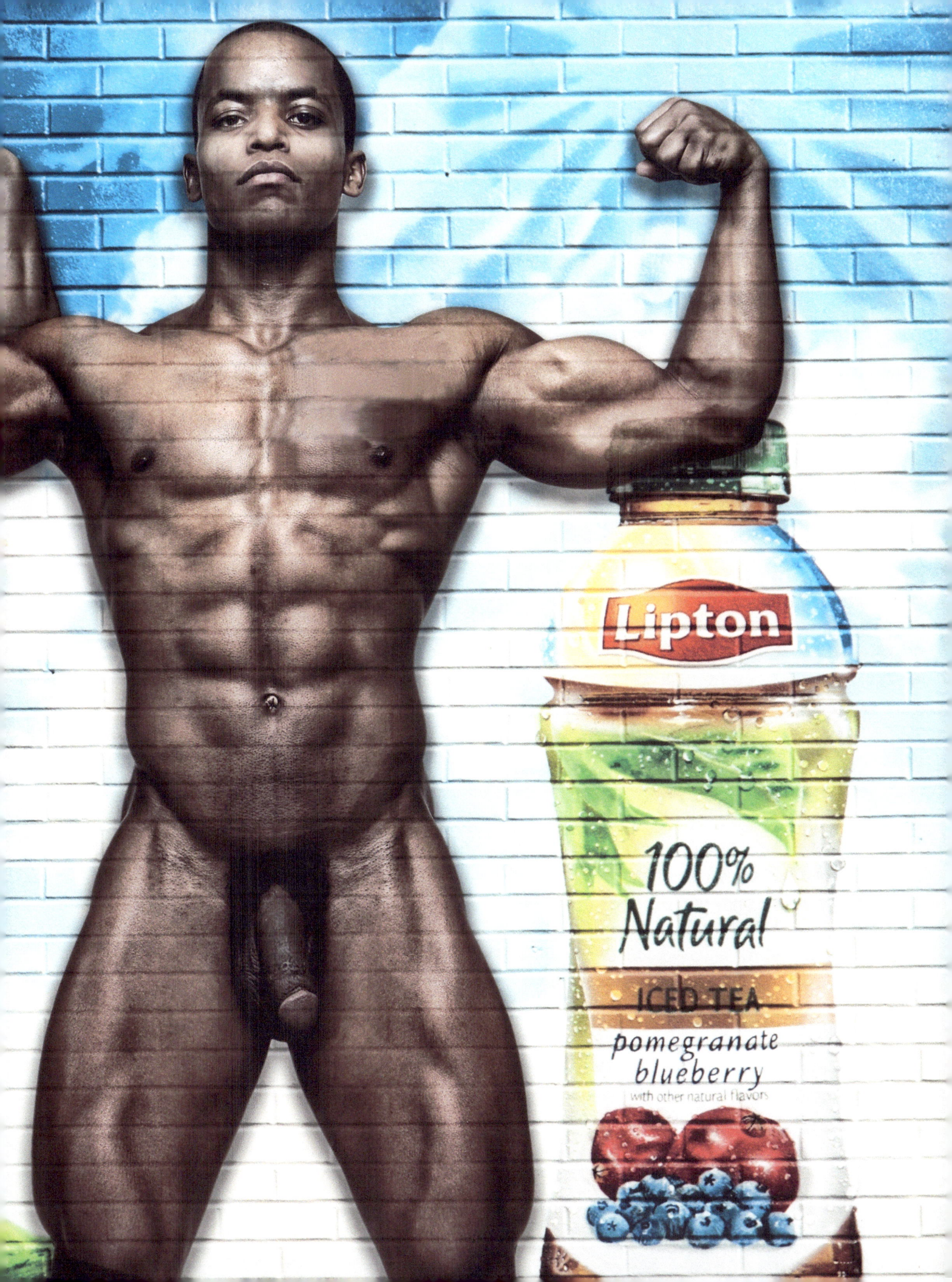

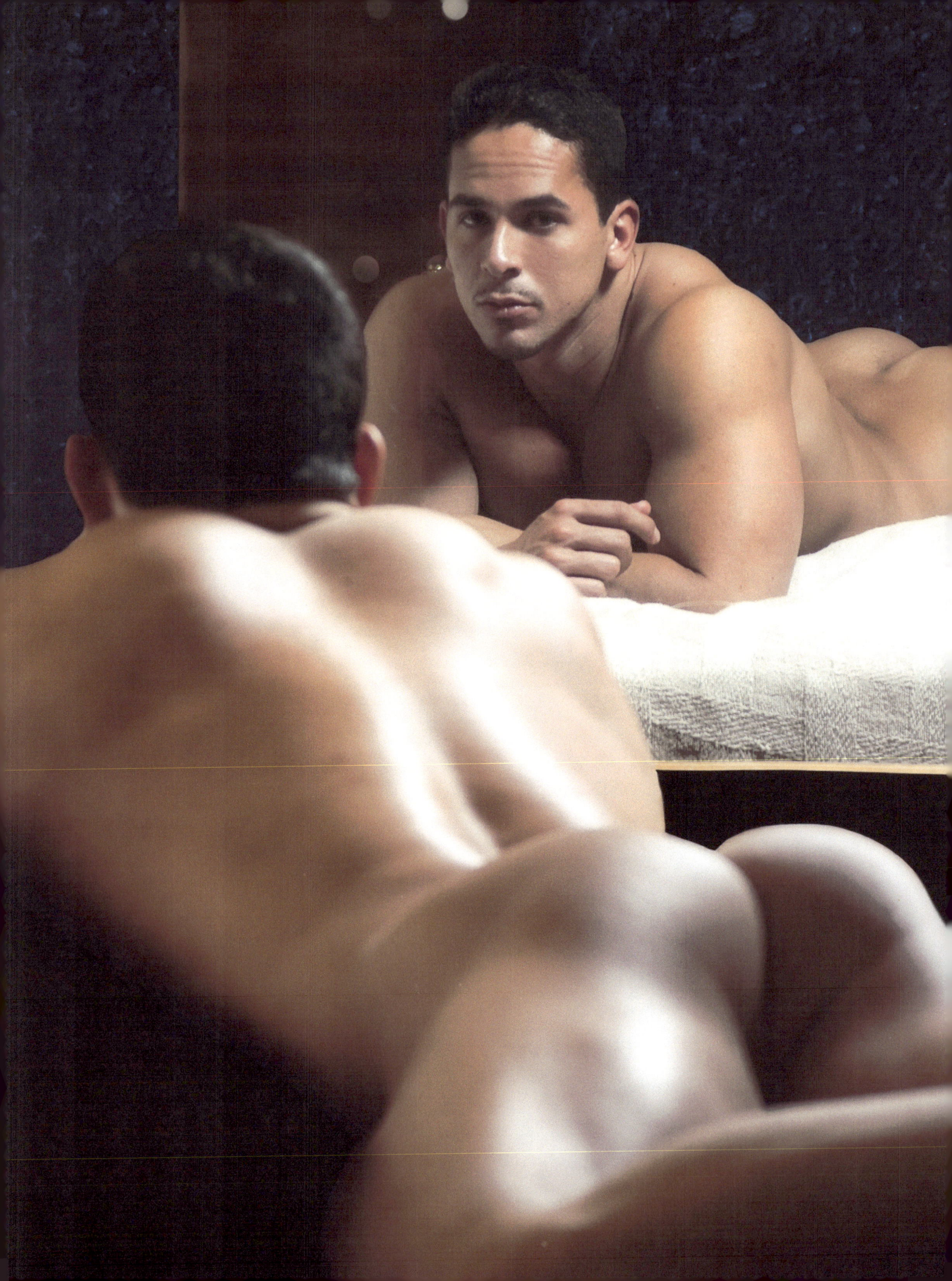

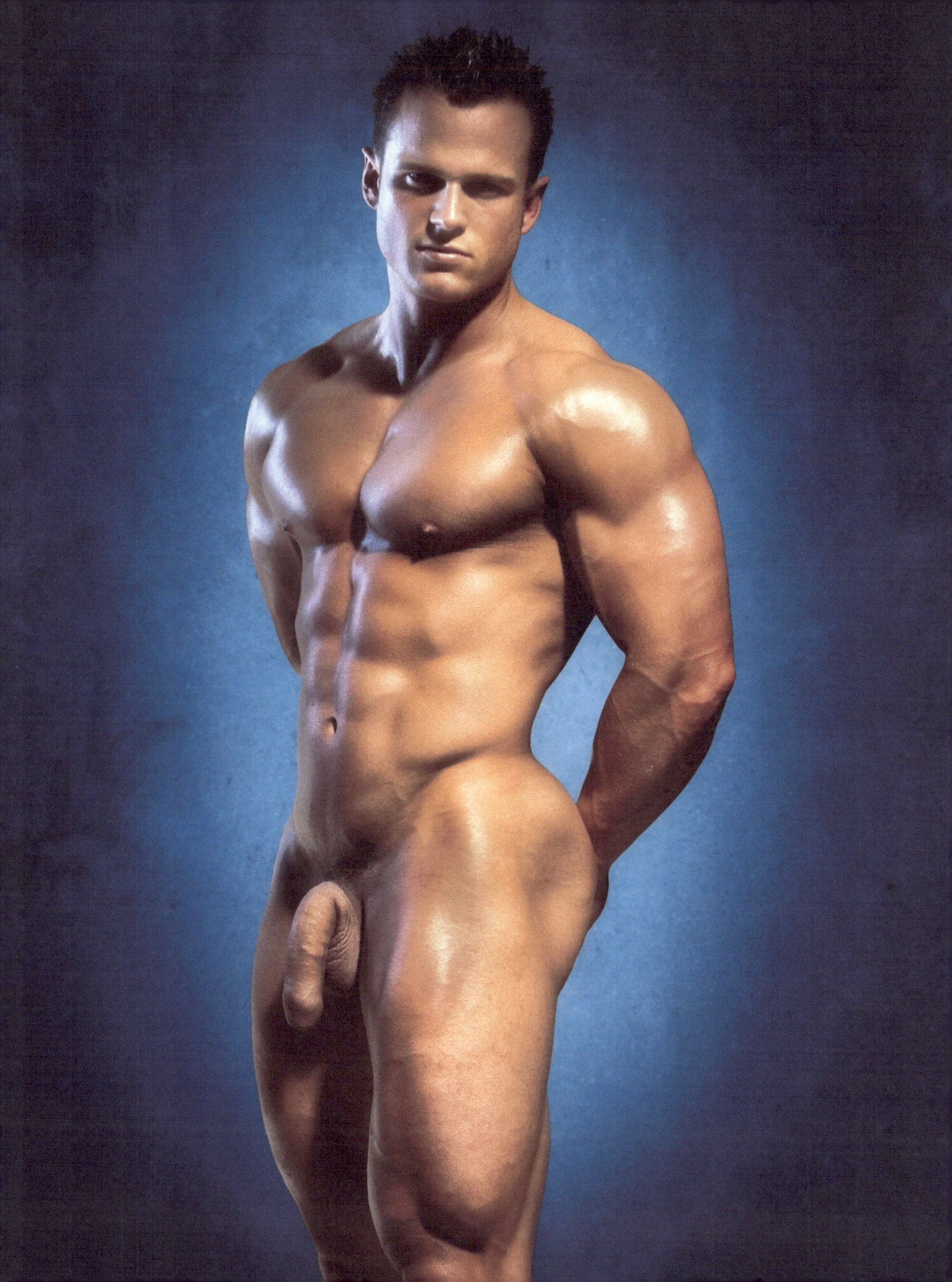

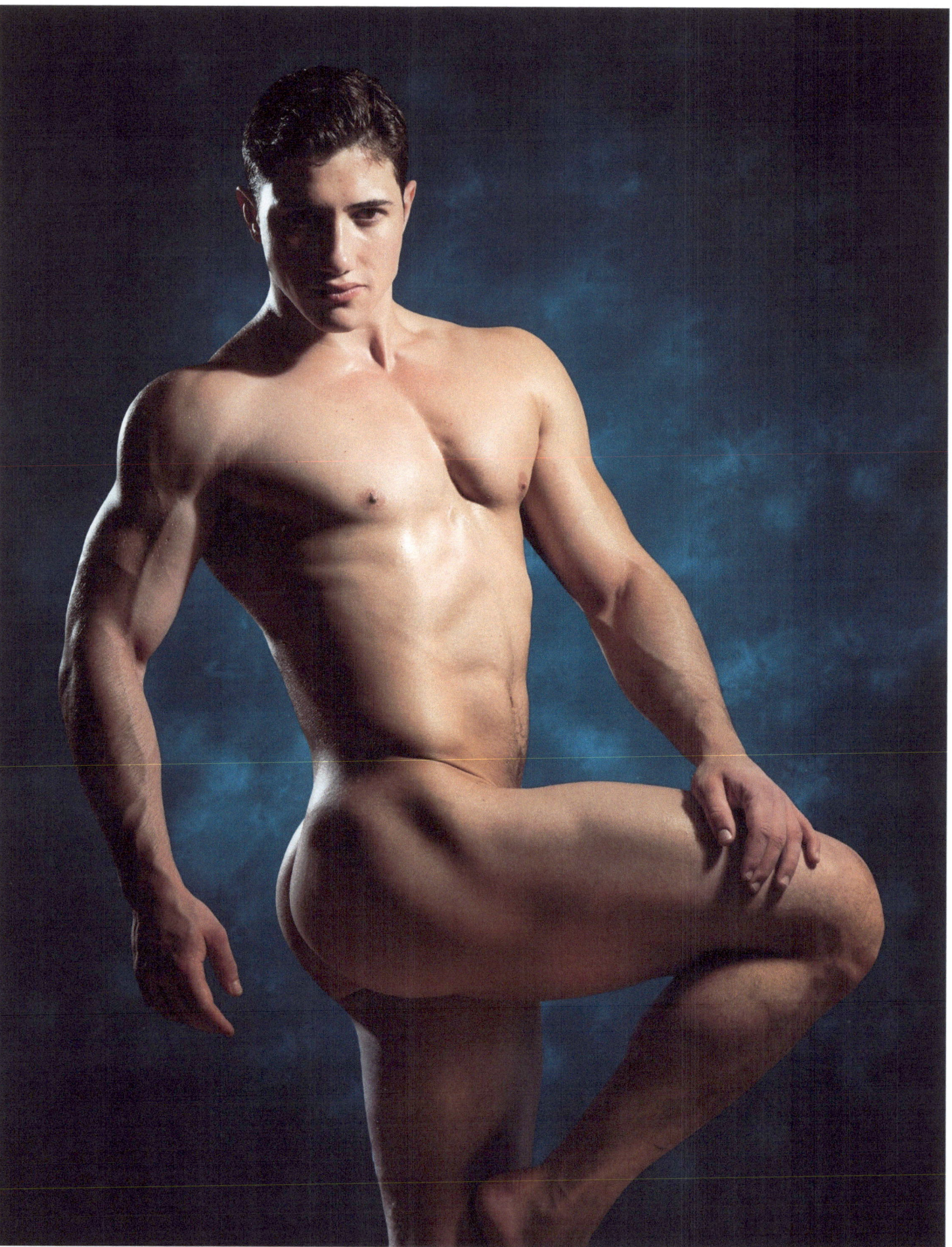

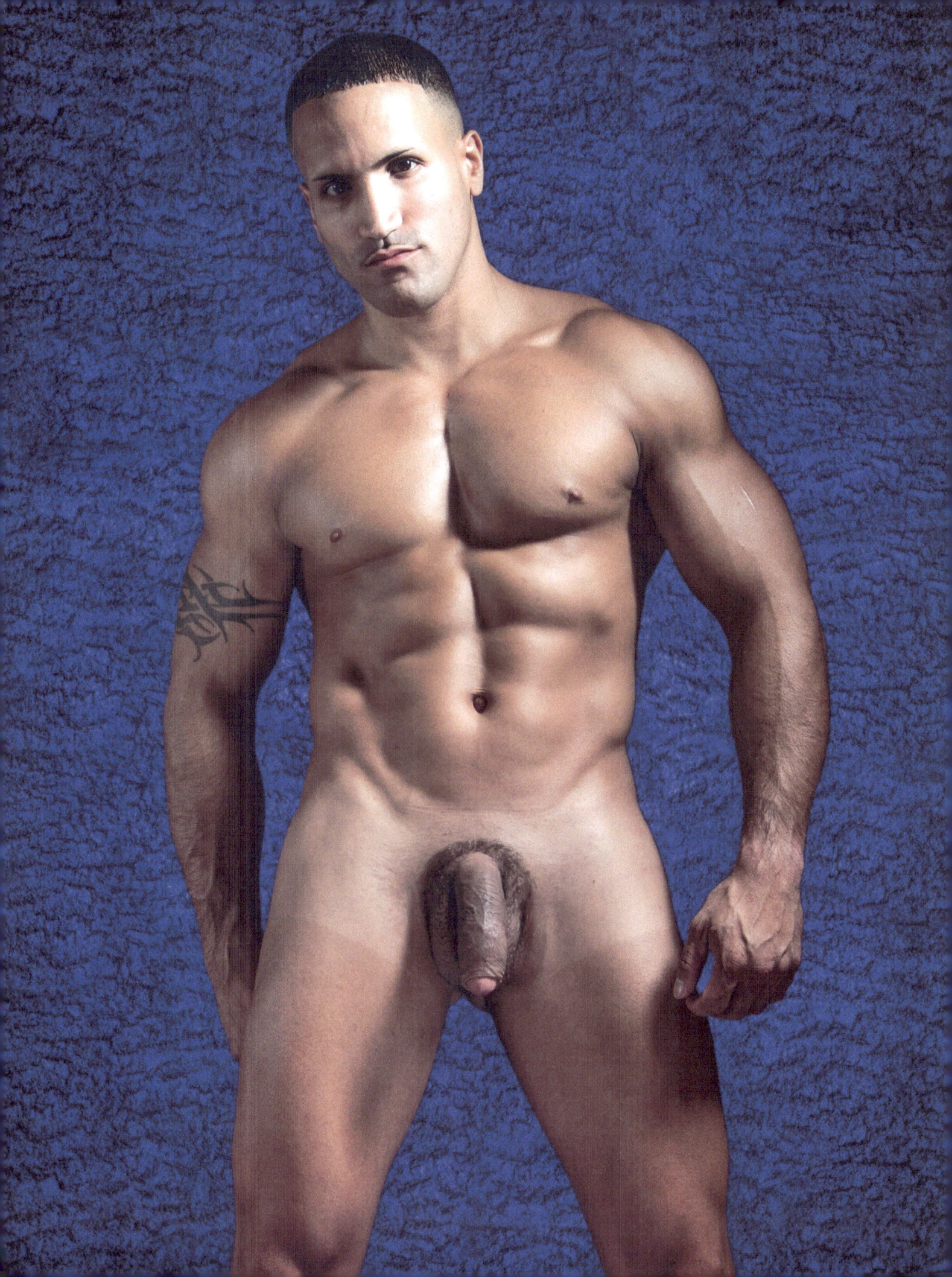

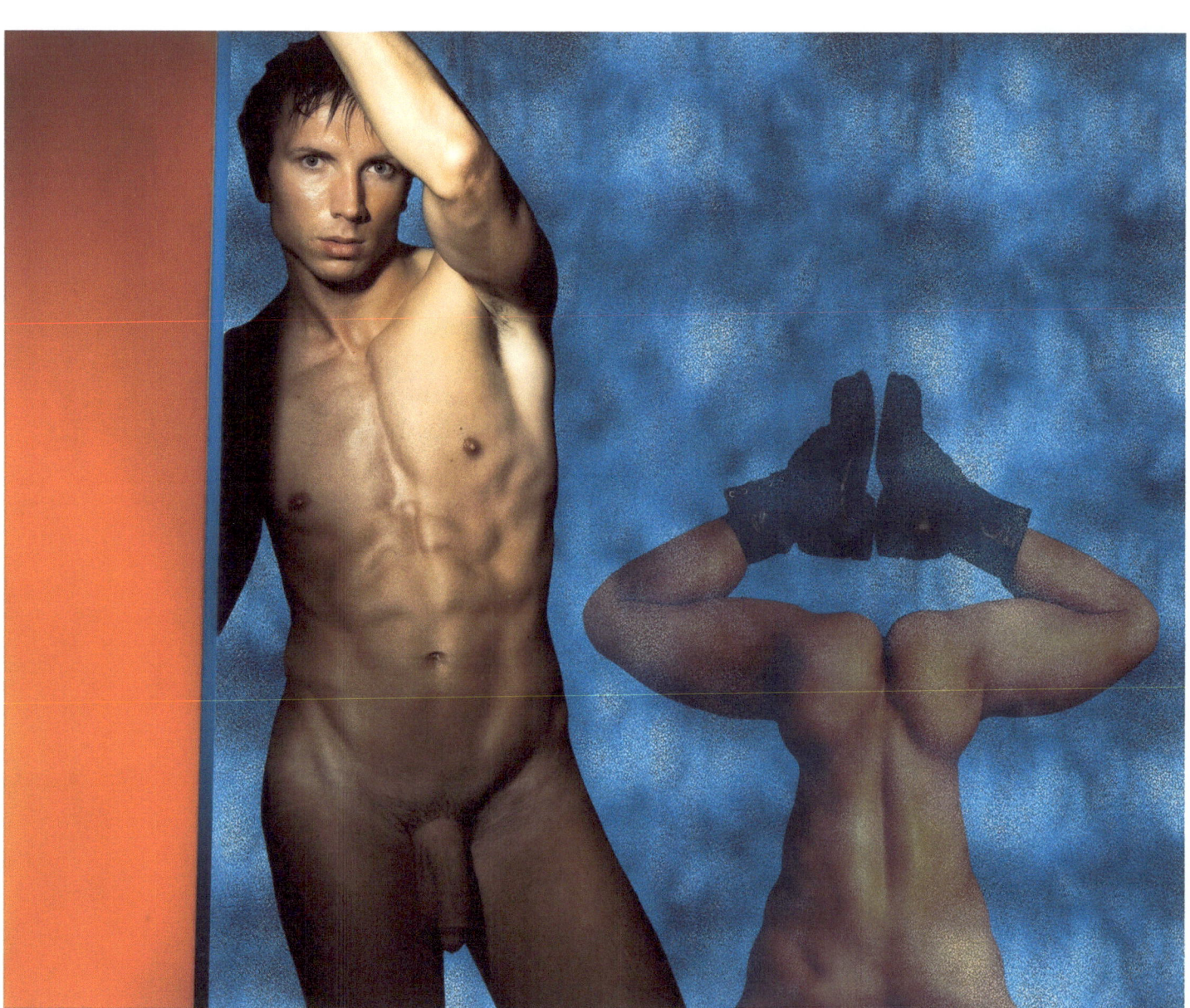

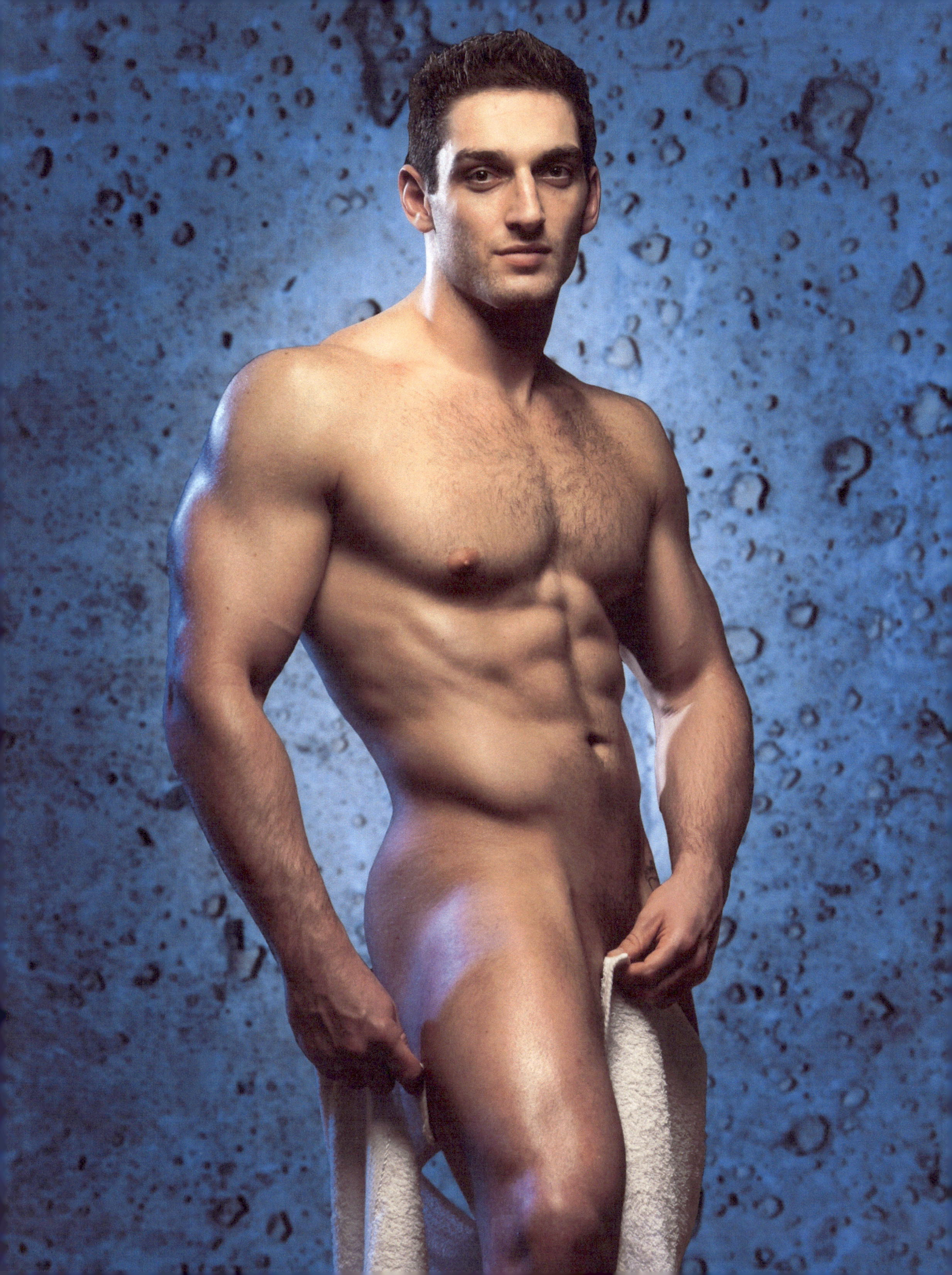

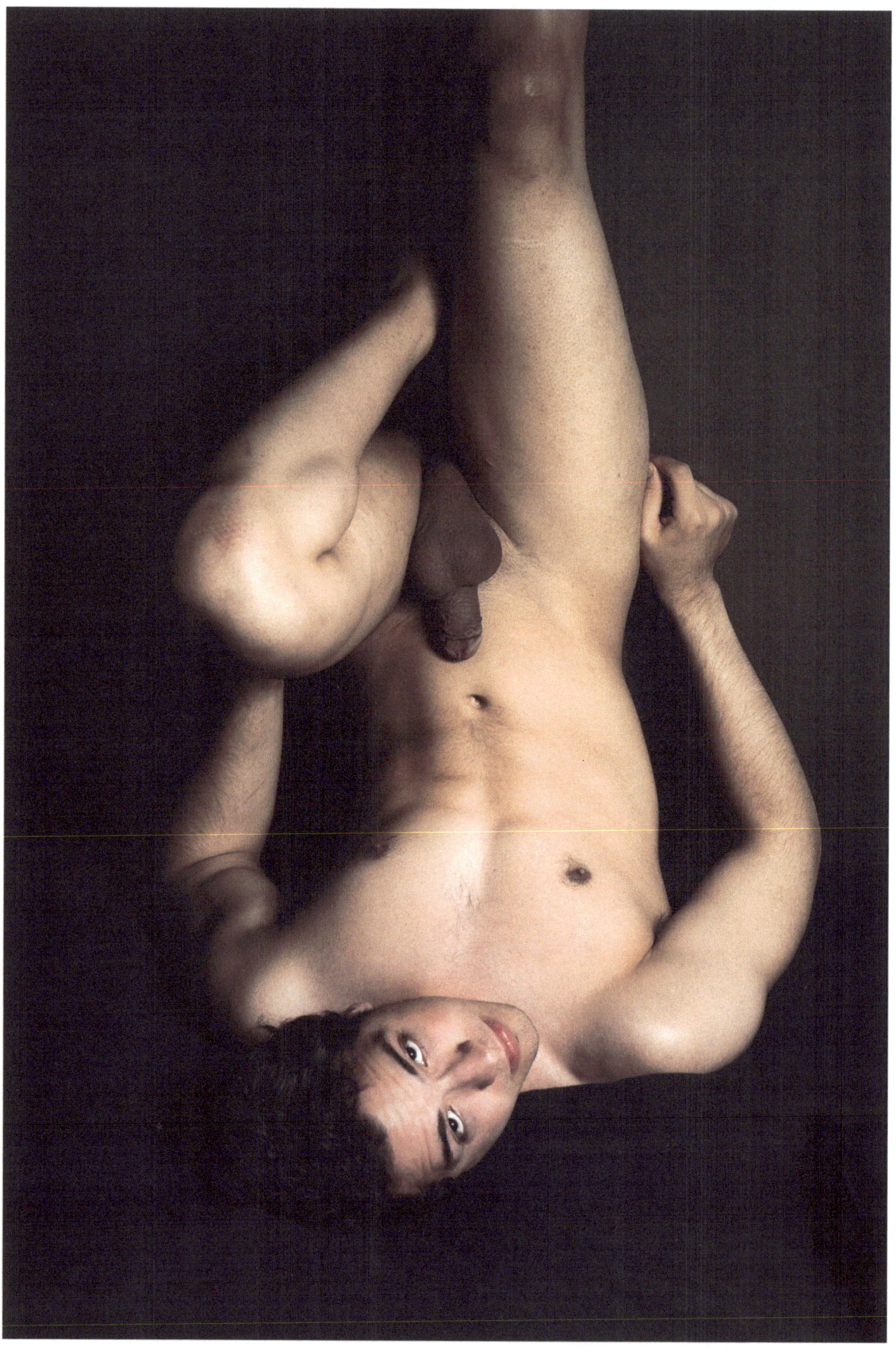

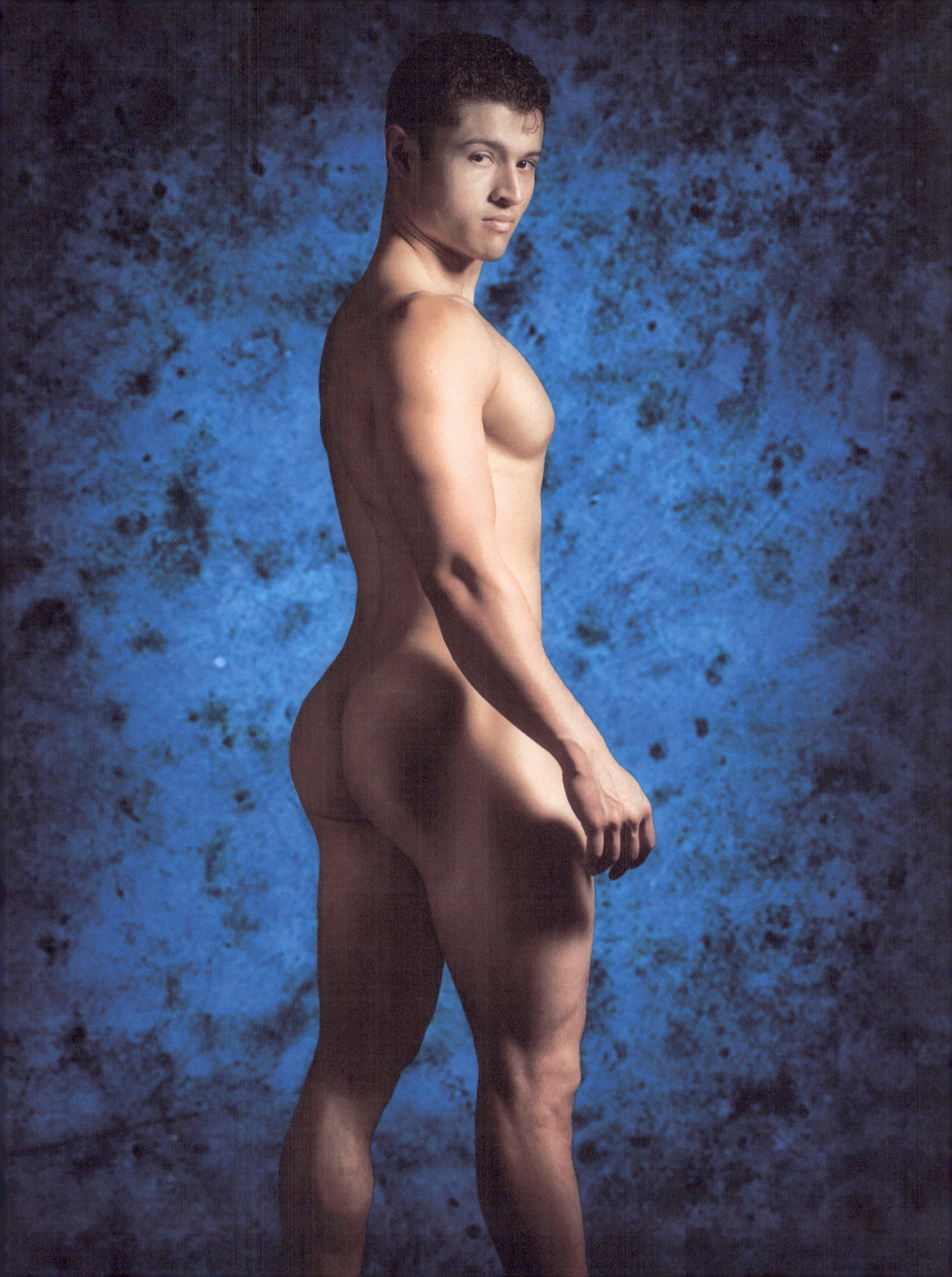

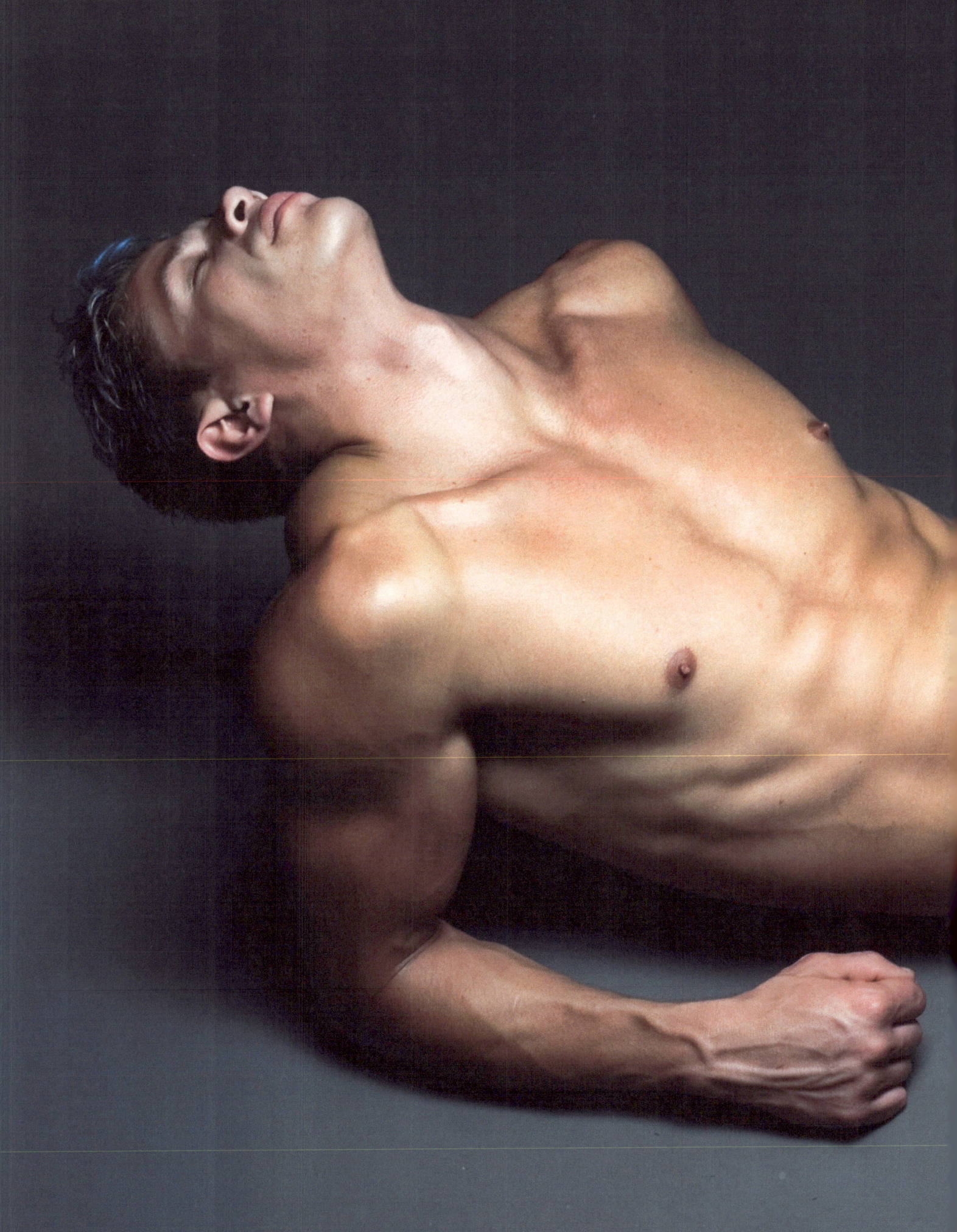

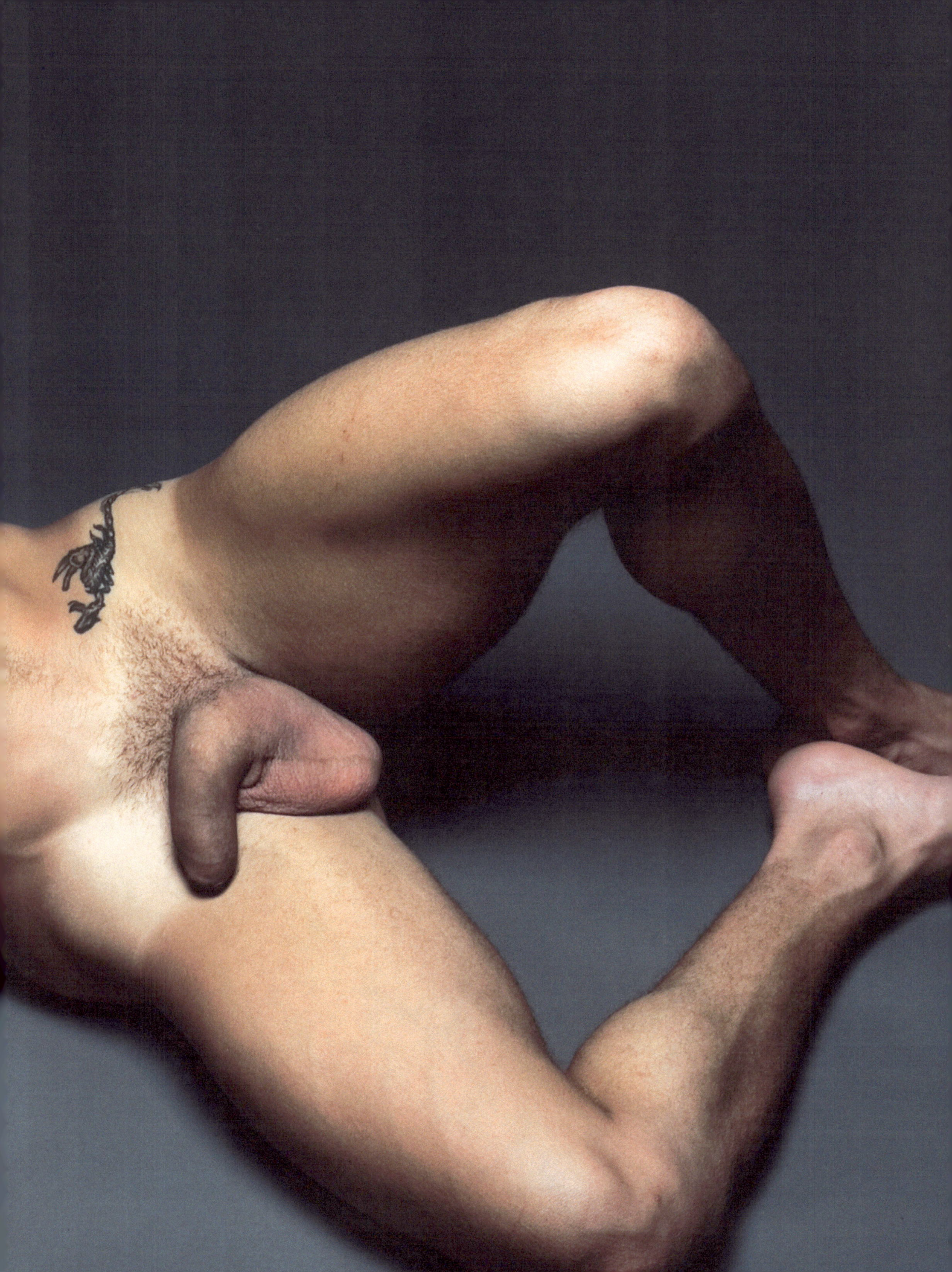

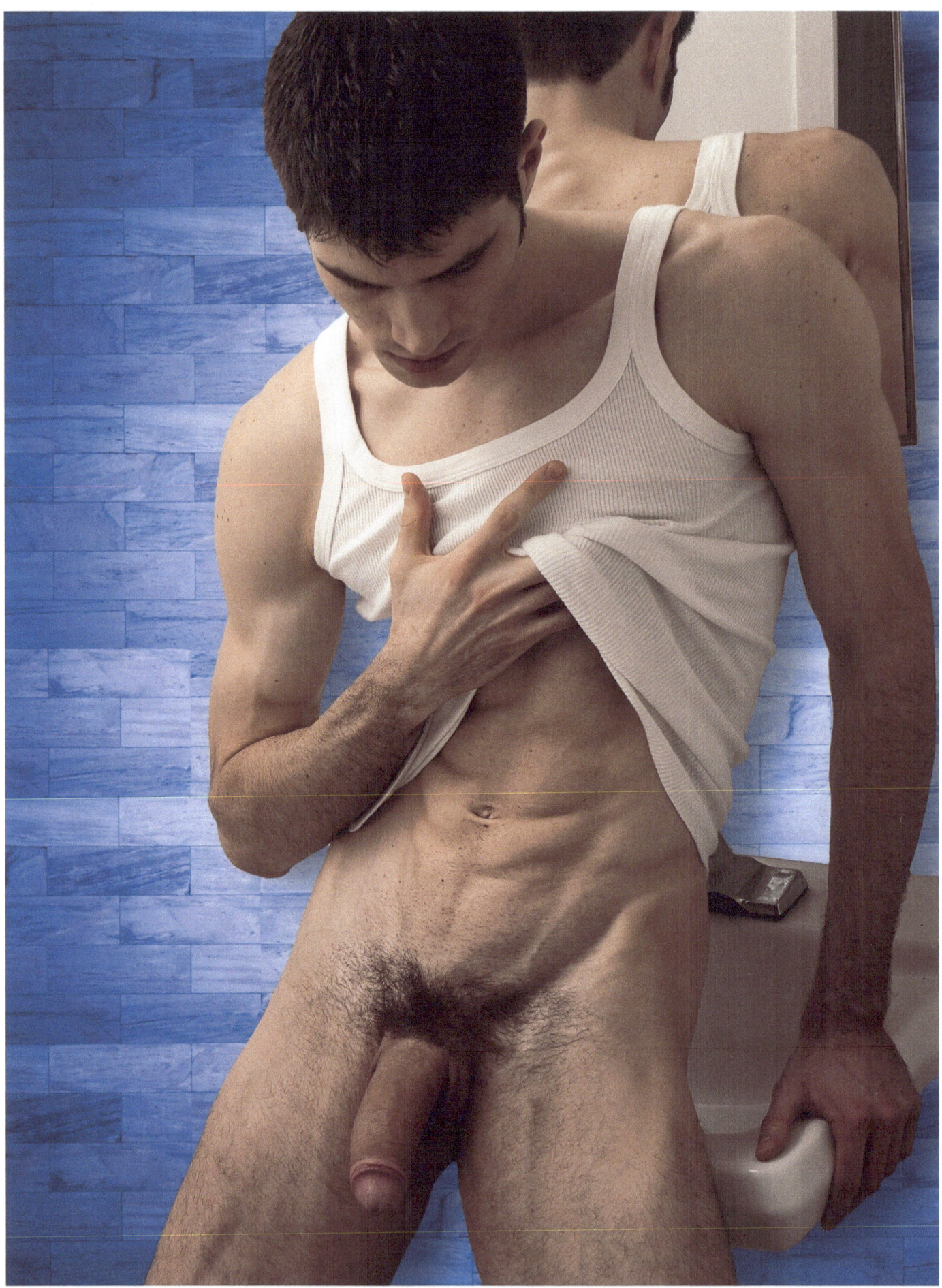

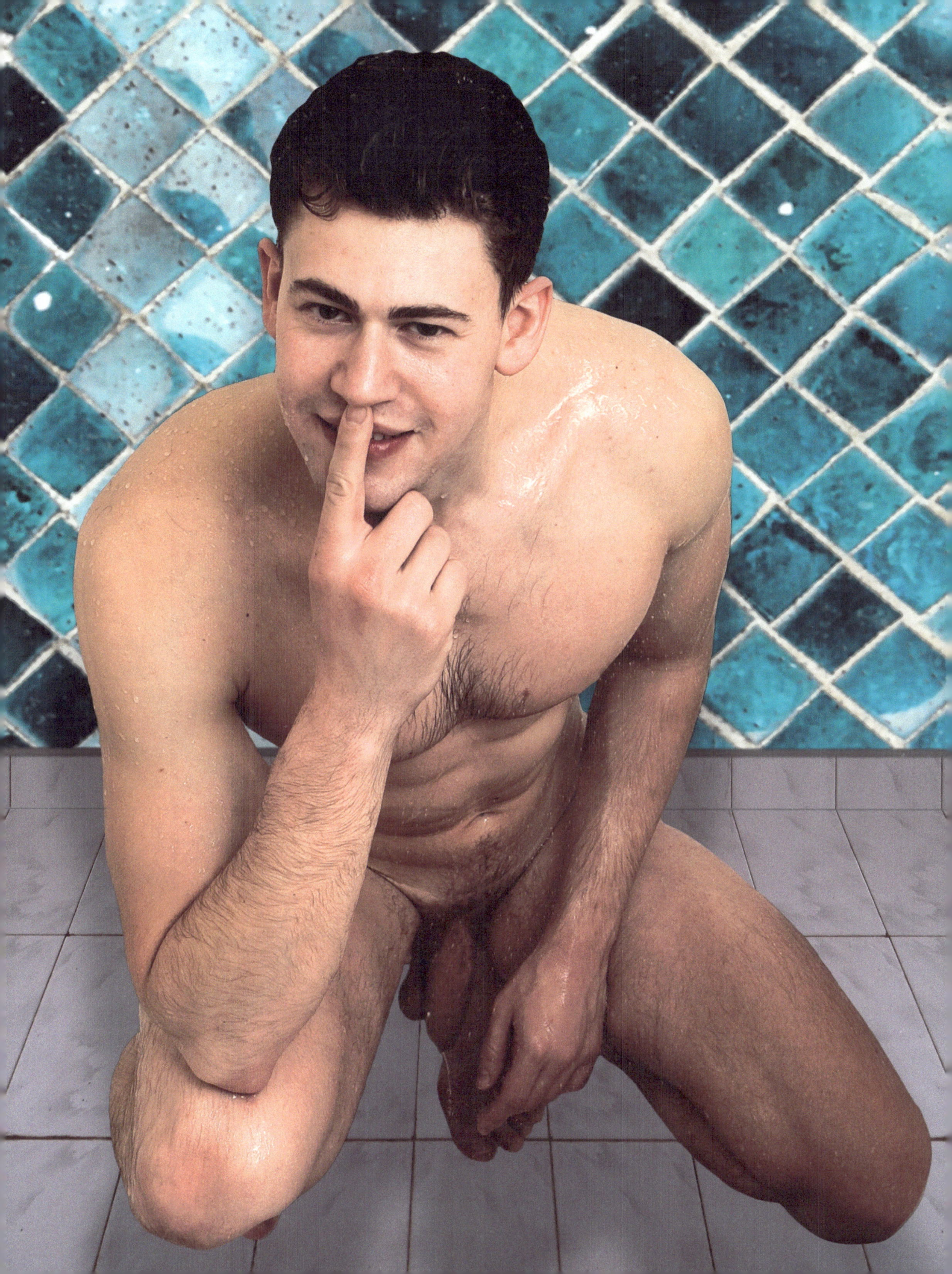

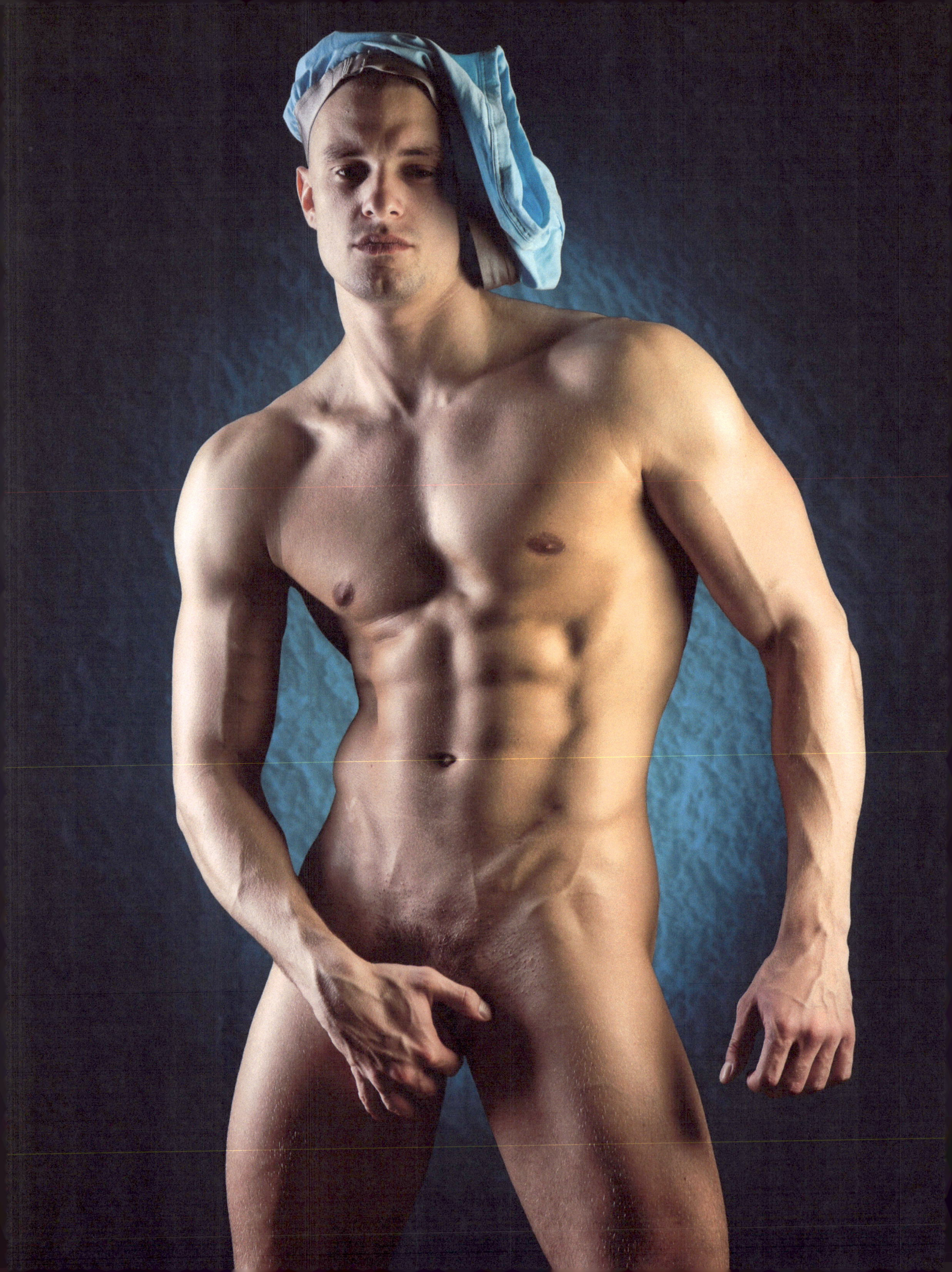

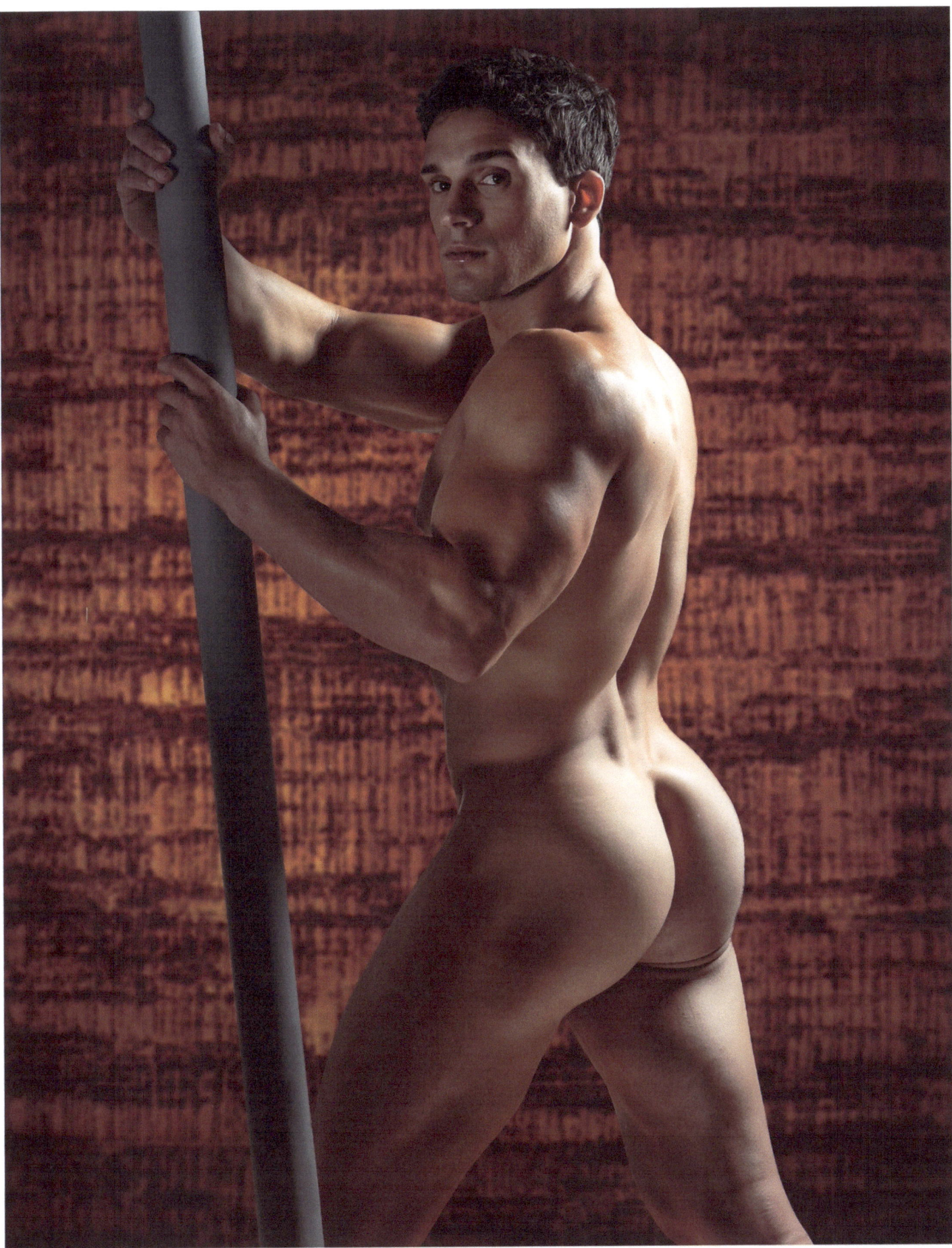

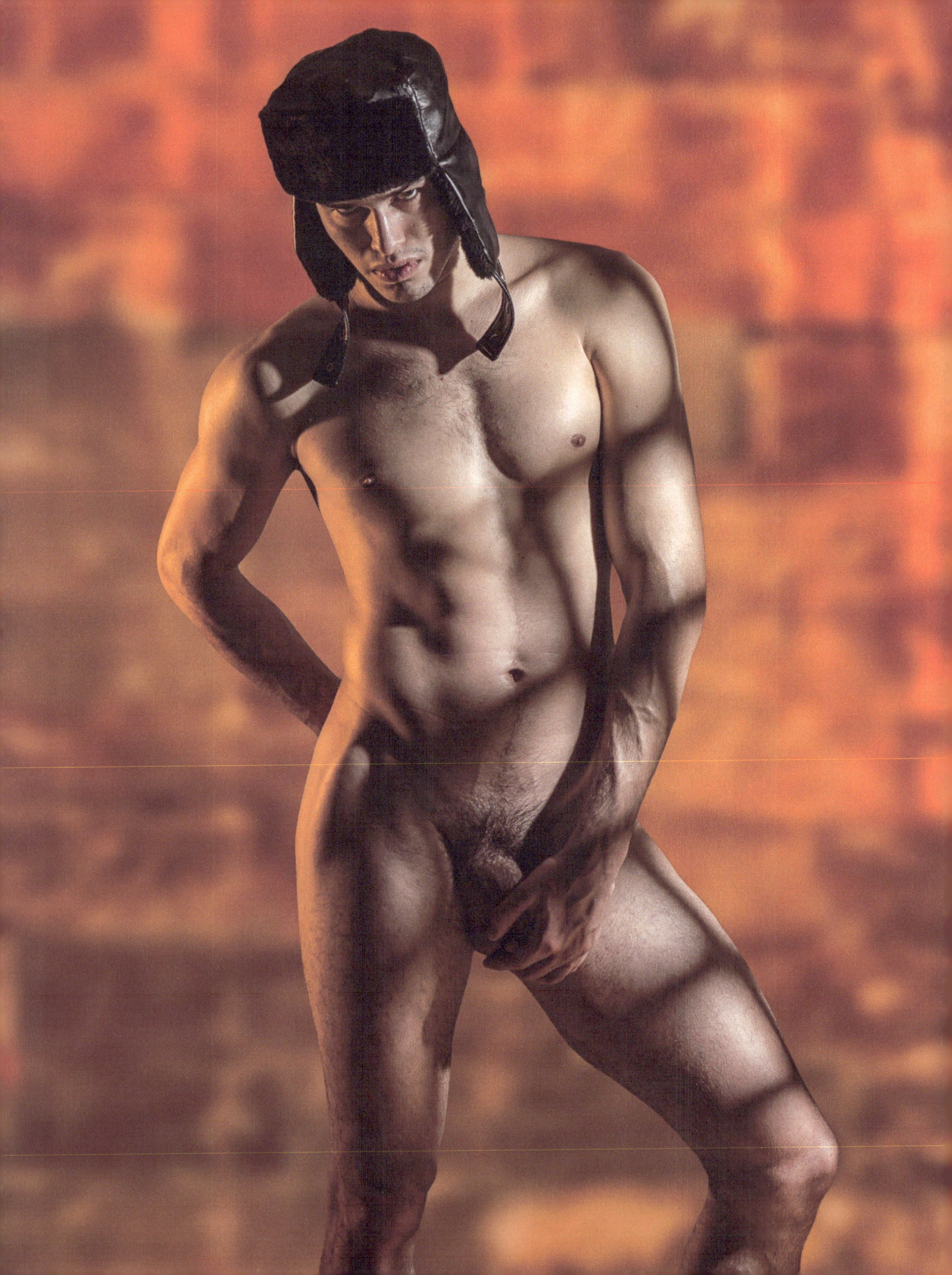

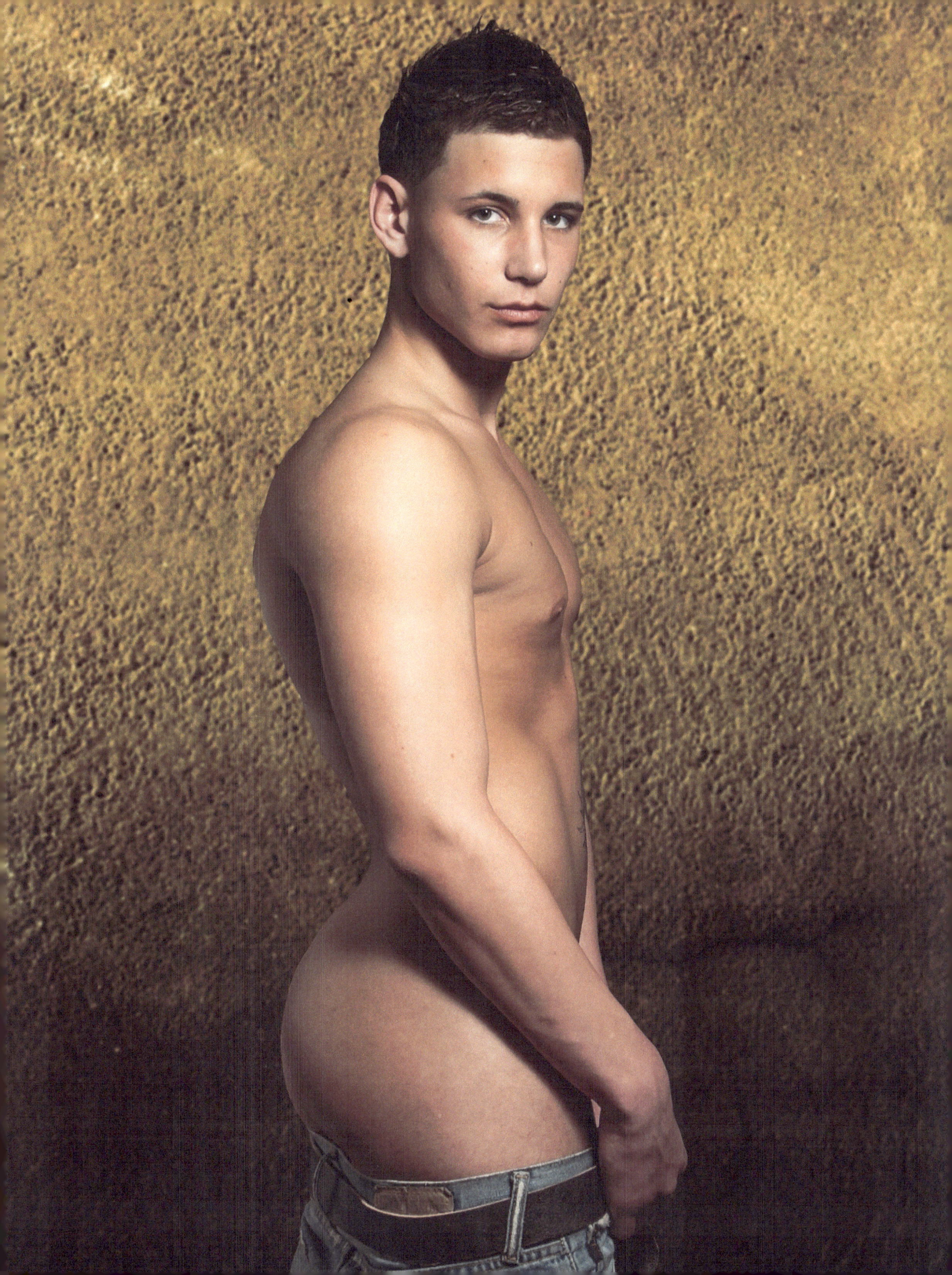

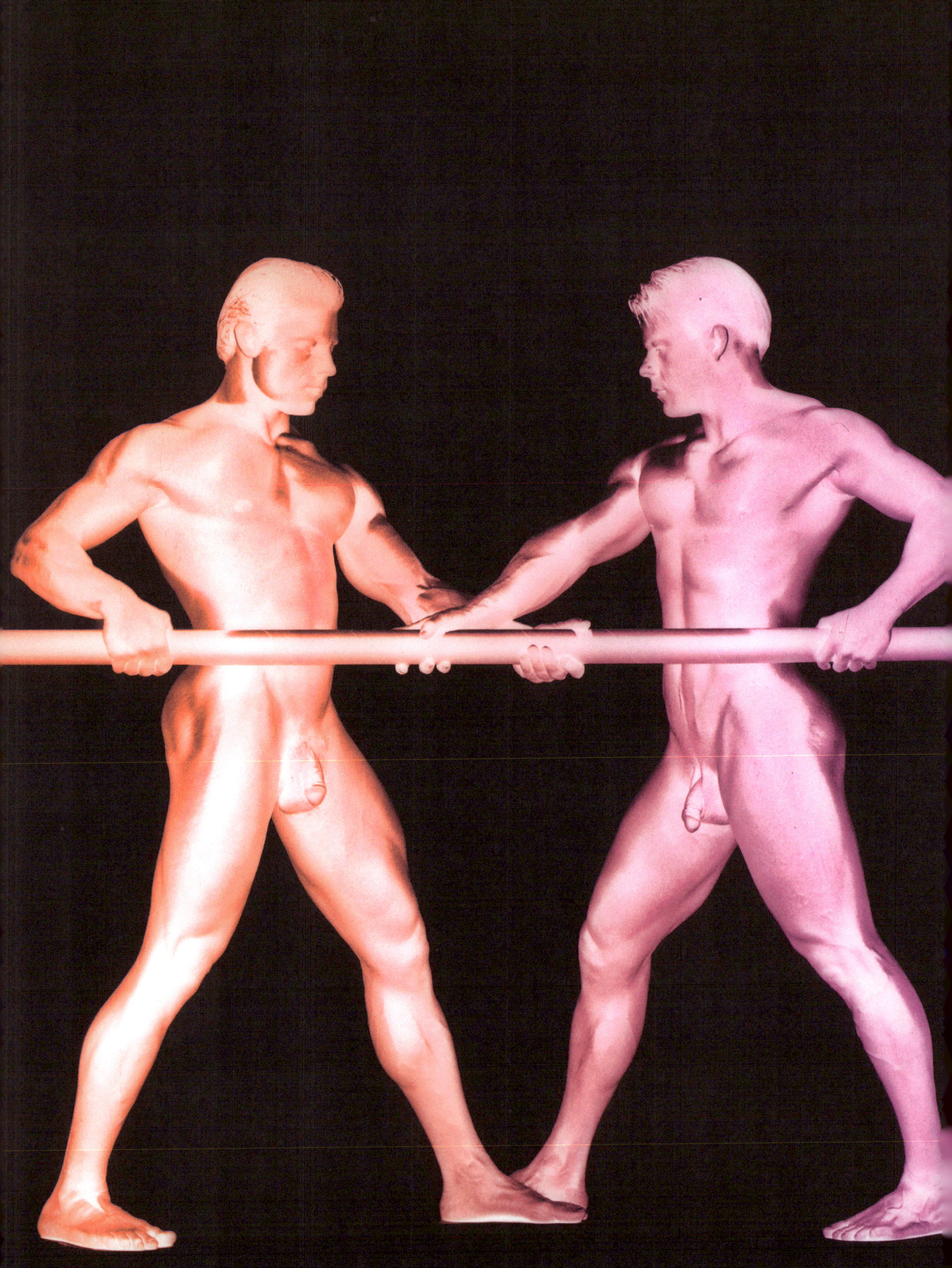

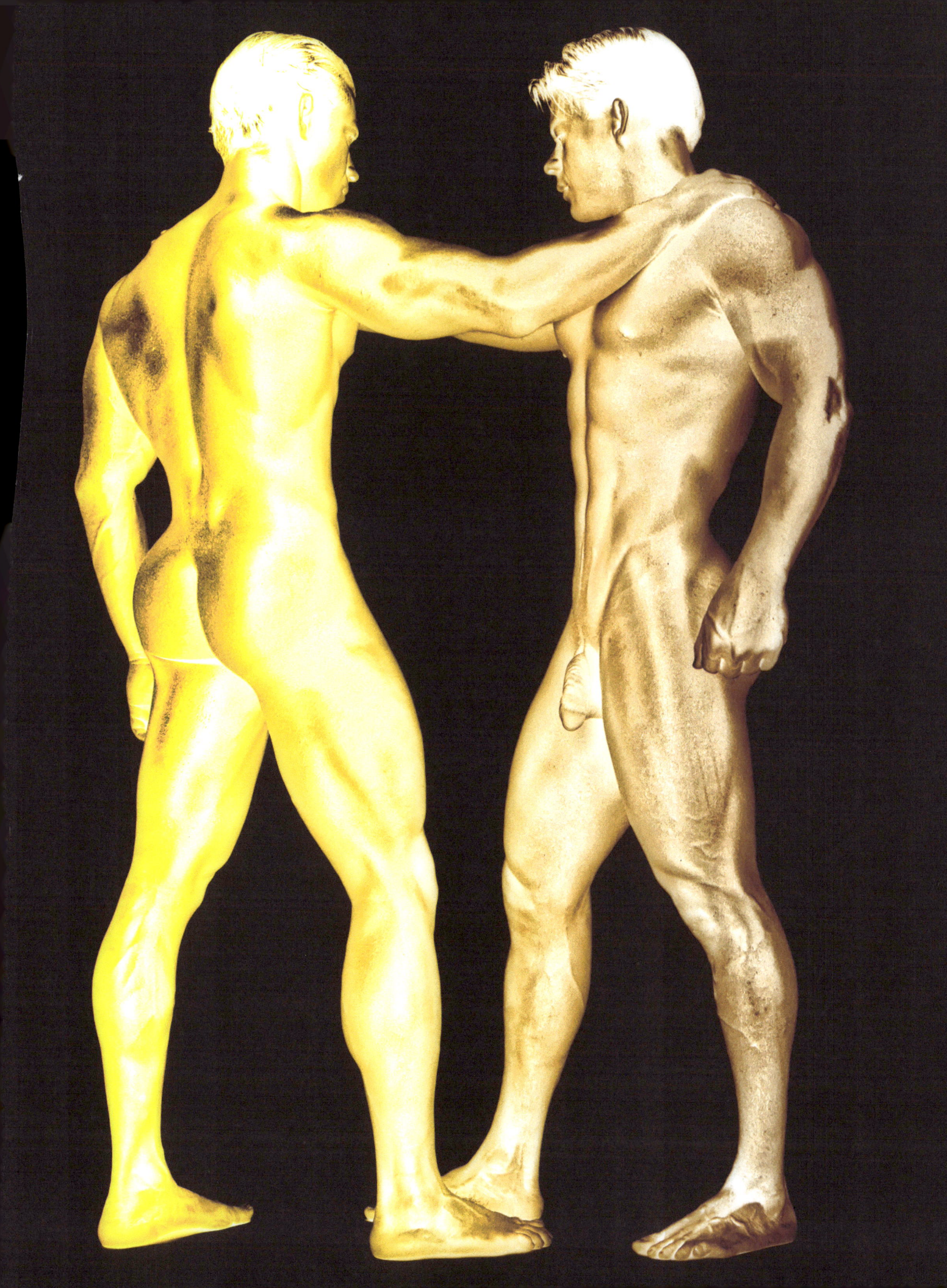

acknowledgments

Very special thanks to Arthur Lambert, Rick Harper
and Trevor Briggs Thanks also to all the Models and
Lucas Entertainment who were involved.

www.ingramcontent.com/pod-product-compliance
Lightning Source LLC
Chambersburg PA
CBHW050717180526
45159CB00003B/1050